Immigration and European integration

MANCHESTER
UNIVERSITY PRESS

European Policy Research Unit Series

Series Editors: *Simon Bulmer* and *Mick Moran*

The European Policy Research Unit Series aims to provide advanced textbooks and thematic studies of key public policy issues in Europe. They concentrate, in particular, on comparing patterns of national policy content, but pay due attention to the European Union dimension. The thematic studies are guided by the character of the policy issue under examination.

   The European Policy Research Unit (EPRU) was set up in 1989 within the University of Manchester's Department of Government to promote research on European politics and public policy. The Series is part of the EPRU's effort to facilitate intellectual exchange and substantive debate on the key policy issues confronting the European states and the European Union.

Titles in the series also include

The governance of the Single European Market   Kenneth Armstrong and Simon Bulmer

The politics of health in Europe   Richard Freeman

Mass media and media policy in Western Europe   Peter Humphreys

The regions and the new Europe   ed. Martin Rhodes

The European Union and member states   ed. Dietrich Rometsch and Wolfgang Wessels

Political economy of financial integration in Europe   Jonathan Story and Ingo Walter

Immigration and European integration

Towards fortress Europe?

Andrew Geddes

Manchester University Press
Manchester and New York
distributed exclusively in the USA by St. Martin's Press

Copyright © Andrew Geddes 2000

The right of Andrew Geddes to be identified as the author of this work has been
asserted by him in accordance with the Copyright, Designs and Patents Act 1988.

Published by Manchester University Press
Oxford Road, Manchester M13 9NR, UK
and Room 400, 175 Fifth Avenue, New York, NY 10010, USA
http://www.man.ac.uk/mup

Distributed exclusively in the USA by
St. Martin's Press, Inc., 175 Fifth Avenue, New York,
NY 10010, USA

Distributed exclusively in Canada by
UBC Press, University of British Columbia, 6344 Memorial Road,
Vancouver, BC, Canada V6T 1Z2

British Library Cataloguing-in-Publication Data
A catalogue record for this book is available from the British Library

Library of Congress Cataloging-in-Publication Data
Geddes, Andrew, 1965–
    Immigration and European integration: towards fortress Europe? /
Andrew Geddes.
        p.   cm. — (European policy research unit series)
    Includes bibliographical references and index.
    ISBN 0–7190–5688–8 (hbk.). — ISBN 0–7190–5689–6 (pbk.)
    1. Europe—Emigration and immigration—Government policy.
    2. Immigrants—Government policy—Europe.   3. European federation.
    I. Title.   II. Series.
    JV7590.G43   2000
    325.4'09'049—dc21   99–42532

ISBN   0 7190 5688 8 *hardback*
       0 7190 5689 6 *paperback*

This edition first published 2000

07 06 05 04 03 02 01 00   10 9 8 7 6 5 4 3 2 1

Typeset by Ralph J. Footring, Derby
Printed in Great Britain
by Bookcraft (Bath) Ltd, Midsomer Norton

For my mother and father and in memory of my grandmother.

Contents

Preface and acknowledgements

Most of this book was written during my time as a Jean Monnet fellow in the 'European Forum' on international migrations at the European University Institute in Florence, Italy, during the academic year 1997–8. I am very grateful to the Forum directors, Professors Christian Joppke and René Leboutte, and the Robert Schuman Centre director, Professor Yves Mény, for the opportunity to participate. I am also grateful to Professors Dennis Kavanagh and Stephen Padgett in the School of Politics and Communication Studies at the University of Liverpool for allowing me to take up the fellowship. The book was finally, finally completed while I was visiting scholar at the New York Center for EU Studies during April 1999, based at the Institute on Western Europe at Columbia University. Thanks go to Professor Glenda Rosenthal and Patti de Groot at Columbia for their hospitality in that wonderful city.

Many friends and colleagues have provided help and assistance during the writing of this book and I'm grateful to them all. Where the book is strong it's because of their help and where there are errors of fact or interpretation it's my fault, loath as I am to admit it. Particular thanks go to Valérie Amiraux, Maria Baganha, Roland Bank, Mark Bell, Michael Bommes, John Crowley, Adrian Favell, Glyn Ford MEP, Robert Geyer, Michael Goldsmith, Elspeth Guild, Virginie Guiraudon, James Hollifield, Sandra Lavenex, Marco Martiniello, Martin Rhodes, Magnus Ryner, Shamit Saggar, Yasemin Soysal and Antje Wiener. I am also grateful to Michelle Harvey, Marian Hoffmann and Yvonne Janvier at the School of Politics and Communication Studies at the University of Liverpool for their help, particularly to Yvonne for printing the whole thing out while I absented myself once again from the department. At Manchester University Press I am grateful to Nicola Viinikka, Pippa Kenyon and the series editors for their assistance and professionalism.

There's also life outside academia, as my football team-mates at Gruppo Sportivo Infoteca in Florence demonstrated – *forza ragazzi*! Football in Florence provided one year's distraction from attendance at home and away matches following the mighty Crewe Alexandra Football Club with David Williams and all the other members of Salford Travelling Alex. After more than 120 trophy-less years we live in hope of eventual success and are reminded that patience is forever a virtue.

On a personal note, I would like to thank my mother and father and all my family. They'd probably never guess, but I'm actually quite grateful for all their support. This book is dedicated with love to them and to the memory of my grandmother, Dorothy Geddes.

Abbreviations

CAR	Cities Against Racism
CCME	Churches Commission for Migrants in Europe
CEC	Commission of the European Communities
CFSP	common foreign and security policy
DGV	Commission Social Affairs Directorate
EC	European Community
ECAS	European Citizens Action Service
ECHR	European Convention on Human Rights
ECJ	European Court of Justice
ECR	European Court Report
ECRE	European Council on Refugees and Exiles
ECSC	European Coal and Steel Community
EEA	European Economic Area
EEC	European Economic Community
EFC	External Frontiers Convention
EMU	economic and monetary union
EP	European Parliament
EPC	European political co-operation
EU	European Union
EUMF	European Union Migrants' Forum
EURODAC	European Data Archive Convention
IGC	intergovernmental conference
ILO	International Labour Organisation
JHA	justice and home affairs
JPC	judicial and police co-operation
LIA	Local Integration/Partnership Action
NGO	non-governmental organisation
OECD	Organization for Economic Cooperation and Development
OOPEC	Office for the Official Publications of the European Community
QMV	qualified majority voting

SAP	Social Action Programme
SEA	Single European Act
SIS	Schengen Information System
SLG	Starting Line Group
TCNs	third country nationals
UN	United Nations
UNHCR	United Nations High Commissioner for Refugees

Introduction

Immigration is a salient issue across the European Union (EU). This point was highlighted once again in 1999 when the crisis in Kosovo displaced around one million people and created a refugee crisis on the EU's doorstep. This needs to be set against the backdrop of restrictive policies in EU member states and attempts to translate these policies into some kind of EU-level framework. At national level, the supposed 'threats' posed by immigration and by immigrants and their children fuel the racist and xenophobic extreme right. At EU level, liberalisation and free movement within the single market have brought with them an emphasis on security and control.

Yet migration has been, is and will be fundamental to EU member states and European integration. The free movement of its citizens is a core component of the building of an economically integrated 'people's Europe'. But who are 'the people'? As it stands, 'the people' does not include those who are legally resident in member states – often the second or third generation descendants of immigrants – but who do not possess the nationality of a member state ('third country nationals', TCNs). Moreover, citizens of member states of immigrant and ethnic minority origin cannot seek EU-level protection against racist discrimination when exercising rights associated with European integration. Migrants helped build and reconstruct European nation states. Just as surely as European integration rescued the nation state then so too did migration, but the language of crisis and threat can disguise the centrality of the contribution that has been made and will be made in the future by migration.

The migration policy picture in contemporary Europe is complex and European integration constitutes another element of complexity which we must account for if we are to chart the supranational challenge to contemporary European migration policy and politics. At their heart, European immigration policy and politics are a *mélange* encompassing restrictive and expansive tendencies in immigration policies and differential processes of inclusion and exclusion of migrants and their descendants.

There have also developed diverse patterns of supranational integration and bilateral and multilateral inter-state co-operation on the control and inclusion/exclusion dimensions of policy. To illustrate this point, the post-1973 movement towards restrictive immigration policies in EU member states was accompanied by the continuation of certain forms of migration (family reunification, asylum-seeking and migration of the highly skilled). Restriction and expansion co-existed and contributed to a particular tension that characterises European immigration policy and politics today. At the same time, the chances for social inclusion of migrants and their descendants differ between migrant groups and across EU member states. Although they are often located at the lower end of the socio-economic scale, immigrants and their descendants are not wholly and uniformly excluded and marginalised: patterns of exclusion and inclusion co-exist and differ between member states and migrant groups.

Since the 1950s, the EU has developed its own migration policy competencies – for free movement of people within its common and single markets and, more recently, for immigration and asylum – which imparts a supranational dimension to discussions of European immigration policy and politics. Articulations between restriction and expansion, between inclusion and exclusion and between intergovernmentalism and supra-nationalism have typified European immigration politics and policy for over thirty years. It is the EU dimension and the reshaping of immigration policy and politics in an integrated Europe that are the focus of this book.

The reshaping and reconfiguration of European immigration policy and politics by European integration are evident in both the 'control' and 'integration' dimensions of immigration/immigrant policies (Hammar, 1985). A distinct supranational dimension has been created by the EU treaty provisions for free movement of people, which has been accompanied by more cautious movement towards closer co-operation with regard to immigration and asylum between member states. This suggests a relation between the national and supranational level that requires closer specification, as well as a determination of the ways in which power and authority for both the 'control' and 'integration' dimensions of policy are diffused through sub-national, non-state and transnational actors. Within these complex relations, states remain *key* actors, but are no longer *the* actors. State power does not itself determine these complex relations; rather state power is something that needs to be explained within an integrating Europe where migration policy competencies are dispersed through structures of governance and market mechanisms.

Why has European integration drawn migration policy into the EU's realm of competencies? This is an important question when it is borne in mind that border controls have been viewed as a key feature of state sovereignty, construed in its modern form as the right to exclude (Caporaso, 1996: 35). This right to exclude has been undermined by patterns of European economic integration that have had freer movement for people, services, goods and capital within the single market as a core objective and, moreover, this integration has been supported by an influential and highly mobile transnational capitalist class (Cowles, 1995). The market-making project and free movement unavoidably made immigration and asylum issues common interests for EU member states, which raised the salience of external frontier control at the borders of the single market and internal security policies within. The 'low politics' of economic interdependence seem to have spilled over into the 'high politics' of border control and state security. Yet this articulation between free movement and immigration/asylum resulting from single market integration did not dictate the form that co-operation between member states would take. Free movement has become *constitutionalised* in the sense that a body of case law and associated institutional competencies have developed at European level that bolster free movement and decisively limit the competence and discretion of member states in this area. It was not inevitable that states would supranationalise their policy response to immigration and asylum in the same way that they did for free movement. There is an important distinction between legal and political-institutional supranationalism and intergovernmental co-operation. This is based on the ability of the EU's institutions to turn a treaty between sovereign states into a body of laws that bind those states (Weiler, 1982; Burley and Mattli, 1993). Constitutionalisation has been applied to free movement but not to immigration and asylum, because they have remained mainly subject to intergovernmental co-operation and been largely unchecked by judicial overview or democratic accountability at either national or supranational level.

A distinction between the EU's regulatory competencies for free movement with associated entrenched institutional competencies at EU level and the largely intergovernmental nature of co-operation on immigration and asylum permits a focus on connections between regulatory competencies, the control and security dimensions of migration policy and the possibilities for democratisation and inclusion of migrants within these new migration policy structures. The ascription of regulatory competence for free movement (applying to EU citizens and tied to core market-making objectives) can be contrasted with a muddled, confused and confusing transfer of competencies for immigration and asylum (applying to TCNs). EU migration policy has assumed diverse forms connected with relative proximity to the functional imperative underpinning market integration and more cautious movement towards co-operation on the control and security dimensions of policy. In turn, this affects the scope for both constitutionalisation, whereby migration policy becomes more rule-governed at the European level (described by international relation specialists as the 'domestification of international politics'), and *institutionalisation*, marked by the empowerment of supranational institutions and their ability to shape policy outcomes.

To what extent can regulatory competencies at EU level be accompanied by new patterns of democratic control and judicial oversight, which reshape our understanding of participation and inclusion? The EU possesses a strong rhetorical and symbolic commitment to an 'inclusive', 'people's Europe', but it is important to ascertain the extent to which EU integration constitutes a threat to democratic accountability derived from the empowerment of unaccountable, expert transnational coalitions of national ministers, officials and technocrats (Kaiser, 1971). A 'new constitutionalism' has been identified, typified by 'the move towards construction of legal or constitutional devices to remove or insulate substantially the new economic institutions from popular scrutiny or democratic accountability' (Gill, 1992: 158). This is accompanied by diminished redistributive functions for nation states because of the shift in the balance of power away from labour and towards capital and an increased emphasis on repressive functions and techniques of population control. This arises because the 'transferring of issues [such as migration] from the domestic to the foreign policy sphere moves them into the *domain réservé* of executive control' (Risse-Kappen, 1996: 57). In this context, the scope for constitutionalisation and institutionalisation is neither an arcane nor a technical point – these are key issues because of the Europeanisation of migration and the consequent emergent institutional context with associated legal, political and institutional sources of power and authority to shape migrant inclusion. This throws into stark relief those analyses of migration that have emphasised 'embedded liberalism' and the role that rights-based politics and the role of the courts have played at national level in opening social and political spaces for migrants and their descendants (Hollifield, 1992; Freeman, 1995). EU-level chances for migrant inclusion are structured by the institutional context and the conceptualisations of the migration *problematique* that underpins it – its close relation on the one hand to market integration and, on the other, to forms of migration deemed to constitute a threat to EU member states.

At the core of this book is the connection it makes between the control and integration aspects of immigration/immigrant policy and politics and the EU-level resonance these issues have acquired. In methodological terms, this book's institutionalist perspective seeks delineation of the transfer of competencies. By doing so, an understanding can be developed of the ways in which the EU's institutional context reshapes understanding of the control dimensions of policy, affects the calculations, motivations, actions and alliance-building strategies of institutional actors, and gives structure to debates about EU-level migrant inclusion/exclusion.

National and, to a lesser extent, transnational influences on migration policy and politics have been explored in the growing literature on European immigration politics (see, for example, Wrench and Solomos, 1992; Collinson, 1993; Baldwin-Edwards and Schain, 1994; Bauböck, 1994; Cornelius *et al.*, 1994; Soysal, 1994; Uçarer and Puchala, 1997; Castles and Miller, 1998; Joppke, 1998). The EU adds a new dimension to debates about policy and inclusion/exclusion of migrants and their descendants. Migration scholars have not always been well placed to analyse the relation between immigration and European integration because the EU often lurks in the background of analyses as either a threat (the so-called 'fortress Europe') or as an opportunity to build an inclusive people's Europe, but is under-specified. It is essential to relate approaches to the analysis of European integration with analyses of European immigration policy and politics in order to develop a more specific understanding about the sources of social and political power created by European integration. It is pointless to pretend that the EU is something it is not, or that it can do things for good or bad that it cannot. This relation between migration and European integration is configured by an inter-relation between patterns of migration and European integration that challenge the nation state. In this sense 'Migration in modern society is a form of geographical mobility which aims at (re-)inclusion in the functional subsystems of the economy, law, politics, health or education and their organisation at a different place' (Bommes, 1998: 1–2). In turn, European integration can be understood as a process by which states cease to be wholly sovereign. The EU cannot be compared to the nation state, wherein debates about the chances for migrant inclusion have usually occurred, because EU competencies are relatively restricted and relate mainly to market-making. European integration is not a rerun of processes of nation state formation and national integration. To analyse it in such terms would provide a convenient but misplaced frame of reference and yardstick for evaluation. Why should we 'mobilise notions of the past in order to explain developments in the future without any effort to justify why these notions might still be appropriate' (Koopmans, 1992: 1049)? To make this misplaced assumption is to adopt a vocabulary of political analysis that can stymie the consideration of patterns of European integration that have nation states as their core building blocks but are not necessarily a process of replication of state functions and capacities. Indeed, analyses of the 'regulatory' (Majone, 1996) and/or 'post-modern' (Caporaso, 1996) EU have drawn attention to the impact of internationalisation of the state, economic liberalisation and deregulation and political decentralisation that derive neither their political, economic, social power nor ideological resonance from nation states alone. Moreover, the EU is not a blank canvas onto which we can sketch normative visions of an inclusive or participatory EU. The transfer of policy competencies that relate in the main to core economic objectives and associated efforts aiming at population control have structured the contemporary EU. The social and political role played by the EU often arises from these economic purposes and the sources of social and political power they create, not vice versa.

Plan of the book

The book's first chapter highlights the ways in which the core themes of contemporary immigration policy and politics – control and integration – have acquired a supranational resonance that bears strong relation to national policy contexts, but cannot be analysed wholly in such terms. This implies the potential for distinct supranational legal and political dynamics to emerge because supranational institutions have acquired power and responsibility for aspects of migration policy. This has been particularly the case for intra-EU migration/free movement, with knock-on effects for immigration and asylum policy that have direct implications for the question posed in this book's subtitle: *Towards fortress Europe*? The notion of fortress Europe looms large over any analysis of immigration and European integration and consumes much of the activist rhetoric on the supposedly malevolent consequences of EU immigration and asylum policy. The construction of the fortress implies two things: first, tight restriction of those forms of immigration deemed to constitute a 'threat' in economic or 'racial' terms to EU member states;[1] second, the social exclusion of settled migrants. The fortress, therefore, tells us something about the external ramparts that keep undesirable immigrants out of the EU and something about internal societal processes of exclusion. This book's perspective on co-existent patterns of restriction and expansion and of inclusion and exclusion leads to doubt being cast on the notion of fortress Europe as a zone of exclusion. Rather than a 'fortress' it may be more appropriate to talk of a 'net' akin to those used on fishing boats with different sized meshes designed to catch certain fish and allow others to slip through. For instance, highly skilled workers from economically developed countries can move relatively easily, while unskilled workers from less economically developed countries encounter formidable obstacles.[2] Immigration policies can be restrictive (brutally so in some cases), while migrants and their descendants are often among the most marginal and marginalised members (or non-members) of society in EU member states. But these patterns of restriction and exclusion are not uniform and are not necessarily a summation of the migrant experience in contemporary Europe.

Having established a perspective on immigration policy and politics and European integration that emphasises the importance and potential effects of policy institutionalisation, close attention is then be paid to the parameters of EU migration policy. This requires analysis of the treaty framework and, particularly, the provisions of the Treaty of Rome (1957),

Single European Act (SEA) (1986), Treaty on European Union (Maastricht Treaty) (1992) and Amsterdam Treaty (1997). Having done this, we can then examine the effects that ascription of competence can have on migration policy outcomes. The underlying emphasis on the importance of the institutional context also implies caution regarding simplistic interpretations of European integration, which take two forms that are particularly relevant to an analysis of immigration and European integration. First is what could be called the fallacy of integrative inevitability, which construes European integration as a process akin to a conveyor belt leading to ever-deeper economic and political integration. European integration is more contingent and conjunctural than allowed for by such naïve teleological federalism. Second, there is what could be characterised as the conspiracy theory of European integration that construes it as a plot to denude EU citizens and immigrants of civil and democratic liberties (there is an element of this in the fortress Europe critique). As will be seen, there are good grounds for being critical of policy co-operation and integration, but meetings of the Council of Ministers are not akin to gatherings of the Ku Klux Klan at which crosses are burnt and policies hatched to protect some mythical white, Christian European heritage. It would be too simplistic to explain EU immigration and asylum policy as entirely driven by anti-democratic and discriminatory impulses. Immigration and asylum policies can be discriminatory and this discrimination can have a racist dimension when it comes to those immigrant and ethnic minority groups deemed to pose the greatest 'threat'. For one thing, however, such blanket denunciations make the mistake of greatly over-stating EU capacities. Given the significant limitations on its institutions' capacity to act, it would be remarkable if the EU could build a fortress. Moreover, the EU relies on national policy implementation, which, as shown in chapter 1, is far from assured. The Council, for instance, is hamstrung by decisional rules that curtail the scope for the development of EU immigration and asylum policy. Moreover, in a negotiating environment based upon unanimity between member states the more reluctant member states can have a decisive effect on the range of possible policy outcomes. Consequently, even if a majority of member states favoured deeper integration and empowerment of EU institutions that could open EU processes to democratic accountability and judicial oversight, the more reluctant member states – such as Denmark and Britain – have sought to block this. Also, it is important to note that the pro-migrant non-governmental organisations (NGOs) that are analysed in chapters 6 and 7 usually call for more, not less policy integration. They tend not to see European integration as the final stage in the process of building the European fortress. Rather, they often see supranational integration with associated empowerment of the European Court of Justice (ECJ), Commission and European Parliament (EP) as a corrective to lowest common denominator restrictive policies made in the Council of Ministers. The problem, therefore, may not be so much that EU member states have developed the structures that they desired for EU-level immigration and asylum policies, but that they have acquired the immigration and asylum policies that a series of inter-governmental compromises have delivered to them. These reflect a clear preference for co-operation on restrictive immigration policies combined with a marked sensitivity and reluctance regarding the possible transfer of competencies to supranational level. A key point is that when negotiations depend on unanimity, then the preferences of a small number of member states can have a decisive effect on the range of possible policy outcomes. This has been characterised as a problem of 'positive integration' that requires unanimity between member states for the development of new EU structures (Scharpf, 1996).

Chapters 2–5 survey the development of the treaty framework for free movement, immigration and asylum. Chapter 2 pays close attention to the development of intra-EU migration policy founded on free movement for EU citizens moving, in the main, for purposes of work. It is vital to study intra-EU migration policy and to identify its origins within the market-making dynamics and economic objectives that have been central to European integration. Economic interdependence and its free movement consequences have also impelled immigration and asylum co-operation and integration. Arguments for expanded rights for TCNs and the development of anti-discrimination legislation that encompasses action against racism and discrimination (analysed in chapters 6 and 7) tend to derive their force from the single market's legal resources and the principle of equal treatment therein, rather than from universalised discourses of personhood. Furthermore, there is a clear disjunction within the single market's legal framework between citizens of the EU, who are entitled to move freely, and TCNs, who are not. The possession of the nationality of a member state underpins this disjunction, as well as the distinction in Community law between EU citizens and TCNs. European integration and its provisions for free movement and EU citizenship have actually affirmed the importance of prior possession of the nationality of a member state.

Chapters 3–5 pay particular attention to the resurgence of integration since the SEA and its effects on immigration and asylum policy co-operation. The plan for the single market, which was the SEA's centrepiece, drew immigration and asylum closer to European integration and blurred the distinction between areas of 'low politics', where interdependence between states is more clearly evident, and 'high politics', which impinges more directly on state sovereignty (Hoffmann, 1966). The economic inter-dependence that underpinned single market liberalisation entailed the dismantling of internal frontier controls between member states. Inevitably, this meant that European integration ran up against issues closely related to national sovereignty such as external frontier control and internal security measures. The 'low politics' of free movement impelled co-operation and integration on the 'high politics' of immigration and asylum.

The characteristics of an emergent EU immigration policy in the post-Maastricht period (i.e. since 1993) are sketched in chapters 4 and 5. In chapter 5, policy development is represented diagrammatically by four concentric circles that illustrate the movement of restrictive external frontier policies outwards from the inner core of EU member states to member states on the edge of the single market, such as southern European countries. Within this inner core, an internal security dimension is being developed. As movement away from this inner core occurs, there are grounds for supposing that the capacity to control immigration may actually diminish, while there may also be less developed legal, social and political frameworks for protection of migrants' rights. Many of the countries within which problems of immigration have become increasingly salient are also countries with little experience of immigration (they were countries of emigration). These countries – such as those of southern, central and eastern Europe – are on a steep policy learning curve and are being rapidly incorporated within the control dimensions of European immigration policy. The removal of internal frontiers between member states shifts responsibility for immigration control from an inner circle of member states to member states on the edge of the single market and to aspiring EU member states that are locked into pre-accession agreements with free movement, immigration and asylum implications. These neighbouring countries have been incorporated within the restrictive policy framework as what could be likened to a buffer zone with a complex web of bilateral and multilateral agreements and intergovernmental processes of co-operation (such as the Budapest process) that regulate construction of this buffer zone.

What effect do these patterns of co-operation and integration have on migrant 'inclusion' as measured by participation, democratic control, judicial oversight and incorporation within the EU's social policy provisions? Can pro-migrant political mobilisations be identified that seek to reshape the parameters of EU immigration and asylum policy and reduce the margin of autonomy for development of restrictive policies largely free from democratic and judicial oversight that the member states have built? If so, what contributes to the possibilities for success or failure of these mobilisations? This changed perspective involves a shift away from migrants as 'objects' of policy – as a 'policy problem' to be solved or managed by member states and EU institutions. Instead, it implies recognition of migrants and their descendants (as well as those who seek to represent their interests) as potential political actors with some ability to shape the institutionalisation of an EU policy context that determines their own chances for inclusion. The initial prognosis – structured by the 'democratic deficit' and the restrictive direction of immigration and asylum policy – is gloomy, but, as is shown, patterns of political activity have developed at sub-national, national and supranational level that direct their attention towards the EU. The key point is that patterns of interest representation are structured by the institutional context established for aspects of migration policy. This policy context is remote and detached from the day to day concerns of migrants living in EU member states, where 'inclusion' tends to have a greater sub-national and national resonance, rather than a supranational dimension. Despite this, there is a developing migration-related issue agenda at EU level, as well as groups that seek to articulate a pro-migrant agenda. It is important to explore the specificities, strategies, calculations and motivations of pro-migrant groups. These groups are actually often sponsored by EU institutions (i.e. the institutions they seek to influence), leading to close relations between lobbyists and the lobbied. The Commission has its own motivations in this respect because it seeks legitimacy as a political actor in the game of European integration and an expanded role for itself where opportunities for integration present themselves. The emphasis is placed on élite, supranational patterns of interest co-option that create scope for the development of a migrants' interest agenda that is structured by the institutional configuration of the EU policy context (including the construction of an immigration *problematique*). This context provides opportunities as well as placing significant constraints upon political action.

Chapter 7 takes this discussion of pro-migrant mobilisations a step further by exploring the EU's social dimension and the rather grand rhetoric that has become associated with the quest for 'social inclusion'. The chapter's frame for analysis of the EU-level interaction between migration and welfare is, however, delimited to a rather more specific consideration of the arguments for expanded rights for TCNs for free movement and thence to the transferable social entitlements that are associated with free movement. The arguments of pro-migrant lobby groups for expanded rights for TCNs in the EU's social dimension stem from the principle of equal treatment in the single market. Pro-migrant groups argue for social inclusion, but the chances for inclusion are mediated by an institutional context established for EU social policy and the emphasis therein on possession of the nationality of a member state before EU-level rights can be accessed. Supranationalism has created rights that traverse borders for EU citizens, but has also reaffirmed the importance of possession of the nationality of a member state and inhibited scope for the development of postnational forms of membership that are inclusive of TCNs.

The final two chapters complement the preceding chapters by broadening the focus, moving beyond the control dimension of immigration policy and enquiring how control policies impact upon migrant inclusion within the spheres of EU responsibility. The stark fact is that despite the rhetoric of 'inclusion' there are over eleven million TCNs who are largely excluded from formal EU provisions. These people find it more difficult to move freely between member states and the EU has not put in place anti-discrimination laws that prohibit racist and xenophobic discrimination against migrants and their descendants (either for those who are citizens of a member state who exercise their rights of free movement or for TCNs). These are pressing issues and are also ones for which the member states have been reluctant to seek supranational solutions because of policy sensitivities closely associated with the exercise of national sovereignty and the bundle of concerns that comprise the immigration issue in contemporary Europe. Chapter 1 pays particular attention to the relation between trends in national immigration policy and politics and the obstacle-strewn path towards deeper European integration.

A note on terminology

Analyses of the EU can often present the reader with a baffling array of terminology. The reason for this is that what we now know as the EU has also been known at various junctures as the European Economic Community (EEC), European Community (EC) and common market. All these terms possessed real meaning at particular points in the history of European integration and all will be used in this book where appropriate. Essentially, this means that before 1993 when the (Maastricht) Treaty on European Union was ratified, I will refer to the EC and post-1993 to the EU. That said, even though the Maastricht Treaty created the European Union, its pillared structure meant that supranational Community (rather than Union) law retained its relevance for core, supranationalised aspects of EU policy such as free movement, but not for immigration and asylum, which were part of the Union but not supranationalised.

'Migrants' is another potentially confusing term. Categorisation can be invidious and bundles together supposed 'migrant' or 'minority' interests that are far from homogeneous but acquire meaning as a consequence of processes of categorisation. That said, a broad distinction can be made between those migrants and their descendants who have acquired the nationality of a member state – and thus become EU citizens – and those categorised as TCNs. The latter do not possess the nationality of a member state and are not usually entitled to benefit from the rights created by European integration. In 1994, out of a total EU population of 370,414,200, there were 11,679,800 TCNs (3.15 per cent) (Eurostat, 1997). These eleven and a half million people could be classed as the EU's 'sixteenth member state', but this would be an inappropriate analogy because they are not usually entitled to the rights of EU citizens, such as to move freely between the member states.

In addition to the TCN population, there are those people of migrant origin living in member states who do have the nationality of the member state in which they reside. In Britain, for instance, the 1991 census revealed the 'ethnic minority' population (whose origins tend to be in south Asia and the Caribbean) to be 5.5 per cent of the total. Because most of these people are British citizens they are also automatically EU citizens, but the EU does not possess legislation against racist discrimination that may be encountered by citizens of immigrant and ethnic minority origin when exercising their rights as EU citizens.

Despite (or perhaps because of) these broad-brush characterisations, it is important to remember the diversity of the migrant-origin population in EU member states and probe the meanings of categories that can provide simple labels for what are actually far more complex social and political realities.

Notes

1   This racial dimension incorporates discrimination based on phenotypical characteristics such as skin colour and, also, the 'new' racism whereby cultural essentialism is used to impute irreconcilability between majority populations (assumed to be culturally homogeneous) and immigrant-origin groups distinguished by aspects of their culture, such as religion.
2   I am grateful to Marco Martiniello for drawing this analogy to my attention.

1

European integration and reconfigured immigration politics

Introduction

This chapter focuses on immigration control and the chances for inclusion of settled migrants and their descendants residing in EU member states and addresses ways in which the EU now impinges on these debates. It puts in place a framework for analysing assumption by the EU of responsibility for aspects of migration policy that used to be determined at national level and for analysing the effects of this assumption of responsibility on European migration politics. By addressing in specific terms the impact of European integration we are better placed to explore the implications of EU developments for national-level models of migratory and post-migratory politics that have heretofore been regarded as paradigmatic and closely associated with national sovereignty. National policy frameworks are not cast in stone. They are challenged internally – a multicultural challenge – and externally – a supranational challenge. The extent of the supranational challenge, which is this book's focus, is closely linked to the distinct sources of legal, political, institutional and social power associated with European integration. At a basic level, the EU's core objective of freer movement for people, services, goods and capital within the single market questions borders, frontiers, national sovereignty, membership and identity, all of which have heretofore been widely construed as delimited by the boundaries of nation states. This cannot be the case in an integrating Europe. Freer movement within the EU's single market means that the ability of EU member states to determine who can and who cannot enter their territory is diminished. The creation of EU citizenship means that nationals of member states acquire rights in all other member states. European integration extends legal rights to EU citizens. But extra-EU migration (immigration and asylum policy) has not been subject to similar supranational legal and political developments. EU immigration and asylum co-operation has allowed member states to slip political and judicial constraints, enhance the autonomy in the *domain réservé* of national executive authorities and

13

their agents of external frontier and population control, and, thereby, seemingly reinforce national sovereignty. A key issue for the EU will be the extent to which immigration and asylum policy becomes subject to similar processes of institutional and legal development at EU level that have characterised the free movement framework. If this were to happen, then European immigration politics would truly have been reshaped.

This chapter's intention is to demonstrate that specificity is required when discussing the effects and implications of EU migration policy integration and co-operation. The EU is not replacing its member states and becoming a new nation state that subsumes them, and nor is it some colossus poised to intervene in all aspects of European migration politics. It does not have this capacity and, indeed, given its distance in both literal and figurative terms from most day-to-day issues of migrant inclusion, it should not have this responsibility. The EU does, though, have distinct functions backed by laws possessed of direct effect in the member states for promoting freer movement within the single market. As it stands, this free movement framework largely excludes over eleven million TCNs. Moreover, the EU currently makes no provision for action against discrimination by race or ethnicity. Free movement, anti-discrimination and fair and just asylum procedures constitute the key components of a 'migrant inclusion' agenda at EU level. It is in these areas that the EU has and is acquiring capacity to act. If the EU is to develop its social and political role further, then arguments for such an expanded role are likely to derive their force from their relation to core market-making objectives that configure the legal, political and institutional context. The EU is not a blank canvas onto which we can sketch our normative visions of an integrated or inclusive Europe wherein social and political spaces have been created for migrants and their descendants. There is a need to be specific about the EU's capacity to act, because specificity leaves us better placed to be realistic about opportunities, constraints and the range of possible policy outcomes with respect to the control and inclusion dimensions of migration policy.

The chapter begins by providing an overview of key issues in contemporary European immigration and asylum policy. It then develops an institutionalist perspective on European integration that recognises the key role of the member states in the development of EU migration policy competencies, while also allowing for distinct legal, political and social effects to arise as a consequence of policy institutionalisation at EU level. The extent and effects of institutionalisation are open questions. There are also significant intergovernmental impediments to the development of a supranational EU immigration and asylum policy role that could dramatically reshape the control and inclusion dimensions of migration policy in contemporary Europe.

It is the control dimensions of migration policy that receive by far the most attention. EU member states often claim to be able to control immigration, but a key implication of European integration is that their ability to control movement of people has diminished because EU citizens can move freely within the Union. Simultaneously, there has been a determined effort by EU member states to police the new external frontiers of the single market and the increasingly frontier-free space within. European integration and the emergence of laws, institutions and policies at EU level that deal with aspects of migration policy constitute the 'Europeanisation' of aspects of migration policy and politics. Europeanisation implies the establishment of supranational authority (laws, rules, institutions and new patterns of political activity) which EU member states have helped establish but which affect policy management in member states. The effect is that the national and European levels become entwined. Debates at EU level cannot be separated from discussion of developments at national level. The governments of EU member states are no longer the sole point of reference for a discussion of contemporary European immigration and asylum policy and politics. State power is something that needs to be explained rather than being identified as the sole cause of supranational and transnational developments. This questioning of state-centric rationalism is not equivalent to a claim that member states have been denuded of power and authority, not least because the member states meeting in the Council of Ministers remain the key decision-makers. At the same time, EU developments point to an emergent EU policy context that possesses legal, political and institutional dynamics with some capacity to shape policy outcomes, particularly for free movement. Moreover, contemporary European migration policy and politics are characterised by a proliferation of actors and the diffusion of capacity to act across levels of government and through market mechanisms (Guiraudon, 1999).

The guests who stayed

The creation of so-called 'fortress Europe' looms large over discussion of immigration and asylum policy and politics and is central to a discussion of EU responsibilities for both the control of migration and the chances for inclusion of settled migrants and their descendants. Yet given the hundreds of thousands of people who cross the borders of EU member states every year, it seems a strange fortress. The ramparts of the supposed fortress rest on a combination of tightly restrictive immigration policies and the social and political exclusion of settled migrants and their descendants. The notion of fortress Europe as a zone of exclusion also brings with it an emphasis on a new and distinct European dimension to immigration policy and politics. The Europeanised fortress reflects, refracts and even intensifies national policies of restriction and exclusion, or so the argument goes. Yet despite the emphasis on restriction associated with the dark vision of the European fortress, European integration has also brought with it liberalisation, freer movement and the transnational-isation of certain rights and entitlements, supported by an autonomous supranational legal and political system at EU level with its own court. This gives some grounds for supposing that the capacity of EU member states to control immigration – to build fortress Europe – is over-stated. Further grounds for scepticism become evident when it is noted that restrictive immigration policies targeted at labour migration since the early 1970s did not lead to the cessation of migration, because family reunification and, later, asylum-seeking continued. A strong discursive commitment to immigration control has been made by national govern-ments. The notion of 'fortress Europe' has become associated more with a politics of symbols – of national and cultural identities and 'ways of life' that are supposedly threatened by immigration and are to be 'protected' – and less with state capacity to control immigration (or match the rhetoric of control with the reality of restriction). This is not the same as saying that immigration policies serve only symbolic purposes, because the effects of these policies can be only too real for those deemed to constitute a 'threat' who seek to enter EU member states. Rather, it is to show that immigration policies are configured by tensions between control and expansion and between inclusion and exclusion. The EU constitutes a new supranational institutional terrain upon which aspects of these tensions will be articulated because of the creation of a European single market and removal of frontiers between member states. The EU policy context is not autonomous and detached from national policy contexts. Percep-tions of the immigration *problematique* at EU level bear strong relation to national policy frameworks that emphasise control and security dimen-sions; but the EU cannot be analysed wholly in such terms. There is something new about the ways in which European integration affects the politics of immigration, although this newness bears strong relation to patterns of immigration policy in EU member states.

If we want to know why the EU has acquired immigration and asylum responsibilities then we have to pay attention to the core market-making dynamics underpinning European integration. Immigration and asylum became increasingly salient issues across the EU in the 1990s. They had been drawn increasingly closer to the mainstream of EU activities with the SEA (1986), the Maastricht Treaty (1992) and the Amsterdam Treaty (1997). Before then, the EU had been highly active in pursuit of free movement for the nationals of member states (intra-EU migration – see chapter 2), but immigration and asylum (extra-EU migration) were viewed as largely being matters for member states. Diverse national patterns of immigration politics bear strong relation to traditions of citizenship and nationhood and render problematic an EU-level response to immigration control and migrant inclusion that necessarily impinges upon questions of membership and identity, regarded as closely linked to national sovereignty (Brubaker, 1992). Yet, from the mid-1980s onwards, it became apparent that a hard and fast distinction between national and supranational was unsustainable. Free movement has been central to the market-making purposes of the common and single markets, but has become connected with immigration and asylum and elicited an EU policy response with a strong security emphasis both at the external frontiers and within the European space created by the single market.

This EU response is connected with a more general salience of immigration issues in the late twentieth century. Five general tendencies in migration at the end of the twentieth century have contributed to this (Castles and Miller, 1998: 8–9). First, the *globalisation* of migration increased the numbers of countries affected. For example, former countries of emigration in Europe, such as Italy, Greece, Portugal and Spain, became countries of immigration (Baganha, 1997). The end of the Cold War and the likelihood of EU membership for central and eastern European countries raised the salience of immigration and asylum policies in EU member states, particularly in Germany. Second, an *acceleration* of migration was associated with movement by increased numbers of people, with attendant policy implications and particular pressure on the frontiers of the EU's southern member states and on those of prospective members in central and eastern Europe. Third, the *differentiation* of migration resulted from the diverse motives for movement, such as highly skilled labour migration (often encouraged – see Salt, 1992), family reunification (which liberal states have been obliged to accept because of national laws and international legal standards) and asylum-seeking (which, although influenced by international legal standards, has prompted tighter criteria for judgement of asylum applications). Fourth, the *feminisation* of migration associated with family reunification stands in contrast to the male-dominated labour migration that sustained 'guest worker' recruitment in many European countries. Fifth, the *politicisation* of migration at national and international level has highlighted the salience of migration issues and the kinds of interdependence it provokes.

Labour migration made an important contribution to western European economic reconstruction and prosperity and led to significant social changes in countries of immigration – characterised as a multi-cultural challenge to the nation state (Joppke, 1996). Yet, even though both immigration and European integration were central to the post-war reconstruction of the west European nation state, it is European integration that tends to get the credit – the 'European rescue of the nation state', as Milward (1992) put it. The substantial input of migrant workers into the establishment of peace and prosperity is part of Europe's hidden history that has actually been as effectively captured in works of fiction and biography by and about migrants/migration than it has by more mainstream analyses of west European politics (King *et al.*, 1995).

The large-scale movement of people in the immediate post-war period resulted from the devastation wrought upon the European state system by the Second World War. The ensuing vast displacement and resettlement of the population were combined with the efforts of west European countries to restore their economies. One consequence was that labour market exigencies in developed capitalist economies of north-western Europe – linked initially with economic reconstruction and then with economic boom – prompted a demand for workers beyond the capacities of national labour markets (Kindleberger, 1967). Recruitment of migrant workers was part of the answer. Workers moved both within and from outside Europe (Castles and Kosack, 1973). Intra-European migrations saw migrant workers move from southern European countries, particularly Portugal, Italy, Spain, Turkey and Yugoslavia, to north-west European countries, especially Belgium, France, Germany, Luxembourg and Switzerland.

Intra-European migrations were supplemented by extra-European migrations, particularly from former colonies. Colonial connections played an important part in structuring migration. It was no coincidence that most migrants from the Maghreb moved to France; that people from India, Pakistan, Bangladesh and former British colonies in the Caribbean moved to Britain (Holmes, 1988; Layton-Henry, 1992; Saggar, 1992); and that people from Surinam and Indonesia migrated to the Netherlands (Entzinger, 1985). Moreover, many who moved from former colonies did so as citizens of the country to which they were moving. For instance, the 1948 British Nationality Act allowed citizens of the British Empire to move to the 'mother country', or at least it did until 1962, when the first of a series of restrictive immigration laws was introduced (Katznelson, 1973). When they came as citizens, migrants and their descendants had the same legal, political and social rights as other citizens, although extension of rights need not guarantee effective utilisation. All citizens are equal in terms of formal access to rights but, as experiences across Europe demonstrate, when it comes to exercising rights then, to paraphrase George Orwell, some citizens are more equal than others (see Layton-Henry, 1990).

Not all European countries had empires from which they could draw labour. Even for some of those that did, colonial links were supplemented by formal recruitment agreements. France's long-standing concerns about the demographic and economic implications of low levels of population growth led to an active recruitment policy in the post-war period (Noiriel, 1988; Weil, 1991; Hargreaves, 1995). France negotiated recruitment agreements with sixteen European and non-European countries. Germany did not have recent colonial connections that could be exploited for labour market purposes so, when labour shortages became a problem in the late 1950s and early 1960s, recruitment agreements with Italy (1955), Spain and Greece (1960), Turkey (1961, 1964), Morocco (1963), Portugal (1964), Tunisia (1965) and Yugoslavia (1968) were concluded. In addition to France and Germany, three other EU member states had eleven recruitment agreements between them: Belgium had four, Luxembourg two and the Netherlands five.

Many migrant workers who moved to Europe were labelled as 'guests', which assumed return to their countries of origin when labour market conditions changed. Immigrant workers were wrongly perceived as a relatively malleable factor of production and the 'rotation' of workers was envisaged, whereby some workers would return to their country of origin after a period working abroad and be replaced by new immigrant workers. Rotation would militate against permanent settlement and circumvent difficult questions about migrant integration into host societies, or so it was thought. The clearest embodiment of this assumption of temporariness was evident in the West German *Gästarbeiter* (guest worker) recruitment scheme. Article 2(1) of the 1965 West German Aliens Law stated that: 'A residence permit may be issued if the presence of the foreigner does not impair the interests of the Federal Republic of Germany'. This legislation linked the presence of migrant workers in West Germany with the interests of the economy. The legislation also introduced a principle of arbitrariness, whereby foreigners had a more precarious status and a vulnerability to techniques designed to encourage them to leave, such as the arbitrary denial of work permits.

But what could countries of immigration do if the 'guests' decided to stay? Switzerland deported unwanted foreign workers (Hoffmann-Nowotny, 1985), but other European countries of immigration tended not to employ draconian measures that would evoke memories of wartime deportations and human rights abuses. Hollifield (1992) argued that it is on this point that economistic approaches to the analysis of immigration slip up, because they neglect the importance of politics, or what he characterises as the impact of 'rights-based politics' rooted in the 'embedded liberalism' of the post-war order (*pace* Ruggie, 1982; Gilpin, 1987). The forced return of migrant workers to their countries of origin would infringe national laws and international standards protecting human rights. This national and international legal framework meant that it was difficult to halt family reunification, although it could certainly be made more difficult. As later chapters demonstrate, this perspective on the importance of liberal politics is severely tested by developments at EU level that distance immigration policy-making from either democratic oversight or judicial control. This is a theme to which we return; it is sufficient to note here that, as currently constituted, EU policy divorces internationalised market relations and ensuing attempts at population control from popular scrutiny and oversight (trends characterised as the 'new constitutionalism' by Gill, 1992).

Restrictions on primary labour migration from the early 1970s onwards did not mean that immigration ended, because 'secondary' migration by families continued apace. Migrant workers and their families began to build new lives for themselves in Europe: they bought houses, their children attended schools, opened businesses and the like. In short, migrants and their descendants became part of the social and cultural fabric of modern western Europe. Migrants and their descendants also of course paid taxes and became entitled to social benefits acquired as a result of legal residence. They were, however, usually denied the right to participate in the political process if they were not citizens of the country in which they resided. Yet, despite facing social, economic and political disadvantages in their new countries, many migrants were still afforded a standard of living and economic and political stability that did not exist in their countries of origin. The result was that the 'guests had come to stay' and Europe's 'new ethnic minorities' were created (Castles *et al.*, 1984; Rogers, 1985). The 'old' ethnic minorities are the indigenous or national minorities such as the Scots, Catalans and Bretons. The 'new' ethnic minorities are post-war migrants and their descendants. Messina (1992) explores the two tiers of 'ethnic conflict' in Europe, although the complex relations between 'old' and 'new' ethnic minorities need not be understood solely in terms of 'conflict' or 'struggle'. Forms of political action that involve mobilisation in relation to ethnic or cultural identities can also be about attempts to seek incorporation into mainstream politics and acquire legitimate status that draw 'identity politics' into the realm of 'normal' liberal politics characterised by bargaining, accommodation and compromise (Koopmans and Statham, 2000).

There is also a distinct temporal dimension located within the shift from an emphasis on immigration control to policies couched in terms of 'immigrant integration'. Immigration policies became increasingly oriented towards restriction of labour migration after the oil price rises of 1973–4. They were supplemented by policies directed towards the social integration of settled migrants. These policies differed substantially across Europe because they were usually refracted through different national traditions of nationhood and citizenship (Hammar, 1985; Brubaker, 1992; Geddes and Favell, 1999). Clearly, permanent settlement undermined economistic approaches to migration analyses couched in terms of 'supply and demand' or 'push–pull' that saw migrants as relatively malleable factors of production. Such approaches failed to account for the various motivations for movement or the diverse social and political implications of settlement (King, 1993; Hammar *et al.*, 1997). A macro-level instance of the deficiency of economistic approaches was their neglect of the importance of prior contact between sending and receiving countries, such as colonial connections. These contacts shaped the development and sustenance of migration networks. At the micro-level, recruitment and settlement patterns did not necessarily correspond with models of comparative economic advantage predicting movement decisions by ego-centred individual economic actors founded upon reasoning about optimal cost–benefit ratios (Portes and Borocz, 1989). Kith and kinship mattered as much if not more than calculations of economic self-interest.

The acceleration of migration

Transport and communications revolutions facilitated increased migration and contributed to discussion of the impact of 'globalisation' (Robertson, 1992). For instance, an 'army of words and images' (Golini *et al.*, 1993: 78) propagated by film, music and television has drawn diverse cultures into closer contact. Martin (1993: 6) wrote of the effects of the communications and transportation revolutions: 'Networks that bring immigrants into industrial countries have been likened to highways: what were once winding paths have become freeways'. Martin goes on to note that the world population increased to around 5.5 billion people during the 1990s and the world workforce to around 2.5 billion. Ninety per cent of this growth occurred in developing countries, which could create jobs for only around half of labour market newcomers. Even though the vast majority of the world's population live and die within a few kilometres of where they were born, simple maths tells us that if only 2 per cent migrate then there would be around an extra two million migrants each year (although only a small percentage of these would want to come to Europe). Writing in the early 1990s, Martin compared Europe with the USA and Japan. US immigration policy was characterised as benign neglect. In Asia immigration was viewed as an economic asset. In Europe the perception of an immigration 'crisis' prompted a crisis response, where restrictive immigration policies have become associated with attempts to reinforce frontiers and counter a globalising 'logic' which implies their diminution (Sassen, 1996). The social construction of the challenges posed by globalisation and immigration to the nation state is a central issue in the politics of both immigration and European integration (Joppke, 1998; Koslowski, 1998; Phizacklea, 1998; Rosamond, 1999). Globalisation and the acceleration of migration have also been seen as contributing to a 'global migration crisis' (Weiner, 1995). Indeed, the politicisation of migration-related issues has frequently prompted connections to be made between migration and various forms of supposed economic, social, political and cultural crisis. Sometimes it can be far from clear what the precise dimensions of these supposed 'crises' actually are. After the end of the Cold War, for instance, there were doom-laden predictions about large-scale east–west migration (Brym, 1991; Heitman, 1991). In fact, east–west migrations did not occur on anywhere near the scale some had predicted, but it was the gloomy predictions rather than actual migration that contributed to the construction of a 'migration crisis'. Codagnone (1998: 55) writes that 'It can be argued that such scenarios have been at least partially instrumental in legitimating and reinforcing the concept of "Fortress Europe" and the restrictive immigration policies derived from this construction'. Similarly, notions of cultural or national identity and the 'threat' posed by immigration by culturally distinct groups viewed through the lens of essentialism underpin much hostility towards migrant-origin communities in western Europe. This has been one factor influencing what has been characterised as 'Islamophobia', whereby Muslim communities en masse can be stigmatised as a subversive fifth column in EU member states (Runnymede Trust, 1997).

By being drawn into the realm of 'identity politics' and the social construction of various immigration-related issues, it becomes clear that the politics of immigration has a significant symbolic dimension. The immigration *problematique* can be configured as much by perception (of 'crisis' or 'threat', derived from what Habermas (1992) calls the 'chauvinism of prosperity') as it can by movement of people itself. Indeed, much contemporary extra-European migration policy is concerned with stopping people moving. National governments may perceive electoral capital in taking a 'tough' stance on immigration, even though they may over-state their ability to control immigration. The failure to attain restrictive targets may, however, actually reinforce the rhetorical commitment to tough and restrictive policies and a ratcheting up of the rhetoric of immigration control while politicians look nervously over their shoulders at the lurking menace of the racist extreme right. Meanwhile, restrictive policies will continue to co-exist with continuation of certain forms of immigration because liberal states can restrict but cannot control migration.

There is a good practical example of the constraints on immigration control. Within the EU, it is the southern member states which have become the focus for much discussion of immigration control (see, for example, Calavita, 1994; Cornelius, 1994; Baganha, 1997; Baldwin-Edwards, 1997). The EU's southern flank has become an external frontier of the single market and Greece, Italy, Portugal and Spain, which are relatively new countries of immigration, having previously been countries of emigration, are subject to migratory pressure at their external frontiers. There are close connections between policies in longer-standing European countries of immigration and those pursued in more recent countries of immigration. 'Older' countries of immigration have sought the imposition of restrictive policies on newer countries of immigration. For instance, Spain's 1985 *ley de extranjería* (foreigner's law) was 'almost entirely the result of external pressure associated with entry into the EC' (Cornelius, 1994: 360). This suggests a process of international policy learning, although the learning curve appears steep, with marked implementation problems (Baldwin-Edwards and Schain, 1994).

Analysing policy implementation problems draws into focus the possibility of developing tightly restrictive policies in southern, central and eastern Europe. Marxist and neo-Marxist approaches emphasise restriction and social exclusion because the changing requirements of capital led to cessation of labour recruitment and prompted a vicious circle of restriction and social exclusion of migrants and their descendants within which racist ideologies played a prominent part. The ultimate endpoint of this vicious circle of restriction and exclusion could even be forced repatriation, some argued (Castles and Kosack, 1973; Castells, 1975; Miles and Phizacklea, 1979; Castles *et al.*, 1984; Bovenkerk *et al.*, 1991; *Race and Class*, 1997).

In contrast, liberal approaches have emphasised expansive immigration policies and the social inclusion of migrants. Freeman (1995) argues that tendencies towards expansive immigration polices are actually a structural characteristic of liberal states because the advocates of expansion, such as business interests, are better organised and have the ear of government, compared with the opponents of immigration, who are not and do not. Hollifield (1992) develops an argument about inclusion by connecting forms of rights-based politics that have developed since the 1960s with the creation of new political and social spaces at national level for migrants, backed by the courts.

The differences between Marxist and liberal analyses of European immigration policy and politics signify the ideological stakes at play and create a dichotomy between restriction and expansion. Yet it is the co-existence of restriction and expansion tendencies that is a central feature of contemporary European immigration politics. And it is practical problems of implementation that go to the heart of the EU's 'management deficit'. The practical difficulties associated with implementing immigration controls imply that theorising on the dynamics of restriction and expansion can neglect some rather more mundane questions. Even though member states may see the EU as an appropriate forum for decisions on free movement and for some aspects of immigration and asylum policy, the EU relies on member states for implementation. If member states cannot match the rhetorical commitment to immigration control with actual implementation, then we should not expect the EU to be any more able to enforce restrictive policies, because we are talking about the self-same national-level implementing agencies. Even if the EU formulated a common immigration and asylum policy (a big 'if', as seen in later chapters) it would face significant constraints on its ability to implement it, because it could not necessarily depend on successful implementation of agreed objectives by implementing agencies. The principal–agent relationship between Union authorities and implementing authorities is characterised by diffuse lines of command, multiple actors and the difficulty of imposing sanctions on non-compliers. Perhaps we should be more surprised when policies are actually implemented than when they are not, or, as Pressman and Wildavsky (1973) subtitled their study of policy implementation in the USA, *How Great Expectations in Washington Are Dashed in Oakland; or Why It's Amazing That Federal Programs Work At All.*

In support of this point, Gunn's (1984: 196–218, quoted in Richardson, 1996b: 280–5) checklist of prerequisites for successful policy implementation illustrates the difficulties faced by the EU when trying to get member states to implement policies. Many of these problems have particular resonance for immigration policies in southern European countries, although their pan-EU dimension makes it difficult to discuss immigration policy and politics in, for instance, southern Europe as though they are wholly distinct from the challenges faced in other member states (Baldwin-Edwards, 1997). Constraints on implementation are as follows:

- External circumstances such as the sheer extent of borders or scale of movement can impose crippling constraints on immigration control. For instance, the cost to the Greek government of policing its external frontiers would be enormous.
- Too much may be expected too soon from countries for which immigration is a relatively new priority and in which administrative and bureaucratic resources are underdeveloped.
- Successful implementation often depends on the availability of additional funding and support from national and sub-national agencies, which may not be forthcoming.
- The policy needs to be based on a valid theory of cause and effect. If a policy is based on a misunderstanding of cause and effect then it is likely to fail. For instance, ever more stringent immigration controls may actually prompt increased illegal immigration, fostered by criminal gangs and encouraged by unscrupulous employers. Southern Europe has experienced a steep increase in the number of undocumented or illegal immigrants. In 1993 there were an estimated 200,000 to 300,000 undocumented immigrants in Spain, even though the 1991 regularisation programme legalised the status of 110,000 people (Cornelius, 1994: 335–44). In the mid-1990s, research by the Organization for Economic Cooperation and Development (OECD) estimated that there were 500,000 undocumented migrant workers in Greece. Greece was an attractive location because even though these undocumented migrant workers were easily exploited, they still earned five or six times more than they would in their country of origin, albeit for less than half the pertaining market rate (SOPEMI,

1995; Fakiolas, 1997: 53–4). Increased restrictions on labour migration may raise the 'cost' of migration but also contribute to increased illegal immigration and a net increase in the sum of human misery.

- The length of the chain between a policy decision being made and being implemented is crucial: the longer the chain then the greater is the scope for objectives to be eroded. Brussels to Brindisi is a long way.
- In areas where implementation has been most successful, the EU has direct powers. When implementing immigration and asylum policy, the EU depends upon national agencies, over which it has little control.
- There needs to be agreement on the objectives of policy. If not, then implementers may adopt a 'tick the boxes' implementation style, where the paperwork is neat and tidy but the policy objectives remain largely unheeded. Moreover, the impetus towards immigration control may not be as strong in southern Europe. Differing labour market factors in southern European countries mean that migrant labour can still be required to an extent that does not apply in the older countries of immigration, of north-western Europe. A Spanish immigration policy-maker remarked that 'Other EC member states talk about the need for a zero immigration policy, but this is completely unrealistic for Spain.... We want them to recognise Spain's objective need for foreign labour. Spaniards won't do certain kinds of jobs, and we need to channel foreign labour to meet those needs' (Cornelius, 1994: 363). Moreover, there may not even be agreement on policy at EU level because of compartmentalisation and a lack of co-ordination. For instance, the Commission has been characterised as a multi-organisation (Cram, 1994), which means that it is not unprecedented for one Commission Directorate to pursue one set of objectives while another Directorate pursues wholly different objectives, with the effect that 'orders of comprehension' can be segmented with separate 'universes of discourse' (Dunsire, 1978: 161).
- Tasks need to be clearly specified and it needs to be clear who has to do what, when and how.
- The absence of perfect communication and co-ordination means that policy objectives can be mangled in the mill of implementation, or ignored. The sheer mass of EU legislation – nearly 150,000 separate laws – means that keeping up with the relevant developments is quite a task in itself.
- If those in authority cannot demand perfect compliance, then implementation is likely to be flawed. Even when sanctions do exist, the 'creative' interpretation of directives can mean imperfect implementation. A fine example of this was the bathing water directive, which attempted to raise water cleanliness standards on beaches in EU

member states. The creative interpretation of this directive by the finest administrative minds in the British Department of the Environment meant that Blackpool, Britain's most popular holiday resort, was excluded from the ambit of the legislation. Italy and Greece admitted that they ignored the results of tests conducted after it had rained. As Richardson (1996b: 287) put it: 'if in doubt – cheat'.

The rhetoric of restriction

If restrictive targets are difficult to attain, then why are they maintained, and commitment to them even intensified? Politicians may want to be seen to build the fortress because when immigration is a salient issue there are likely to be votes in seeking, as former French interior minister Charles Pasqua put it, 'zero immigration' (Hargreaves, 1995: 1). Pasqua later watered down this commitment to 'zero illegal immigration', but the first statement revealed the desire to be seen as 'tough' on immigration and immigrants. Moreover, policy failure – as measured by failure to attain restrictive objectives – need not lead to a re-evaluation of policy, rather it may harden commitments to restriction that are even less likely to be attainable. It is a sad fact that there are few votes in being nice to immigrants.

   A rationale for building the European fortress can also originate from the justification of the activity and budgets of state security agencies. Security can be viewed as:

> a practice, a specific way of framing an issue. Security discourse is characterised by dramatizing an issue as having absolute priority.... 'Security' is thus a self-referential practice, not a question of measuring the seriousness of various threats and deciding when they 'really' are dangerous to some object.... It is self-referential because it is *in* this practice that the issue becomes a security issue. What we can study is the practice that makes this issue into a security issue. (Wæver, 1996: 106–7)

A strong security rationale underpins the development of EU immigration and asylum policy. This arose in part from established patterns of internal security co-operation, such as the Trevi Group of EC interior ministers and officials, set up in 1975. A post-Cold War re-evaluation of the role of security agencies in EU member states called for new threats to justify budgets and activity: illegal immigration was one issue that fitted the bill and could be subsumed within a more general emphasis on internal security in an EU where internal frontiers between member states were being dismantled and the distinction between external and internal security was becoming blurred (Bigo and Leveau, 1992; Anderson and Den Boer, 1994; Monar and Morgan, 1994; Anderson *et al.*, 1996). The 'securitisation' of migration emphasises the links between market relations embodied within the free movement framework and the control of population. Micro-level power relations determine the system of power relations that form the basis of capitalist class relations. Of particular importance are the modern technologies of surveillance, discipline and punishment. Attention is directed towards the practices of security agencies and the implementation and effects of new technologies of population control. From this perspective it makes less sense to analyse the articulation between liberalisation (free movement) and securitisation (involving techniques of population control) and to see security concerns as a knock-on effect of single market integration. Rather, processes of securitisation and the control of population are the foundation stones of liberalisation, with the effect that migration becomes a part of the security issue marked by the intensification of co-operation between security agencies (Foucault, 1979; Huysmans, 1995; Bigo, 1996, 1998). Securitis-ation perspectives are particularly valuable because they 'make politicians, activists and academics aware that they make a choice when they treat something as a security issue' (Wæver, 1996: 108).

The politicisation of asylum

While the focus on security and restriction has been a guiding light for immigration policies across the EU, new factors have come into play since the end of the Cold War that affect perceptions of the immigration 'problem'. These are particularly associated with increased asylum-seeking, the ways it has become conflated with an immigration *problematique*, and then construed as a problem of numbers of 'bogus' asylum-seekers to which the answer is stringent controls. According to the international legal standards and national laws defining the rights of asylum-seekers, they are not immigrants *strictu sensu*, because movement is not voluntary, but rather is motivated by the fear or reality of persecution (Zolberg *et al.*, 1989). The politicisation of asylum and its conflation with immigration has resulted from the perception that many asylum-seekers in EU member states are disguised economic migrants seeking to circumvent stringent controls on labour migration (particularly by unskilled or semi-skilled workers). The EU asylum framework that has developed since the mid-1980s allows member states to slip domestic legal and political constraints by developing European co-operation, within which the scope for political and judicial control is far weaker than at national level and within which the relation to international standards can appear tenuous.

   Asylum-seekers' rights are outlined in the 1951 United Nations (UN) Convention on Stateless Persons (more commonly known as the Geneva Convention) amended by the 1967 New York Protocol. These protect the rights of people fleeing persecution on the grounds of race, religion, nationality or membership of a particular social group or political opinion

(Goodwin-Gill, 1996). After the Second World War, liberal asylum regimes were put in place in western Europe. The Federal Republic of Germany's was particularly liberal. Article 16 of the 1949 Basic Law stated that the 'Politically persecuted enjoy the right of asylum'. What distinguished German provisions and made them particularly expansive was that Article 16 gave individuals the right to seek asylum, rather than recognising the right of the state to grant it (Joppke, 1997).

Across western Europe, asylum was not considered too much of a problem in the 1950s, 1960s and 1970s because the numbers involved were small. Many of those who did seek asylum were lauded as brave escapees fleeing from totalitarian regimes in central and eastern Europe. Attitudes began to change in the 1980s. First, 'jet-age asylum-seeking' (Joppke, 1997: 262) allowed easier access to European countries for those fleeing post-colonial trouble spots in Africa and Asia. Second, the convulsions resulting from the end of the Cold War added an east–west source of displaced persons to more long-standing south–north patterns of movement. This was particularly evident at the height of the 1991–2 civil war in the former Yugoslavia. The number of asylum applications made to EC member states increased dramatically and reached its peak in July 1992 when 80,000 asylum applications were made in that month alone. Since that time, the number of applications has fallen. In the first six months of 1996 they totalled 107,144 (data from Greece, Ireland, Luxembourg and Portugal were not available, but the numbers of asylum applicants in these countries were small). Germany received over half the applications: 57,849 in the first half of 1996, 3 per cent down on the first half of 1995. The next three member states in terms of total applications all recorded much more substantial falls: in Britain it was down 25 per cent to 14,860; the Netherlands saw a 30 per cent fall to 10,052; and numbers of applicants in France fell by 32 per cent to 7,846. In 1996, states in the former Yugoslavia ranked first as sources of applicants, with Turkey in second place and Romania third (Eurostat, 1997). The conflict in Kosovo of 1999 re-ignited the European asylum crisis by displacing around one million people. Not long before the conflict began, ethnic Albanian asylum-seekers in Britain had been demonised as criminals and welfare scroungers (Kaye, 1998). The conflict elicited a swift, albeit temporary, about-turn from newspapers that had previously produced racist coverage of the asylum issue, but also revealed a continued reluctance to host refugees. Indeed, the US base at Guantánamo Bay in Cuba was even suggested as a suitable haven that would certainly discourage asylum claims being lodged either in the USA or in western Europe.

Germany's liberal asylum laws, its geographic location at Europe's crossroads and its prosperity has made it an appealing destination. Germany also had long-standing ties with Yugoslavia, from where it had recruited many guest workers. This meant that many of those fleeing the Yugoslavian civil war had kith or kinship connections with Germany. Indeed, in the early 1990s, Germany received more asylum claims than all other EU member states combined: in 1992 it had 65 per cent (438,000). The policy of distributing asylum-seekers across the country meant that some claimants were placed in towns or cities where hostility towards asylum-seekers spilled over into attacks and even murder (Hockenos, 1993). The decline in the numbers of applicants in Germany and other EU member states indicated a measure of economic, social and political stabilisation in central and eastern Europe; equally importantly, it reflected more stringent procedures in receiving countries. In July 1993 Germany amended its liberal asylum laws. The new law allowed for deportations at Germany's borders when asylum applications were deemed manifestly unfounded. The recognition of 'safe third countries' and 'safe countries of origin' allowed for a fast track system and (more often than not) rejection. These changes brought Germany into line with restrictive asylum policies in other EU member states. At EU level, Germany has pushed for more equal distribution of asylum applications and maintained an interest in what has been called 'burden-sharing', but is now referred to as 'sharing the balance of responsibility' (chapters 4 and 5 contain more information on the German government's stance on EU treaty reform).

Joppke (1997: 263) noted the insidious effects of the conflation of asylum and immigration: 'In all cases, the erosion of the old distinction between political refugee and economic migrant has been the main casualty of the new era of mass asylum-seeking'. 'Economic' asylum-seeking can arise from the Geneva Convention's lack of adaptability to the cases of people whose movement has been caused by economic crisis, environmental calamity or persecution by non-state actors, all of which are forms of persecution not covered by it. Whether 'genuine' or 'bogus', the harsh discourse and practice of anti-immigration politics has been redirected towards the soft target of asylum-seekers. Rather than prompting an expanded definition of asylum-seeking – unlikely given the increased numbers of asylum-seekers – EU member states have mooted the creation of a system of temporary protection for asylum-seekers and refugees to replace what they see as the 'outdated' international legal standards of the Geneva Convention.

Building the European fortress?

The connection between free movement within the single market and its impact on immigration and asylum policy means that 'fortress Europe' is linked with single market liberalisation. Freedom of movement for some begets tighter control over movement by others. Yet, despite the emphasis on restriction, immigration can continue or even increase. This expansion need not arise from the characteristics of liberal polities and inherent tendencies towards expansiveness; rather it may be that 'control' in the strong sense of the term is beyond the capacity of member states to implement. Restriction and expansion can co-exist because EU citizens are free to move between member states, while secondary immigration, asylum-seeking, undocumented migration and the migration of highly skilled workers mean that the cessation of large-scale recruitment of migrant labour has not ended immigration *per se*. National laws, supra-national laws and international standards have all affected the capacity of EU member states to control immigration. This is not to say that national immigration laws are not restrictive – because clearly they are – or that they do not lead to harsh and brutal controls, but that the commitment to restriction need not imply the attainment of restrictive targets. Immigration policies can be restrictive and politicians may volubly expound their intention to 'control' immigration, but immigration continues. The co-existence of restriction and expansion led Cornelius *et al.* (1994) to note convergence between countries of immigration in terms of: first, the adoption of restrictive policies; second, public responses to immigration (generally hostile); and third, measures designed to promote the integration of immigrants and their descendants. But they also noted a 'gap' between restrictive targets and their attainment. This 'gap' is filled by anti-immigration/immigrant sentiment.

As well as telling us something about restriction, the supposed 'fortress' also implies the social exclusion of settled immigrants. This exclusion can arise from racist ideologies, which use phenotypical or cultural differences to consign migrants to subordinate positions in the economic, social and political order (Bovenkerk *et al.*, 1991). Yet a focus on the exclusion of migrants can neglect that these patterns do not apply across all migrant and migrant-origin groups and that differential processes of inclusion and exclusion co-exist. The context for inclusion/exclusion at national level is strongly influenced by differing national historical traditions which have influenced responses to immigration.

At EU level, the chances for exclusion/inclusion will be structured by: the migration policy competencies of the EU that determine its capacity to act; the EU's commitment to 'social inclusion' and the ways in which the EU's institutional context can structure debates about inclusion; and the motivations, calculations and alliance-building strategies of institutional actors and NGOs in the migration policy area at EU level. 'Inclusion' at EU level will be structured by and channelled through the market-making rationale of European integration and associated structures for population control, with some spillover effects for TCNs in the areas of free movement, anti-discrimination and social rights. These have become Europeanised issues. We can also ask, to what extent can migrants and migrants' organisations shape their own chances for inclusion?

Migrants can and do organise and mobilise sub-nationally, nationally and transnationally, but when we probe the particular characteristics of supranational pro-migrant political activity we find a close relation between the institutional context and resultant patterns of political activity. In short, élite patterns of European integration have prompted élite patterns of political activity at EU level. These particular character- istics of the impact of the EU's institutional context on pro-migrant lobbying and social rights are analysed in chapters 6 and 7, where the difficult path from migrants as 'objects' of policy to migrants as political actors is analysed, as well as the role played by élite institutional processes that shape possibilities for inclusion.

The EU policy context

Having sketched salient trends in national-level immigration and asylum politics and policy, we are better placed to ask what difference the EU makes to European migration policy and politics. A basic observation that needs to be restated is that the EU *qua* EU cannot control immigration because it relies on the member states to implement policies. Nor can the EU intervene to seek 'migrant inclusion' in the member states, because its capacity to act in this area is limited. We can, though, examine ways in which EU responsibilities for migration policy create a legal, political and institutional context with the potential to affect national policy responsi- bilities and establish a supranational policy context with some scope to shape policy outcomes. But we need also to be specific. For instance, any analysis of the inclusion of TCNs within the EU's provisions requires clear specification about what it is they are to be included in. The legal, political and social resources underpinning a claim for inclusion derive much of their force from the EU's market-making objectives and the body of case law that has developed to bolster this core purpose. The institutionalisation of market-making backed by processes of consti- tutionalisation that turns treaties between member states into laws that bind those states is a key feature of the EU. It would be wrong-headed to conceive of the EU as a social and political actor without first noting that its social role and political role stem from its economic purposes. Institutional analysis can demonstrate how the development of an EU policy context establishes possibilities for a measure of institutional autonomy derived from the endowment to supranational institutions by treaty of legal and political authority. This has been the case for free movement for EU citizens (not for TCNs). Immigration and asylum, in contrast, have been dealt with mainly through inter- governmental co-operation, which constrains the scope for supranational constitutionalisation (treaties into laws) and institutionalisation (capacity to act).

The distinction at EU level between a supranationalised free movement policy and a largely intergovernmental immigration and asylum policy does not mean that the two are disconnected and can be analysed separately. They are, in fact, inextricably linked, because freer movement for EU citizens has brought with it tighter controls on movement by non-EU citizens, as a result of 'structural' and 'contextual' dynamics (den Boer, 1996). Structurally, single market liberalisation focused attention on the implications for immigration and asylum policy of a Europe without internal frontiers within which people, services, goods and capital could move freely. Contextually, continued migratory pressures raised the salience of immigration-related issues at both national and European level. Although neither of these factors dictates the forms that policy co-operation and integration take, the relation between debates about member state immigration and asylum policy and politics and the development of EU responsibilities requires an approach that is sensitive to 'thick' horizontal national-level policy contexts and the emergence of a thinner vertical dimension at EU level. This vertical dimension is contextualised by the tension between restrictive/expansive and inclusive/exclusive tendencies in national-level immigration policies and politics. The EU's competencies derive from a free movement/immigration and asylum policy nexus resulting from the overlap between liberalisation and securitisation.

This also suggests interdependence and interplay between national and supranational levels, as well as the diffusion of power through market mechanisms. The entwinement of the roles of national and supranational institutions needs to be explored when assessing EU policy development. This allows circumvention of a potential dichotomy arising from the response to the question of whether it is member states or supranational institutions that control the scope and direction of European integration. Underpinning this question is a macro-level international relations dispute about processes of European integration between neo-realist state-centrism and a 'neo-functional' emphasis on the importance of supranational institutions, such as the Commission, as the driving force of European integration. In fact, the question of whether or not it is member states or supranational institutions that are in charge may not be particularly interesting, because the answer is likely to be 'both sometimes' (Putnam, 1988). In key situations – what Peterson (1995) calls the 'history-making decisions' – the member states remain in control. In other situations – what Wincott (1995) calls day-to-day integration – the ceding of competence to supranational level has given the Commission, ECJ and, to a lesser extent, the EP a sufficient margin of autonomy to become significant actors, with the power to shape policy outcomes. This suggests conceptualisation of an EU migration polity reflecting national policy preferences measured along the axes of immigration control (well entrenched at national level), immigrant integration (diverse responses in member states) and market-making (substantial endowment of supranational capacity to act) that contribute to a free movement/immigration *problematique*. The EU context can play a role in shaping debates about immigration control, immigrant inclusion and free movement of migrants because of specific policy competencies ceded by treaty.

Instead of pursuing an intergovernmental versus supranationalism line of analysis, it is more useful to examine the actual and potential effects of the institutionalisation of an EU migration policy context. This suggests that European integration is not just about the member states and that it is certainly not just about the EU. It is far more helpful to take both these levels into account and assess their interdependence and the effects of this interdependence on scope for action. This will necessarily bear strong relation to policy contexts in the member states, but cannot be analysed solely in terms of national policies and inputs without taking account of the potential for supranational dynamics to play some role in determining outputs, particularly in the area of free movement. This perspective on institutionalisation encompasses both the transfer of com-petencies to supranational level and the reshaping of expectations among social and political actors about relevant institutional arenas.

Institutionalisation can be conceptualised as a three-stage process (the 'isation' suffix does suggest a process, although the stop–start history of European integration means that process-oriented accounts need to be treated with caution): first, the *accommodation* at EU level of member states' policy preferences; second, the formal transfer of *competencies* (laws, rules, practices and decision-making capacity); third, *expectations* of social and political actors about the relevant location of decision-making power and authority (Stone-Sweet and Sandholtz, 1998). The task is to be specific about national policy preferences, about processes of preference accommodation, about the subsequent extent of transfers of competence, and about the potential effects on expectations about capacity to act. Intergovernmental and supranational approaches both offer insight into migration policy in an integrating Europe and it seems that no book on European integration is complete without a survey of supranational and intergovernmental approaches to analysis of European integration. The purpose of this section has been to suggest that we should draw from both these approaches to highlight the potential for institutionalisation at EU level of a policy context with some capacity to affect migration policy outcomes in the realm of both free movement and immigration/asylum. The chapter now goes on to outline in more detail an institutionalist perspective on the relation between migration and European integration.

Supranationalism

Supranational accounts of European integration highlight the importance of the establishment of legal, institutional and political competencies at European level that create the potential for supranational leadership. Neo-functional accounts of European integration developed in the 1950s were influenced by the idealistic functionalism of writers such as David Mitrany (1943), who saw the continued existence of nation states as inimical to world peace. From a strongly normative perspective, functionalists argued that many of the responsibilities of nation states should be ceded to international organisations, where they could be managed in such a way as to obviate conflict. Mitrany opposed regional integration in Europe because he thought global co-operation would reduce the potential for conflict. 'Pure' functionalism fell into abeyance soon after the end of the Second World War, when European nation states were quickly restored and became the foundation blocks of the international order.

Instead, the focus of functionalist analysis turned towards what was known as neo-functionalism and its attendant emphasis on incrementalism and 'spillover' effects (Haas, 1964; Lindberg and Scheingold, 1970; Holland, 1993; Schmitter, 1996). Neo-functionalists highlighted the role of the Commission as a driving force of European integration and identified the role of interest groups as central to a refocusing of political activity from national to supranational level (Coombes, 1970; Edwards and Spence, 1994; Ross, 1995; Grant, 1995). The centrality of the Commission to neo-functional spillover derived from its policy proposal and implementation roles. Moreover, as European integration continued apace, driven by the technocratic Commission, interest groups would instigate political spillover by redirecting their activity to supranational level. A process of 'geographical spillover' would also occur as neighbouring countries became drawn into the web of interdependence and eventually joined the EU. The EU did of course expand from six to fifteen members between 1957 and 1995, with the likelihood of further expansion to maybe twenty-five member states by early in the twenty-first century. Neo-functionalist spillover has been construed as implying a degree of inevitability about European integration. Writing from a neo-functionalist perspective, Haas (1960: 376) emphasised the contingent nature of the conceptualisation when writing that that there was no: 'dependable, cumulative process of precedent formation leading to ever more community-oriented organisational behaviour, unless the task assigned to the institutions is inherently expansive, thus capable of overcoming the built-in autonomy of functional contexts and of surviving changes in the policy aims of member states'.

Neo-functionalism drew attention to the potential effects of institution-alisation, as well as the relevance of transnational political mobilisations in the generation of political spillover and the Europeanisation of policy issues. Its weaknesses were that, first, its technocratic emphasis on the role of the Commission led to an overly simplistic distinction between tech-nical and political issues, which appeared to rest on the assumption that technical experts could solve the problems of Europe. This technocratic emphasis is difficult to sustain, because even boffins possess political value preferences that influence judgements on supposedly technical matters. Second, neo-functionalism appeared undone by events. Even in the early days of European integration, the French National Assembly's rejection in August 1954 of plans for an integrated European Defence Community with a European army and a political community dented supranational ambitions. Third, neo-functionalism was criticised for under-estimating resistance from national bureaucracies and being too optimistic about member states' willingness to transfer resources to supranational level. By the mid-1960s, when the French government pursued an 'empty chair' policy in the Council of Ministers, it became clear that national interests could not be written out of the equation and that 'Politics follows its own logic, not simply those of economics and technology' (Wallace, 1990: 7). The 'empty chair' crisis was resolved only by affirm-ation of a country's right to impose a national veto if it felt a 'vital national interest' was imperilled by supranational action. Fourth, the notion of 'spillback' seemed as relevant during the 1970s, when some actually doubted whether the EC had a future, although even during this period of supposed stagnation economic interdependence between member states continued to grow.

On the plus side, neo-functionalism's main strength was its recognition that European integration created scope for the emergence of distinct institutional dynamics at supranational level, resulting from the endow-ment of legal and political capacities. A further strength was to suggest that the redeployment of political activity alongside the transfer of competence could reinforce integration and that pro-integration alliances could develop between key societal interests and supranational institu-tions. These observations become particularly pertinent when we examine the development of co-operation on the control and security dimensions of immigration and asylum and strategies employed by lobby groups seeking to represent migrants' interests in EU decision-making.

Intergovernmentalism

In contrast to the postulated supranational and Commission-led techno-cratic dynamics of neo-functionalism, intergovernmentalists were influenced by realist and neo-realist approaches to analysis of international relations, which emphasised the centrality of states (for example, Morgenthau, 1967). European integration, in the words of a famous book on the subject, actually 'rescued' the nation state and did not herald its demise (Milward, 1992). This means that 'the unique institutional structure of the EC is acceptable to national governments only insofar as it strengthens, rather than weakens, their control over domestic affairs' (Moravcsik, 1993: 507). National governments have their feet on the accelerator and (importantly) the brake, not the Commission, the ECJ and certainly not the EP. European integration has not denuded state sovereignty, it has reinforced it: 'The EEC regime ... has served not only to preserve the nation states, but paradoxically to regenerate them and to adapt them to the world of today ... it has strengthened the nation state's capacity to act at home and abroad' (Hoffmann, 1982). Integration arises from inter-governmental preference convergence because: 'Each government views the EC through the lens of its own policy preferences; EC politics is the continuation of domestic politics by other means' (Moravcsik, 1991: 47; see also Moravcsik, 1998).

The influences from domestic politics to supranational and inter-national politics can be systematic. For instance, states with extensive domestic social welfare programmes tend to have a stronger commitment to foreign aid, while those with weaker programmes are less supportive. As a result, 'features of domestic politics have regular, predictable and widespread effect' (Lumsdaine, 1993: 302). Countries that favour a principle domestically are likely to favour it internationally. An implica-tion of this is that EU member states with restrictive immigration policies are likely to pursue this preference at supranational level. Moreover, the existence of divergent 'immigrant integration' paradigms suggests difficulty melding a common European-level policy. However, decision-making procedures at supranational level associated with the development of positive integration can hinder the translation of national policy preferences into a common European policy. For instance, the member states all have a welfare state in some shape or form, but the idea that a European welfare state will emerge is far-fetched. Rather the market-making impetus underpinning European integration has prompted a limited extension of the EU's role into social policy, but primarily to deal with public goods problems and externalities.

It has been argued that a weakness of intergovernmentalism is that while it provides an approach to the analysis of intergovernmental preference formation, it tells us less about institutional dynamics that can arise as a consequence of intergovernmental deals. Intergovernmentalism has a methodological predisposition to emphasise intergovernmental deals and a consequent tendency to highlight their importance. A basic divergence emerges between intergovernmentalists, who view the EU as a passive structure, and those who emphasise the emergence of supranational patterns of governance. A focus on supranational governance suggests a challenge to intergovernmentalism, which arises from the observation that rather than strengthening nation states, the creation an EU policy context may actually weaken them:

> This is because in the context of multi-level, multi-arena and nested games, *the uncertainty principle* is of enormous importance. States may well be rational actors although state politicians may act rationally in their own interests rather than those of the state, but so are domestic and (increasingly) *transnational* interest groups. If they too act rationally, they will know that the ability of any one state to influence, let alone control, the EU policy process is extremely limited. Hence it is often rational for them to seek supranational solutions, in their own right. The Europeanisation of policy-making power to a supranational level, albeit one in which the states have a very powerful role – has done as much to weaken states as policy actors as to strengthen them. (Richardson, 1996a: 21–2)

This points to the importance of the ways in which powers and authority are now shared within a multi-level or multi-tier European polity and requires that we become specific about the distribution of legal and political power, authority and capacity to act in particular policy sectors.

Multi-level approaches

Multi-level approaches are particularly associated with the establishment of new patterns of governance at EU level (Marks *et al.*, 1996). These governance perspectives typically focus on the establishment of regulatory capacity at EU level for management of private–public relations (Majone, 1996). The EU is characterised as 'a unique system of non-hierarchical, regulatory and deliberative governance' (Hix, 1998: 38). Multi-levelness also imparts a degree of complexity, derived from deliberation and co-operation between various levels of state and non-state officials. Governance perspectives place emphasis on the provision of guidance, steering, control and management (Kooiman, 1993) within a polycentric rather than state-centric system (Jahtenfuchs, 1995: 115). It has been succinctly described as 'governance without government' (Rosenau and Czempiel, 1992) or, because of the complexity and the uncertainty surrounding outcomes, 'the post-modern state' (Caporaso, 1996).

A methodological implication of these perspectives on multi-levelness is that the EU cannot be analysed by relying entirely upon the familiar reference points of comparative political analysis or international relations. The EU is 'not a "re-run" of the processes and policies that earlier made the national state' (Schmitter, 1996: 14). Multi-level perspectives challenge a vocabulary of political analysis that takes the state as its point of reference. Schmitter (1996: 132) notes that:

Our language for discussing politics – especially stable, iterative, 'normal' politics – is indelibly impregnated with assumptions about the state. Whenever we refer to the number, location, authority, status, membership, capacity, identity, type or significance of political units we employ concepts that implicitly refer to a universe featuring sovereign states.

European integration demonstrates that policy and politics need not be played out between nation states. Other levels of government and non-state actors (such as business and lobby groups) involve themselves in social, economic and political processes that acquire transnational dimensions and a supranational resonance with associated legal and political capacity. It has been argued that the EU constitutes an emergent polity and that the techniques of comparative political analysis allow investigation of its characteristics (Hix, 1994). However, developments in migration policy show that, although states remain key actors, the diffusion of power and competence through structures of governance and through market mechanisms creates a proliferation of transnational and non-state actors in immigration control (Guiraudon, 1999). Retention of the nation state and its forms of political organisation as our sole frame of reference are likely to mean that we cannot adequately account for these kinds of developments.

Multi-level perspectives also challenge zero-sum understandings of sovereignty as something that in absolute terms states either possess or do not. By this zero-sum reasoning, European integration denudes state sovereignty because it could not do otherwise. Non zero-sum understandings of sovereignty construe it as the ability of states to achieve desired objectives. By this reasoning, states can integrate and actually enhance their sovereignty. For instance, if a member state decides that it is more likely to achieve restrictive immigration policy targets within an integrated EU policy framework, then it would be prepared to cede elements of national sovereignty to secure this. 'Logically this would lead one to say that a successful national government in a federal European state has more control than a less successful national government in a confederal state' (Marks *et al.*, 1996: 351). Once decisions to integrate have been made, member states lose elements of control because of the empowerment of supranational actors. In essence, multi-level perspectives serve as a useful heuristic device that capture in a self-evidently comprehensible term the changing political contours of contemporary Europe. The downside is that, although it is self-evident what the term implies, it can be rather vague unless accompanied by close specification of its relevance to particular policy sectors. Europeanised policy sectors clearly involve the distribution of authority between sub-national, national and supranational authorities, but unless particular conditions are specified for particular areas of integration, then cause and effect can become muddled and multi-levelness can become tautological. The key issue is to demarcate the allocation of responsibility and demonstrate how policy areas such as migration have been reshaped by the emergence of an EU context. Institutional perspectives help do this.

Institutionalising policy

Although characterised as having become 'almost a fad within social theory during the 1980s' (Grendstad and Selle, 1995: 6; see also March and Olsen, 1989; Steinmo *et al.*, 1992), 'new institutionalism' in its various guises (Hall and Taylor, 1996) has provided powerful insights into European integration (see, for example, Bulmer, 1994; Garrett and Tsebelis, 1996; Pollack, 1996). These institutional approaches derived from broader trends in social science that reacted against behaviouralism's emphasis on the motivations of individual actors, which rendered politics epiphenomenal and political institutions tertiary phenomena. North (1990: 126) defined institutions as 'the rules of the game in a society or, more formally, ... the humanly devised constraints that shape human action'. North's emphasis is on institutions as constraints. This contrasts with other approaches that emphasise the ability of actors to play a part in shaping institutional contexts. In general terms, institutionalism emphasises the importance of examining ways in which 'prior institutional choices limit available future options' (Krasner, 1988: 71) and involves recognition that the capabilities and preferences of individuals cannot be understood except in relation to the wider institutional framework (see also Evans *et al.*, 1985; March and Olsen, 1989; Powell and DiMaggio, 1991; Cammack, 1992).

Institutionalist perspectives have provided valuable insights into immigration politics. For instance, attention has been directed towards 'institutional repertoires' in countries of immigration that structure immigration policy and politics (Soysal, 1994). A key insight is that certain kinds of immigration policies and administrative practices lead to certain kinds of ethnic and immigrant group activity, not the other way around. Consequently, whether or not ethnic or cultural identities play a part in politics is a political question that requires assessment of the institutional context. Institutional contexts are thus conceptualised as independent variables imparting structure to policy development and political activity that occur within socially constructed systemic parameters established by the rules of the political game, the institutional contours of particular policy sectors and a discursive context.

Institutionalism has been criticised for possessing a conservative predisposition by emphasising constraints. To overcome this shortfall, it is important to emphasise reflexivity and the ways in which 'Institutions do not merely reflect the preferences and power of the units constituting them; the institutions themselves shape those preferences and that power.

Institutions are thus *constitutive* of actors, as well as vice versa' (Keohane, 1989: 161, emphasis in original). *Structuration* perspectives emphasise interplay between structure and agency (Giddens, 1979), with emphasis placed not on institutions as 'static edifices' but as processes of structuration within which agency and structure become entwined. 'Structuration implies a process of continuing interaction between agent and structure, in which structures which are generally constraining can also change and be changed in certain conditions' (Cerny, 1990: xi). As a result, the motivations, choices and strategic calculations of political actors are framed by institutional contexts, which shape opportunities for action. Ireland's (1994) analysis of immigrant political mobilisation in France and Switzerland concentrates on political opportunities provided by institutional contexts. Opportunities for immigrant political mobilisation were structured by the immigrants' legal situation, social and political rights, citizenship and naturalisation laws, policies in areas such as education, housing and social assistance, and the roles of trade unions, political parties and religious and humanitarian organisations that acted as 'institutional gatekeepers' controlling access to participation. At EU level, pro-migrant political activity draws from a more limited range of resources that are closely linked to European integration's market-making purposes.

As well as the insight that institutionalist perspectives can provide into the conditions structuring political activity, they also have important implications for analysis of the EU policy process. For instance, 'historical institutionalism' criticises intergovernmental approaches for failing to move beyond the analysis of intergovernmental bargains and for not exploring the consequences of integration that occur once inter-state deals have been agreed and signed. 'Actors may be in a strong initial position, seek to maximise their interests and nevertheless carry out institutional and policy reforms that fundamentally transform their own positions (or those of their successors) in ways that are unanticipated or undesired' (Pierson, 1996: 126). The basic observation is that, in a structured polity, the impact of institutional rules put in place at time t_0 cannot be foreseen, with the effect that earlier decisions can have unintended consequences at time t_1 and so on. The result is that 'gaps' open in member states' control of the EU, leading to a measure of autonomy for supranational actors. These gaps emerge because 'Member states are often pre-occupied with short-term outcomes. Their decisions are certain to produce all sorts of unanticipated consequences. The preferences of member states may also shift, leaving them with formal institutions and highly developed policies that do not fit their current needs' (Pierson, 1996: 147). Once gaps are opened they are difficult to close, because of supranational resistance, institutional barriers to change which mean political institutions are 'sticky', and high sunk costs and barriers to exit, which mean that even sub-optimal decisions become self-reinforcing over time.

The extent of EU-level institutionalisation depends upon the development of a legal context through the EU's treaty basis and subsequent development of this legal context (i.e. through constitutionalisation). It is also necessary to underpin analysis of the formal legal definition of a policy context with consideration of perceptions of policy problems to be solved/managed. The immigration *problematique* is a complex of issues associated with movement of people (and its prevention) and the legal, economic, social and political consequences of entry, residence and settlement. These issues acquire particular characteristics in different countries of immigration as a result of the institutional context through which the phenomena associated with movement of people are refracted and by an EU dimension created by free movement. A broad measure of agreement between EU member states can be detected concerning immigration policies that are designed to restrict entry, but on immigrant integration policies there are markedly diverse national frameworks. Formal, legalistic analysis can neglect the importance of probing the social constructions of immigration-related issues.

The importance of EU-level constitutionalisation and institutionalisation is that they render 'the international system a bit less like anarchy, a bit more like a constitutionalized domestic polity' (Caporaso, 1996: 35). This is a key issue throughout the book, because liberal writers such as Hollifield (1992) emphasise the role of courts and rights-based politics at national level in creating social and political spaces for migrants and their descendants in western Europe. A key task is to explore the prospects for the opening of such social and political spaces at EU level. The whole methodological framework set out in this chapter rests on the centrality of political institutions and the ways in which a Europeanised migration issue agenda – incorporating immigration, asylum, free movement, transferable social entitlements and some (albeit limited) scope for anti-discrimination measures – structures the chances for migrant inclusion. Transferred competencies have also refocused political action stemming from perceptions among social and political actors about shifts in the location of power and authority and altered strategies to influence power-holders. Chapters 6 and 7 explore pro-migrant activity by NGOs operating at EU level and emphasise the particularities of debates about 'inclusion' and their relation to the Europeanised migration policy context. To some extent, the framework of future policy development is still up for grabs. By applying Lowi's (1972) fourfold classification of policy-making patterns, immigration and asylum can be seen as a 'constituent' policy sector, within which the rules of the game remain matters for negotiation but are already fairly well structured by national responses to the control and security dimensions of policy. It is also vital to emphasise that immigration and asylum, as Europeanised issues, are closely linked with intra-EU free movement, which has assumed a regulatory character associated with the entrenchment of legal, institutional and political processes. Arguments for the inclusion of migrants tend to derive their potency from the sources of legal, social and political power created by free movement.

Conclusion

This chapter's approach to the analysis of EU immigration and asylum policy attempts to circumvent some of the binarisms that can pervade analyses of European integration and European immigration politics: restriction versus expansion, inclusion versus exclusion, intergovernmentalism versus supranationalism. The task is to be more specific about the implications of European integration, because aspects of migration policy have acquired an EU resonance where they are refracted through new institutional structures that bear close relation to those in member states, but cannot be wholly analysed in such terms. Close attention was paid to institutionalisation and the sensitivity to both the strong national policy contexts (a horizontal dimension) and nascent multi-levelness at EU level (a vertical context). It is the extent of this non-state empowerment and its effects on the strategies, motivations and choices of political actors that are the core questions addressed in this book. The next chapter explores the development of a supranationalised intra-EU migration policy (free movement). In later chapters this is contrasted with more limited co-operation and integration of extra-EU migration policies (immigration and asylum). This prompts the question of whether or not free movement has created institutional dynamics that offer the prospect for the supranationalisation of immigration and asylum policy, as well as expanded rights for TCNs. As will be seen, the recent history of the slow and cautious movement of immigration and asylum policy competencies from national to EU level shows that European integration is not inevitable with policy sectors located on some kind of trajectory towards supranationalisation. Rather, it is contingent and conjunctural and calls for analysis that explores the social, economic and political factors impinging on key conjunctures at which decisions about the direction and scope of European integration have been made. Only by doing this is it possible to comprehend the possibilities that exist for the 'inclusion' of migrants and their descendants (whether or not they are citizens of member states) within the remit of EU responsibilities for free movement, social entitlements and action against racial and ethnic discrimination. Initially, however, it is important to outline the development of a free movement framework, as is done in the next chapter.

2

The supranationalisation of free movement

Introduction

Free movement is central to the contemporary EU, while immigration and asylum are not. Free movement chimes with the EU's fundamental market-making purposes, but has brought with it immigration and asylum policy co-operation and limited integration. These connections between free movement and immigration and asylum demonstrate the blurred distinction between 'low' and 'high' politics that arises because of the ways pressure can build for integration in policy areas that impinge directly on state sovereignty as a result of integration in areas where national sovereignty issues are less pronounced and where economic interdependence is more clearly evident. Analysis of events since the signing of the Treaty of Rome also indicates that these interdependencies need not dictate the institutional form taken by co-operation and integration on migration policy. We should not blithely assume that the EU is locked into some kind of trajectory of which the endpoint is a common immigration and asylum policy. European integration is more contingent and conjunctural than this teleological federalism allows. Despite the supranationalisation of intra-EU migration policy, there remain substantial obstacles to immigration and asylum policy integration. Free movement for people has, though, created legal and political sources of power and authority that have implications for TCNs, albeit that they are largely excluded from the rights of free movement, as things stand.

Free movement in the common market

The Treaty of Rome's provisions for free movement for people, services, goods and capital were central to the common market that was, in turn, to be the keystone in the arch of European integration and ensuing political integration, or at least that was the plan. The establishment of a legal and political framework guaranteeing free movement also required the establishment of supranational legal and political competencies to ensure that free movement arrangements were given full effect. The corollary of this was that member states' competencies and discretion were limited by the encroachment of supranational authority, which developed to ensure attainment of the EU's market-making goals. Member states could not control immigration absolutely because nationals of other member states moving for purposes of work could move freely (and enforce this right through the courts).

This section of the chapter explores the development of a supranationalised free movement policy framework within which freedom of movement has developed within the common market. It also shows that TCNs are in the main excluded from these provisions, irrespective of the acquisition of 'legal resident' status in a member state. If TCNs are to be included within the free movement provisions of the EU, then the legal, political and institutional framework established for free movement plays an important part in structuring inclusion. Free movement was not originally intended to be a generalised right of free movement open to all people; rather it was to be free movement *for workers* (Commission of the European Communities (CEC), 1977). Free movement was a functional right related to the economic purposes of building the common market. Neither was the freedom to move to be extended to TCNs, irrespective of how long they had lived in a member state. Free movement was to be for nationals of member states moving for purposes of work. Free movement for TCNs was a tangential issue because conditions of entry, residence and movement by TCNs were issues that resided squarely within the domain of competence of the member states. During the late 1950s and 1960s, it was also far from clear that the 'guests' (migrant workers) had actually come to stay. When it became apparent that permanent settlement had occurred, the member states displayed little intention to broaden the free movement framework to include within its scope legally resident TCNs. Immigration and asylum policies were squarely within the domain of national competencies, while the problems associated with melding diverse national policy paradigms highlighted problems of 'positive' integration requiring unanimity among member states. Immigration and asylum were sensitive national issues for which the Treaty did not endow the Community with competence. Member states were prepared to resist Community encroachment into these areas. The result was that TCNs were largely excluded from the provisions of the Treaty. The question of the rights of TCNs still loomed large at the end of the 1990s and was an important part of the issue agenda of pro-migrant NGOs.

Free movement provisions were made in the Treaty of Rome, signed in March 1957, that established the EEC and put in place the legal, institutional and political structures of the EC.[1] The EC's market-making objectives and technocratic origins have led European integration to be perceived as an elite-driven process emphasising efficiency in relation to capital rather than democracy in relation to participation and popular legitimation, despite the oft-quoted ambition to create a 'people's Europe'. A market-making rationale and fundamental economic purposes were central to the EC; the politics, it was thought, would follow once the complex web of interdependence had been woven.

When tracing the origins of free movement, it is actually possible to delve a little further back and observe its origins in the European Coal and Steel Community (ECSC) created by the Treaty of Paris, signed in April 1951. The ECSC was the EC's forerunner and was itself indicative of far broader integrative intentions among the six founding states (Belgium, France, Germany, Italy, the Netherlands and Luxembourg) than its rather narrow focus on the coal and steel industries appeared to imply. Article 69 of the ECSC Treaty provided that member states were obliged to remove restrictions based on nationality upon employment in the coal and steel sectors for workers who were nationals of one of the six member states and held a recognised qualification. The Treaty of Rome built upon the Treaty of Paris' establishment of a common market for coal and steel with labour market provisions by seeking to create a broader customs union.

It is important to be specific about actual provisions while keeping in mind the broader points that we are interested in: first, connections between free movement, immigration and asylum; and second, the ways in which the legal and political components of the institutional context established to manage free movement potentially have effects on the rights of migrants and TCNs in EU member states, with particular relation to free movement and anti discrimination.

The Treaty of Rome's most relevant free movement provisions were contained in Title III, Part II (Articles 48–66). Of particular relevance are the separate chapters dealing with workers (Articles 48–51), the self-employed (52–58) and the provision of services (59–66) (Handoll, 1995; Martin and Guild, 1996; O'Leary, 1996). Article 48(1) stated that free movement for workers was to be attained by the end of a transitional period finishing on 1 January 1970. The functional character of the right of free movement is quite clear in the English language version of the Treaty of Rome establishing the common market. The six signatories referred to 'workers' to indicate that the provisions applied to employees. As Plender (1988: 194) noted, this reference was even clearer in the German and Dutch versions of the Treaty, where the words *Arbeitnehmer* and *werknemer* are used. Three types of economic activity were defined by the Treaty as giving rise to a right of free movement, these being work (Article 48), self-employment (Article 52) and service provision (Article 59). The importance of these Treaty provisions and their centrality to free movement within the common market should not be underestimated because if the common market was to succeed, it was vital that free movement for workers within the common market be facilitated, or at least not unnecessarily impeded. To reinforce this point, the ECJ has established a consistent body of case law enforcing these rights and shown its ability to shape the parameters of supranational economic and political integration, or what international relations scholars call 'the domestification of international politics', which 'describes the process by which that system becomes less anarchic and more rule governed' (Caporaso, 1996: 38).

The legislation introduced in the 1960s to give practical effect to the Treaty of Rome focused on free movement for people who were nationals of member states, their dependants and those covered by agreements between the EC and third countries. This meant that the Treaty covered some TCNs, if they were a dependant of a Community national or covered by provisions of an agreement that the EC was to strike with countries such as Algeria, Morocco, Tunisia and Turkey. The Treaty's provisions did not cover TCNs *qua* TCNs. Possession of the nationality of a member state was the basis for access to Community rights. This raises problems with regard to post-national perspectives on citizenship and membership and ideas about entitlement derived from universal rights of personhood (Soysal, 1994). The specificities of supranational integration illustrate that inclusion beyond the nation state was difficult to secure for non-nationals because of member state sensitivities about immigration and their own nationality laws. This was despite the fact that in Article 48(1) of the Treaty of Rome the words 'nationals of a member state' did not actually appear. Article 69 of the Treaty of Paris had been more specific, because it referred to 'workers who are nationals of Member States'. Plender (1988: 197) noted that it was possible that the drafters of the Treaty of Rome 'wished to leave open, in 1957, the possibility that the Community might develop a common market in labour corresponding with the common market in goods; accompanied by a common external policy towards labour from third countries and freedom of movement within the Community for established immigrants'. The key point is that they have not adopted such a policy, yet.

Irrespective of whether there was serious intent to broaden the provisions to include settled immigrants, the enactment of the free movement provisions made it clear that TCNs were not covered. Instead, attention was directed towards ensuring the effective operation of free movement for nationals of EC member states. Central to this was outlawing discrimination on the grounds of nationality for people moving for purposes of work. Article 48(2) of the Treaty of Rome stated that freedom of movement entailed the abolition of discrimination based on nationality between workers of member states as regards their employment, remuneration and other conditions of work and employment. Non-discrimination on the basis of nationality is the oil in the cog of free movement. Article 6 of the Treaty of Rome stated that any discrimination on the grounds of nationality was prohibited, and that the Council of Ministers could adopt rules designed to prohibit such discrimination. No provisions were made for the prevention of discrimination on grounds of race or ethnic origin until the Amsterdam Treaty in 1997. Even then, such forms of discrimination were not explicitly prohibited.

Member state competencies with respect to intra-EU migration were severely diminished and even where there was scope for prevention of the exercise of the right of free movement there were limitations on the exercise of this discretion. Article 48(3) of the Treaty of Rome outlined some limitations on the right of free movement for workers that were related to public policy, public security or public health. Directive 64/221 had dealt with the grounds for expulsion of EC nationals from another EC member state.[2] Member state discretion was constrained because the ECJ defined very narrowly the circumstances in which these powers could apply. In the *Bouchereau* case the Court ruled that there must exist 'a genuine and sufficiently serious threat to the requirements of public policy affecting one of the fundamental interests of society'.[3] This meant that a member state's discretion to expel non-nationals was limited. The free movement framework empowers individuals who are nationals of an EU member state and gives them recourse to national courts and the ECJ to protect their rights of free movement.

Article 48(3) details other key practicalities. It specifies that workers must be free to accept offers of employment; move freely within the territory of a member state for the purpose of taking up an offer of employment; stay in a member state for the duration of that employment; and remain in the territory of a member state after having been employed there. Aside from the limited public policy, public health and public security concerns that could be used by member states to prevent free movement, the only other significant limitation on free movement for workers was that it did not apply to employment in the public service. Most member states reserve the right to appoint their own nationals to key public service jobs. The Treaty did not actually define 'public service' – this was left to the ECJ (Plender, 1988: 209–13)

A key effect of the free movement framework was that it empowered supranational institutions and created scope for constitutionalisation. Member states' discretion was limited because, for certain categories of people (EC nationals moving for purposes of work), they could no longer determine who could and could not enter their territory. State capacity to control immigration by EC nationals moving for purposes of work was effectively ended. Article 49 gave the Council competence to issue directives or make regulations which set out the measures required to bring about, progressively, free movement for workers. Directives and regulations are the principal instruments of EC law; they possess direct effect and are supreme, which means they over-ride national law.[4] A key feature of a supranational community is that its laws over-ride those of its member states. EC law creates rights and entails obligations guaranteed by laws that exist 'above' member states and which member states are obliged to uphold. Most of the powers established by the Treaty of Rome for free movement were exercised in the form of directives. Directives were used because the powers contained in the Treaty of Rome were fairly substantial and the use of directives gave member states a degree of latitude when implementing them (Hartley, 1978: 7). Directives leave the actual method of implementation to the discretion of national governments and their bureaucracies. Regulations are supposed to be implemented in a uniform manner across member states (although the EU does face problems with implementation, as discussed in chapter 1).

The nuts and bolts

The Council adopted the most important implementing regulation for free movement of workers in 1968. Regulation 1612/68 of 15 October 1968 provided for 'the right to take up activity as an employed person'.[5] Until 1968, member states were still able to control entry, residence and access to employment. After this, they were no longer able to do so because their competence in this area was ceded to supranational level. TCNs were not covered by Regulation 1612/68, because Article 1 made it clear that the provisions applied to nationals of a member state. The possibility was expunged that a more general right of free movement open to all people legally resident in an EC member state could develop. Nationality laws were – and still are – none of the EU's business, as a declaration attached to the Maastricht Treaty attested. This does present some difficulties. For instance, definitions of entitlement to nationality can differ between member states. Germany, for instance, has emphasised 'blood' descent, which led to an expansive notion of German nationality for ethnic Germans that exceeded the borders of what was, when the EC was founded, West Germany. The 1949 *Grundgesetz* (Basic Law) defined a German as 'a person who possesses German citizenship or who has been admitted to the territory of the German Reich as it existed on 31 December 1937 as a refugee or expellee of German stock'. German nationals could be taken to mean those holding German citizenship (the narrow definition) or those falling within the broader definition provided for by the Basic Law, which included people deemed German by nationality law but who did not actually live in the Federal Republic of Germany (a broader definition). In a declaration attached to the Treaty of Rome, the Federal Republic of Germany stated that it preferred the second definition. This meant that free movement for workers within the common market also applied to people in what was East Germany, in parts of Silesia and

Upper Prussia, which were part of Poland and the former Soviet Union, respectively, and to expellees and refugees of German descent. Similarly, the provisions made in the 1948 British Nationality Act prompted an expansive notion of nationality encompassing British passport holders living in countries of the Empire/Commonwealth. This position was changed by the 1981 British Nationality Act, which emphasised acquisition of citizenship by descent (*jus sanguinis*).

After it had been made clear that free movement for workers applied to nationals of a member state, the forty-eight articles of Regulation 1612/68 outlined in detail the rules for nationals of a member state. These covered their right, irrespective of their place of residence, to take up employment within the territory of any other member state. The right to take up employment was to be on the same terms as those afforded to nationals of that member state, that is, the application of the principle of non-discrimination on grounds of nationality. This applied to conditions of employment and work, remuneration, reinstatement and re-employment. Migrant workers who were EC nationals were also given the same social and tax advantages, the same access to training in vocational schools and retraining centres, and the right to equal housing treatment with national workers. If workers were to exercise their right of free movement, then it was also essential that their families could join them, otherwise incentives to move would be diminished. Article 10 of Regulation 1612/68 provided for family reunification. Migrant workers had the right to be joined by their spouse as well as by descendants under the age of twenty-one years who were dependants, as well as by dependant relatives in the ascending line of the worker (parents, grandparents). Member states were also required to 'facilitate the admission' of other members of a worker's family if they were dependant on the worker or living under the same roof.

These details can appear arcane, but their effects are very important because they illustrate the connections between market-making and free movement and the distinct sources of legal, political and social power created at the EU level. If we want to identify a piece of EU legislation that goes right to the heart of questions about border control and national sovereignty, then we need look no further than Directive 360/68 of 15 October 1968.[6] This required that member states abolish restrictions on the movement and residence of their nationals and their families and give workers the right to enter, reside in and leave member states. Upon production of a valid passport or identity card, migrant workers would be issued with a 'residence permit for a national of a Member State of the EEC', which would have five years' duration and be automatically renewable. Article 2 of Directive 360/68 stated that the family of a migrant worker who was not a national of a member state had the same residence, work and welfare rights as the migrant worker on whom they were dependant. This meant that some TCNs could move within the Community, but this was because they were dependants of an EC national. Council Directive 148/73 made similar provisions for self-employed persons.[7]

Social security entitlements were also important within the free movement arrangements, because workers would be reluctant to move between member states if their entitlement to social benefits were jeopardised. Territorial principles rooted in national systems of welfare provision underpinned west European welfare states (Bommes and Geddes, 2000). TCNs did, however, acquire social entitlements as a result of legal residence. It is important to distinguish between territoriality (residence) and nationality as the bases for entitlement. Although they have been nationally based, welfare states in member states have also tended to operate on the basis of territoriality, which means that legal residence and contribution prompt entitlements. However, access to EU-level social entitlements derived from the right of free movement depended on possession of the nationality of a member state. European integration brought with it an element of deterritorialisation for member state nationals moving for purposes of work, while affirming nationality as the basis for access to these entitlements. The effects were that most TCNs could not move freely and, thus, were not entitled to what were otherwise transferable social entitlements. The broader point here, and one to which we will return, is that the treaty framework provides us with a rather specific set of migration-related issues that have become Europeanised in the sense that an institutional and legal context at EU level has developed with the capacity to shape policy. The issues that are Europeanised relate to the market-making fundamentals of European integration, from which TCNs are largely excluded. Arguments about the inclusion of TCNs are similarly structured.

To continue with the nuts and bolts, Article 51 of the Treaty of Rome provided that the Council, acting by unanimity on a proposal from the Commission, could adopt measures for social security provision for migrant workers that were nationals of an EC member state. These powers to adopt measures apply to: first, aggregation of entitlements when acquiring and retaining the right to benefit and calculating the amount of benefit under the laws of the member states; and second, payment of benefit to persons resident in the member states (Handoll, 1995: 21–2). The main implementing regulation was 1408/71, on the application of social security schemes to employed persons, to the self-employed and to members of their families moving within the EC, which also covered stateless persons and refugees. Regulation 574/72 laid down procedures on the application of 1408/71.[8] Both have, as Eichenhofer (1997: 12–13) notes, been the subject of hundreds of ECJ decisions. Certain welfare rights were placed on a 'personal' rather than 'territorial' basis and became portable within the common market. Social entitlements became portable for nationals of EC member states moving to other member states for purposes of work, but TCNs were largely excluded from these provisions.

Other parts of the Treaty of Rome also had free movement implications. Article 127 established the principle of non-discrimination on the basis of nationality in the provision of vocational training. Article 100 gave the EC powers to approximate (i.e. render more compatible) national measures impinging on the functioning of the common market. Article 235 allowed the EC to attain one of its objectives where the Treaty has not provided the necessary powers. The Council must act unanimously on a proposal from the Commission and consult the EP before taking the appropriate measures.

Over time, rights of free movement have been extended to other categories of persons, such as students, pensioners and other economically non-active persons, so long as they would not be dependent on the receiving state and had adequate health insurance. This helps illustrate the point that free movement was not a generalised right; rather it was a right extended to those who fell within one of the categories of people entitled to move freely. The need for further refinement of the free movement framework was made clear by the report of the High Level Panel on free movement of persons, chaired by the French politician Simone Veil. The Commission responded to the report of the High Level Panel with its 1997 action plan for free movement of workers, which sought to improve and adapt the free movement rules. It did this by proposing: that the labour market be made more transparent by, for instance, encouraging cross-border dissemination of information on employment opportunities; that structures for assisting migrant workers to adapt to their new countries be strengthened; that education schemes to improve knowledge among EU citizens of the right to free movement be developed; and that projects to support free movement within the provisions of Article 6 of the European Social Fund be supported (CEC, 1997a).

Agreements with third countries

Some TCNs have acquired rights of free movement as a result of agreements between the EU and third countries (Guild, 1992; Peers, 1996). For instance, the European Economic Area (EEA), created by the Treaty of Oporto in May 1992, extended rights of free movement to nationals of Austria, Finland, Iceland, Norway, Liechtenstein and Sweden. The EEA was seen as a halfway house to EU membership, as indeed it was for Austria, Finland and Sweden, which acceded to the Union in January 1995. Attitudes were rather different in Switzerland, which refused to join even the EEA.

Association Agreements which the EU has developed with third countries such as Turkey, Morocco, Algeria and Tunisia involve reciprocal rights and obligations applying to EU nationals and the nationals of the third country. Guild (1998) shows that a key feature of EC law is its creation of a triangular relationship between individuals, member states and the EU. Although the principle of direct effect was a judicial invention and the empowerment of individuals was not necessarily its main intention, individuals have been empowered within this triangular relationship, while the discretion of member states has been limited. But does this triangular relationship also apply to TCNs? In general terms, it would seem that it does not, because TCNs *qua* TCNs are excluded from EU provisions as they do not possess the nationality of a member state. However, the provisions of Association Agreements between the EU and third countries mean that for some TCNs a more limited triangular relationship with implications for competence and discretion can develop. The basis for this argument is that Agreements with third countries have direct effect and their provisions must be interpreted in accordance with the equivalent principles of the Treaty of Rome. A series of ECJ decisions since 1986 have affected the rights of TCNs covered by these Agreements, although not all the judgements point in the same expansive direction (Alexander, 1992). The provisions of the 1964 Agreement with Turkey have been used as the basis for the case for the creation of a 'Resident's Charter' that would allow permanently settled TCNs to enjoy the same free movement rights as EU citizens (Starting Line Group (SLG), 1998). It has been argued that if this Agreement gives rights to some TCNs (Turks) then it is unfair that not all TCNs benefit (see chapter 7 for more details).

Between 1957 and 1986, the EC entered into Association Agreements with Turkey, Algeria, Morocco and Tunisia. An Agreement with Yugoslavia became effective in 1983, but was revoked for obvious reasons in 1991. Each Agreement established an Association Council, with representation from both the Commission and the Council of Ministers, as well as the relevant governments. The decisions of these Councils are legally binding on all parties. The Agreement with Turkey (supplemented by an additional protocol signed in 1970) includes provisions for workers under the heading of 'Movement of Persons and Services'. In 1980, the EC–Turkey Association Council provided that Turkish workers would benefit from the gradual elimination of employment restrictions, the same social security benefits, free access to the labour market for family members after five years' residence, equal educational, vocational and apprentice-ship opportunities and a prohibition on future restrictions on Turks' access to employment. In the *Demirel* case, the ECJ ruled that Article 12 of the 1964 Agreement and Article 36 of the 1970 protocol covering progressive extension of rights of free movement for Turkish nationals did not have direct effect because they were general programmes, insufficiently precise and unconditional, and not specific plans for action.[9] However, in the *Sevince* case the ECJ decided that provisions made in the Association Council covering the entitlement to free access to the employment of their choice once residence requirements had been met were sufficiently precise to have direct effect[10] (Guild, 1992: 3–11; Handoll, 1995: 323–9).

The *Demirel* case was also interesting because the ECJ ruled that it had no jurisdiction to determine whether national rules on family reunification were compatible with the principles of the European Convention on Human Rights. This meant that Demirel, a Turk resident in Germany, was unable to challenge a national ruling forbidding him from being joined by the rest of his family for a lengthy period. Handoll (1995: 329) argues that 'leaps of judicial imagination' could have prompted more ambitious interpretations of Demirel's rights under the terms of the Association Agreement, but that the ECJ was not prepared to take such bold steps, which 'would be seen as trespassing on sensitive national preserves'. In other areas it did display some boldness. In the *Kus* case, a Turkish worker without a residence permit following his divorce from a German woman was entitled to renew both his residence and work permits because he had legally entered Germany and, upon entry, lawfully obtained residence and work permits. The right to continue employment was, therefore, held to have direct effect.[11] This was described as 'a stunning example' of ECJ policy-making (Ireland, 1995: 252).

Separate Co-operation Agreements were signed with Algeria, Morocco and Tunisia in 1978.[12] All three made provisions for co-operation in the 'Field of Labour'. Workers from any of the three Maghreb states were to be free from discrimination on grounds of nationality regarding their working conditions or remuneration. Workers of Algerian, Moroccan or Tunisian nationality were also to receive social security treatment free from discrimination based on nationality in relation to the nationals of the member state in which they were employed. In the *Kziber* case, the ECJ ruled that the provisions of the Morocco Agreement in respect of social security entitlements had direct effect.[13] A similar decision was made with regard to non-discrimination. It has been argued that as the provisions of each of the Agreements with the three Maghreb countries are virtually identical, the decisions made in relation to Moroccan nationals apply also to nationals from the two other countries (Guild, 1992).

The ECJ has also dealt with what is known as the 'posted worker' problem, where workers from one member state are sent for employment to another member state. Court judgements on this issue and the 1996 Posted Workers Directive have implications for TCNs, although it is the right of establishment that is the key issue and has served as the basis for ECJ rulings. In the 1990 *Rush Portugesa* case, the right to post workers was affirmed by the ECJ. A Portuguese contractor had sent Portuguese workers to France while the transitional arrangements governing Portuguese accession to the EC (which occurred in 1986) were still in place.[14] The French Labour Inspectorate fined the Portuguese employer for not having secured work permits for the Portuguese workers in France. The ECJ used Article 59 of the Treaty of Rome (the right of establishment) to argue that Portuguese enterprises were entitled to equal treatment and the requirement that its workers had work permits was contrary to that right. There were also posted worker implications for TCNs. In the *Vander Elst* case, a workforce of mixed Belgians and Moroccans was sent to France.[15] The French Labour Inspectorate fined the employer because the Moroccan workers were TCNs and did not have French work permits. The ECJ again upheld the right of establishment. A 1997 Commission directive on the posting of workers in the framework of the provision of services included TCNs within its remit.[16] The original proposal had been presented in 1991, but was held up because of a dispute between those countries with contractors sending posted workers, which wanted to maintain what they saw as competitive advantages associated with low labour costs, and those receiving them, which feared 'social dumping'. This has been particularly evident in the German construction industry, where cheap labour from other EU member states, such as Britain and Portugal, undercuts the domestic workforce and draws into stark relief the relation between free movement, migration and welfare in an integrating Europe (Hunger, 2000).

Another key issue for the EU is eastwards enlargement. This has clear free movement implications, but the Association Agreements and other pre-accession agreements signed with central and east European states have sought to restrict the free movement implications in the pre-accession phase while incorporating these aspirant member states within the Union's immigration and asylum policy provisions (Lavenex, 1998b).

Immigration and asylum

The constitutionalisation and institutionalisation of a free movement context has not been accompanied by similar developments for immigration and asylum. While the EC pressed ahead with creation of the free movement framework during the 1960s and 1970s, immigration and asylum policy remained beyond the remit of supranational institutions. There was some intergovernmental co-operation outside of the Treaty of Rome between member states on internal security issues, but little inclination to seek a common policy in response to immigration and asylum, which were mainly matters for national governments. A key factor was, of course, the absence of a substantive legal basis in the Treaty of Rome for immigration and asylum policy, as well as an absence of political will among member states to establish such competencies.

An example of member state opposition to the development of migration policy responsibilities at supranational level occurred when the Council blocked the Commission's 1976 proposal for a directive against clandestine immigration.[17] The EP sniped from the sidelines and argued that the absence of EC competence made it more difficult to ameliorate growing social tensions in member states. As is its wont, the EP made an ambitious call for immigration and asylum responsibilities to be exercised at EC level, combined with policies for immigrant integration and action against racism and xenophobia. What actually did occur was of far less significance. The 1977 Joint Declaration by the EP, Council and the Commission on fundamental rights affirmed respect for the 1950 European Convention on Human Rights, but was a costless declaration with no legislative teeth to deal with substantive issues related to TCNs, or to tackle racism and xenophobia.[18] As with many EU denunciations of racism and xenophobia, the declaration was essentially symbolic and not backed by attribution of competence to act.

There was the possibility that more substantial and wide-ranging migration policy development affecting national immigrant integration policies could arise from a Council Resolution of 1974 establishing the Social Action Programme (SAP).[19] The Council Resolution called for the achievement of equality for EC nationals and TCNs in relation to living and working conditions, wages and economic rights, as well as promoting consultation between the EC and the member states on immigration policies vis-à-vis third countries. The SAP was an attempt to counterbalance the market-based purposes of the EC with activity in the areas of social policies and citizens' rights. In December 1974 the Commission published its action programme, which envisaged a migrants' charter covering equality of treatment in living and working conditions, the granting of civil and political rights, the control of illegal immigration, and co-ordination of immigration policies (Handoll, 1995: 352). The Council preferred a less expansive understanding of the term 'migrant workers' that encouraged (i.e. rather than legislated for) the achievement of equality, consultation on migration policies and co-operation on illegal immigration. When the Commission sought to put the first SAP into effect, it faced Council opposition over proposed legislation to extend social provisions to include TCNs (see chapter 7 for more details).

European citizenship

The EU has been motivated primarily by a market-making imperative, but as Meehan (1993) has shown it is incoherent to suppose that European integration is just about economics. The EU's social and political role does, though, derive largely from its economic purposes. To neglect this is to risk misconstruing the nature of the EU and adopting a perspective within which the EU can solve the problems of Europe by acquiring responsibility for activities and purposes for which it has not been designed and for which it is not necessarily suited.

The development of EU social policy has raised questions for analysis, because the legal, political and social components of the widely used Marshallian framework have acquired an EU resonance as a result of European integration (Marshall, 1964). Debates about citizenship have become Europeanised in the sense that questions about membership, democracy, social inclusion and participation have acquired a European dimension resulting from the dismantling of frontiers between member states and the development of rights for nationals of member states who cross national borders. That said, one risk of utilising a Marshallian perspective is that it could lead us to suppose that we are witnessing a rerun of processes of nation state formation; but the EU does not have powerful agents of socialisation such as its own church, army or schools. It has its single market, its economic and monetary union (EMU) and regulatory competencies. EU institutions have played a prominent role in developing an EU citizenship agenda prompted by an overlap between instrumental and idealistic motivations: more democracy and account-ability would be good for Europe and at the same time be good for supranational institutions because supranational institutions would acquire a greater role. The debate about European citizenship fits nicely within this kind of context whereby the core purposes and social and political effects of European integration are considered, as well as the motivations of EU institutions.

At the Paris summit meeting of the heads of government held in October 1972, the Belgian and Italian governments proposed that local voting rights be extended to EC nationals residing in another member state, but this was rejected. The December 1974 Paris summit meeting of heads of government asked the Commission to prepare reports on the establishment of a passport union and the granting of special rights to citizens of EC member states.[20] The heads of government also asked the Belgian Prime Minister, Léo Tindemans, to prepare a report that would examine the meaning of 'European Union'. The Tindemans report stressed the importance of countering the image of a technocratic Community detached from the concerns of the nationals of member states. Citizen-ship was seen as one way of bringing the Union closer to its people.[21] These rights were not seen as replacing national citizenship; rather they were seen as complementary and creating added value. Tindemans proposed, for instance, that the protection of consumer and environmental rights be a priority. He also called for an attempt to create some form of European solidarity through use of symbols, such as a European flag. The citizen-ship agenda had not exactly moved to centre stage, but substantive and symbolic aspects of the agenda, as discussed in the Tindemans report, began to be taken more seriously. However, it was not until 1992 that the Maastricht Treaty created EU citizenship, and even then it was a limited package.

Another risk in utilising a Marshallian perspective on citizenship is that the sequential progression he postulated that linked legal, political and social rights has broken down in EU member states with respect to immigration. Many migrants received legal and social rights before they acquired political rights. There was discussion of the extension of local voting rights to foreigners and greater involvement of foreigners in local communities. In its 1976 proposal for an Action Programme in Favour of Migrant Workers and their Families, the Commission had called for extension of local suffrage. As a first step, greater involvement for non-EC nationals in the life of local communities was proposed through local consultative councils based on Belgium's well developed system of Consultative Commissions for Immigrants. An EP resolution supported the Commission's proposal for the granting of special rights[22] but, once again, 'member state sensitivities precluded progress' (Ireland, 1995: 240).

In June 1984 the Fontainebleu European Council set up an *ad hoc* committee to examine the creation of a people's Europe.[23] Its proposals with regard to the free movement of people and wider opportunities for employment and residence fed into the Commission's 1985 White Paper on creating the single market (see chapter 3). These concerns with building some kind of people's Europe were clearly directed at the nationals of the member states. This was confirmed in the Commission's 1988 *Communication on a People's Europe* (CEC, 1988a) and a 1988 proposal for a directive on local voting rights for EC nationals in their member state of residence.[24]

The structure of EU citizenship as a complement to rather than a replacement for national citizenship was outlined in a memorandum circulated by the Spanish government that sought a move in status for nationals of member states from 'privileged foreigner' to 'European citizens'.[25] The Maastricht Treaty built on the Spanish government's proposals and included provisions for EU citizenship derived from prior possession of the nationality of a member state. Citizens of the EU were to have the right to move freely (Article 8a(1)), although this freedom would remain associated with people belonging to one of the categories (workers, the self-employed, students, pensioners, etc.) already entitled to such rights. Article 8a(2) allows extension of these categories, but only upon the basis of Council unanimity.

The scope of EU citizenship created by the Maastricht Treaty was circumscribed by practical considerations (Meehan, 1993; O'Keeffe, 1994; Closa, 1995; Wiener, 1997). EU citizenship sprang from the market-making purposes of the common and single markets and was intended to oil the wheels of free movement. If the EU were to become a democratic federation it would need its citizens, but as it stands the EU is not a democracy and its citizenship provisions are not particularly extensive. Promoting EU citizenship is a way of closing the democratic deficit and emphasis has been placed upon the constructive potential of EU citizenship in building some kind of community of Europeans (Howe, 1995; Wiener and Della Sala, 1997). The realisation of a *Gemeinschaft* imparting common European values, beliefs, a shared destiny and ties of solidarity could, however, prompt new forms of exclusion (Kostakopoulou, 1997, 1998).

Maastricht also made it clear that EU citizenship was to be a right derived from prior possession of the nationality of a member state. This has reinforced the importance of member state nationality laws. This could be construed as paradoxical because key citizenship rights, such as social entitlements, are often acquired as a result of legal residence in a member state rather than acquisition of the nationality of that member state (Bommes and Geddes, 2000). In Germany, for instance, restrictive nationality laws have made it difficult for migrants and their descendants to acquire German citizenship, while the labour market and welfare state have served as vehicles for inclusion and renegotiation of the terms of inclusion (Bommes and Halfmann, 1995; Bommes, 1998). Yet, despite inclusion within provisions for social rights at national level, access to entitlement at EU level largely depends on first acquiring the nationality of a member state. Clearly, the form of 'post-national membership' created by European integration is circumscribed by the emphasis on acquisition of nationality for those who are not citizens of a member state. Without the nationality of a member state, the 'freedoms' created by European integration are largely meaningless.

Discussions of EU citizenship prompt invocation of 'inclusion'. It is rather ironic that the creation of EU citizenship reinforced the exclusion of TCNs by affirming the importance of prior acquisition of nationality for access to free movement rights and access to social entitlements that at national level did not depend upon acquisition of nationality. Ironic it may be, but irrational or inexplicable it is not – nationality of a member state has been central to acquisition of rights associated with European integration.

International obligations

Those who stress a post-national dimension that reconfigures the European politics of immigration and claims-making by migrants emphasise the importance of international agreements for migrants and the ways these agreements contribute to post-national forms of membership; these in turn create a universalised discourse of entitlement that renders national citizenship 'inventively irrelevant' (Soysal, 1998: 210–11). As a result, it has been argued, rights traverse borders and claims for membership no longer take nation states as their sole point of reference. Yet free movement in the EU has privileged nationals of member states and offered little substantive entitlement to TCNs. Moreover, claims for inclusion are made in respect of an organisation that constitutes 'a form of regional governance with polity-like features to extend the state and harden the boundary between themselves and the rest of the world' (Wallace, 1996: 16). The exclusion of TCNs and the specificities of regional integration suggest a supranational critique of post-national perspectives.

Have international legal standards offered scope for the protection or advancement of the rights of TCNs within the EU? This question prompts examination of the relationship between EU member states, the free movement framework and international human rights standards that EU member states are pledged to uphold. Arguments for 'postnational membership' (Soysal, 1994) or 'rights across borders' (Jacobsen, 1996) are countered by those who contend that international legal standards were at best 'soft law' and, at worst, irrelevant and that the developments that did occur arose as a result of national legal standards (Joppke, 1997, 1998; Guiraudon, 1997, 1998). Joppke (1997: 261) writes that 'the protection of human rights is a constitutive principle of, not an external imposition on, liberal nation states. The international human rights regime set up after World War Two is, after all, the externalization of principles that liberal states have internally long adhered to'.

After the Second World War, the newly created UN was central to the construction of international human rights standards. Several UN legal instruments have relevance for migrants and TCNs, but there are two important differences between UN legal standards and EC law. First, UN agreements are more expansive in their scope because they do not tend to distinguish between nationals and non-nationals when rights are granted. Second, the highly significant downside is that, even though they can claim moral force of the 'international community', they carry little legal weight as a practical source of redress, because they are neither supreme nor possessed of direct effect in the way that EC law is. Even though the potentially expansive principle of non-differentiation between nationals and non-nationals is a key aspect of instruments such as the Universal Declaration of Human Rights (1948), the International Covenant on Civil and Political Rights (1966) and the International Convention on the Elimination of All Forms of Racial Discrimination (1966), the practical effects on EU member states are minimal. A good example of the lack of impact is the 1990 International Convention on the Protection of the Rights of All Migrant Workers and Members of Their Families, which covers civil, political, economic, social and cultural rights. The aim of the 1990 Convention was to provide a core of human rights for migrant workers that it was hoped would encourage legal immigration and discourage illegal immigration. Hune (1994: 79) argues that 'although there are inherent weaknesses in human rights legislation with regard to the universality of application for both men and women', the 1990 Convention 'advances human rights theory' because it 'obligates States Parties who ratify to extend the application of human rights to a vulnerable group of non-nationals within their own national boundaries and jurisdiction'. It addresses the rights of legal and illegal/undocumented migrants and also deals with rights of family reunification and 'equality of treatment'. Part II of the Convention consists of one article, which outlines the principle of non-discrimination and provides that no distinctions of any kind, such as those based on sex, race or colour, can be adopted by signatories. Bold intentions have little effect when EU member states show little inclination to ratify ambitious international declarations. By mid-1998 the Convention had not even mustered the twenty signatures from States Parties among UN members needed for it to enter into force. In its 1994 *Communication on Immigration and Asylum Policies*, the Commission invited EU member states to sign the 1990 Convention, but by 1998 none had done so (CEC, 1994a: 43). Hune (1994: 89) points to ignorance of the Convention's existence as a factor, and also notes that states may fear that the Convention would prompt increased migration. EU member states are also likely to oppose the proposed extension of rights to undocumented and irregular migrant workers.

Another organisation with clear migration policy responsibilities is the International Labour Organisation (ILO), which was set up by the UN to monitor workplace standards and seek improvements, but again without real teeth. Convention 97, of July 1949, on the Position of Migrant Workers, establishes the principle of non-discrimination between migrant workers and workers who are nationals. Convention 143, of June 1975, Migrations in Abusive Conditions and the Promotion of Equality of Opportunity and Treatment of Migrant Workers, extends the principle of non-discrimination and provides for action against illegal migration. Conventions apply to all workers, irrespective of nationality and whether or not their countries of origin have ratified them. Both, however, apply only to workers who are legally resident in the territory of the contracting states. Provisions for implementation and supervision of ILO conventions are weak and based on government reports and on complaints made to the ILO, which are then investigated by expert committees.

A key legal standard in the European context is the European Convention on the Protection of Human Rights and Fundamental Freedoms (ECHR), which was adopted by the Council of Europe in 1950. By 1997 the Council of Europe was the largest pan-European organisation, with forty members, covering all major policy areas except defence. All EU member states are signatories and pledged to abide by the standards of the European human rights framework. Within the Council of Europe,

conventions and agreements are prepared and negotiated before cul-
minating in a decision by the Committee of Ministers, composed of
representatives of all forty member states, which establishes the text of a
proposed treaty. A convention usually requires ratification at national
level. An agreement can be signed by a member state without having to
seek national ratification. The ECHR established the European Court of
Human Rights in Strasbourg (not to be confused with the European
Court of Justice in Luxembourg).

The European Commission on Human Rights was established to
monitor implementation of the ECHR. In 1958 it noted that: 'a state
which signs and ratifies the ECHR must be understood as agreeing to
restrict the free exercise of its rights under general international law,
including the right to control the entry and exit of foreigners to the extent
and within the limits of the obligations which it has accepted under that
Convention' (quoted in Plender, 1988: 227). There is, though, a key
difference with EC law, because the ECHR is international law and
depends for its effect on national ratification. This means that national
legal contexts are central to an evaluation of impact. When seeking to
account for the impact of international legal standards on EU member
states, a distinction has been made between 'monist', 'quasi-dualist' and
'dualist' legal systems (Baldwin-Edwards, 1991: 203–4). Monist systems,
like those in Belgium, France, Greece, Luxembourg, the Netherlands,
Portugal and Spain, incorporate treaties automatically after approval by
the competent state bodies. International laws can be invoked in national
courts if the treaty is 'self-executing' and does not require national
legislation. Quasi-dualist systems, like those of Germany and Italy, require
a transforming legislative act prior to incorporation into national law. In
dualist systems, like those in Britain, Ireland and Denmark, implementation depends upon separate national legislation. The result is that
international conventions and treaties have different effects in different
EU member states, depending on national legal systems.

Article 1 of the ECHR provides that contracting states have to secure
the Convention's rights and freedoms to 'everyone within the jurisdiction',
not just to nationals of that state. This means that the rights granted by
the ECHR are available to TCNs in EU member states. All EU member
states have ratified the Convention, have allowed the right of individual
complaint, and recognised the jurisdiction of the European Court of
Human Rights. Article F of the Maastricht Treaty stated that: 'The Union
shall respect fundamental rights, as guaranteed by the ECHR ... and as
a result from the constitutional traditions common to the Member States,
as general principles of Community law', but this is a non-justiciable
declaration and does not constitute accession by the EU to the ECHR.
There was some discussion during the negotiation of the Amsterdam
Treaty about whether the EU should accede to the ECHR. Even though

most member states favoured accession, the view of the ECJ was that accession would be problematic within the existing legal framework of the EU and without an explicit treaty commitment to accession (Hix and Niessen, 1996).

The ECHR does not apply specifically to immigration. If challenges to national immigration laws have been made which draw from its provisions, then the foundation for these claims has tended to be derived from one of six Convention articles:

- Article 3, prohibiting inhuman or degrading treatment;
- Articles 5 and 6, protecting the liberty of the person and ensuring the right to a fair hearing;
- Article 8, providing for respect of family and private life;
- Article 12, covering the right to marry;
- Article 14, establishing the principle of non-discrimination (on grounds that include race, colour, language, religion and national origin). A 1996 judgement of the European Court of Human Rights (*Gaygusuz v. Austria*) established that Article 14 of the ECHR prohibited discrimination against resident TCNs on grounds of nationality for access to social security entitlements.[26] This demonstrated the potential for the ECHR to tackle discrimination on grounds of nationality that the EU currently does not.

Other Council of Europe conventions have implications for migrants, but these usually apply only to persons who are nationals of a signatory state.[27] For instance, the European Convention on Establishment (1955) deals with admission, expulsion and the legal status of physical persons who are nationals of one signatory state in the territory of another. The European Social Charter (1961) protects a wide range of social and economic rights and, in certain circumstances, applies to foreigners so long as they are nationals of another signatory state. This means that the European Social Charter applies to TCNs working in an EU member state, so long as they are nationals of a member state of the Council of Europe. For instance, Turks working in an EU member state are covered. The European Convention on Social Security (1972) makes provision in Article 73 for social security for migrants and aliens to secure their acquired rights and the principle of equality of treatment. The European Convention on the Legal Status of Migrant Workers (1977) protects migrant workers in their migration to work in another country and covers such things as recruitment, travel to and establishment in that country. The 1992 European Convention on the Participation of Foreigners in Public Life at Local Level noted in its preamble that 'the residence of foreigners on the national territory is now a permanent feature of European societies'. The Convention deals with such issues as the right of association.

The most ambitious part of the Convention is Article C, which provides for the right of foreigners to vote and stand in local elections. Denmark, Finland, Ireland, the Netherlands and Sweden are the only EU member states to have granted voting rights to all non-citizens meeting residence requirements. The Convention aimed to improve the participation of foreigners in their local communities. By October 1998, eight Council of Europe states had signed the Convention (Cyprus, Denmark, Finland, Italy, the Netherlands, Norway, Sweden and Britain) while in only four states had it actually entered into force (Italy, the Netherlands, Norway and Sweden).

In 1997 the European Convention on Nationality was opened for signatures. The Convention made it very clear that each state had the right to determine under its own law who its nationals are (Article 3). It then proceeded to lay down a series of principles on non-discrimination, acquisition of nationality, loss and recovery of nationality, procedures relating to nationality, multiple nationality, state succession and nationality, and military service. By October 1998, sixteen of the forty Council of Europe member states had signed the Convention, but only Austria and Slovakia had actually ratified it.

Given the absence of direct effect, what impact have international legal standards had on migrants' rights in EU member states? Guiraudon (1998: 12) is sceptical and prefers to focus on national-level political-institutional structures as facilitating or militating against the extension of rights to migrants. Writing in the late 1990s, she noted that since the European Court of Human Rights began operating in 1959, 'less than half a dozen decisions have involved the civil rights of foreigners (2.5 per cent of the decisions) and they were all issued in the preceding ten years', that is, between 1987 and 1997. Ireland (1995: 247) is equally sceptical when he describes international standards as 'soft law ... vaguely worded and with no real enforcement mechanisms, their goal is really to pressure governments to change their policies'. Niessen (1994: 5) acknowledged the difficulties faced by individuals or groups seeking to draw from international legal standards when he wrote that: 'conventions are often too much a compromise and offer too little. States also often undermine the significance of conventions ... by frequently using the possibility offered in conventions to make reservations with respect to certain parts. In addition, states tend not to recognise supervisory mechanisms such as, for example, the right of individual complaint', with the effect that the usefulness of these conventions may be diminished in the eyes of the people whose rights are supposed to be protected. However, he goes on to argue that conventions do offer significant resources to individuals and NGOs: 'They offer protection in addition to national laws and practices, provide for friendly settlements and remedies for victims, oblige states to adapt their legislation to international norms, have a preventative effect on state's behaviour and offer possibilities of having public and parliamentary debates on the efforts of states to comply with international human rights standards'.

While EU member states have acknowledged their obligations under international treaties, it remains the case that they can legitimately discriminate on behalf of their own nationals and the nationals of other EU member states. Discrimination against TCNs is in accord with the principle of international law that it is for a state to decide who can or cannot become its citizens and obtain access to associated rights and obligations. The strong connection between nationality and the right of free movement within the EU means that international legal standards have been largely tangential to the operationalisation of the EU's free movement framework. A discourse of universal entitlement does provide political conviction, a lobbying resource and moral force to the arguments of pro-migrant NGOs, but the political sensitivities associated with immigration and asylum policy coupled with moral equivocation by member states have militated against expanded rights for TCNs within the EU.

Conclusion

This chapter has explained the origins in the period between 1957 and 1986 of a strongly institutionally structured (in terms of supranational legal and political competencies) EC-level free movement framework and virtually non-existent extra-EC migration policies. There was substantial encroachment upon national prerogatives by supranational legal and political authority to promote and protect the rights of EC nationals moving for purposes of work. There was no legal basis for establishment of supranational legal and political authority to deal with immigration and asylum issues. Even when immigration became more salient and its relationship to free movement more clearly evident, member states were still reluctant to extend the competencies of EC institutions, as is shown in the next chapter.

Free movement for workers within a common market was a central aspiration of the Treaty of Rome and it was highly unlikely that the EC's economic purposes could be attained without it. Immigration and asylum policy were not closely associated with this economic imperative. Instead they were linked to issues of high politics that were associated with state sovereignty and bedevilled by the difficulties of securing positive integration. When immigration became more salient from the mid-1970s, member states displayed determination to maintain national jurisdiction. Livi-Bacci captures this disjunction by referring to a 'positive ideology' of European integration and a 'negative ideology' of immigration (Livi-Bacci, 1993). Despite the vital contribution made by migrant workers to

European economic reconstruction, by the 1970s there was a drive towards restrictive immigration legislation. The 'problem' of immigration (as defined) was to be 'solved' by restrictive immigration policies adopted and enforced at national level coupled with immigrant integration policies that bore strong relation to national traditions of citizenship and nationhood.

Despite this apparent disjunction between intra- and extra-EU migration, it is not possible to separate free movement entirely from immigration and asylum policy. Freer movement for EC nationals within the common market raised questions associated with entry, movement and residence by TCNs and these questions became even more salient in the aftermath of the SEA (1986). This could be characterised as some kind of generic spillover effect, but member state opposition to supranationalisation draws attention to the difficulties of securing policy integration. It does, though, suggest that low and high politics cannot be neatly separated because the pursuit of market development and free movement drew immigration and asylum closer to European integration.

Notes

1 There are three founding treaties of what is now known as the European Union: the Treaty of Paris (1951) creating the European Coal and Steel Community; the Treaty of Rome (1957) establishing the European Economic Community; and the Treaty of Rome establishing the European Atomic Energy Commission (1957). Our attention is mainly focused on the Treaty of Rome establishing the EEC.
2 *Official Journal* L56/850, 1964.
3 Case 30/77 *Bouchereau* [1977] European Court Report (ECR) 199.
4 A famous ECJ decision established the supremacy of EC law by stating that: 'The Community constitutes a new legal order of international law for the benefit of which states have limited their sovereign rights, albeit within limited fields, and the subjects of which comprise not only Member States, but also their nationals.' *Costa* v. *ENEL* [1964] ECR 585.
5 *Official Journal* L257/13, 1968.
6 *Official Journal* L257/13, 1968.
7 *Official Journal* L172/14, 1973.
8 Updated versions of both 1408/71 and 574/72 are in the *Official Journal* L28, 1997.
9 Case 12/86 *Demirel* [1987] ECR 3719.
10 Case C-192/89 *Sevince* [1990] ECR I-3641.
11 Case C-237/91 *Kus* [1992] ECR I-6781.
12 Council Resolutions 2210/78 (Algeria), 2211/78 (Morocco), 2212/78 (Tunisia). All 27 September 1978.
13 Case C-18/90 *Kziber* [1990] ECR I-199.
14 Case C-113/89 *Rush Portugesa* [1990] ECR I-1417.
15 Case C-43/93 *Vander Elst* [1994] ECR I-3803.

16   *Official Journal* L18/1, 21 January 1997.
17   *Official Journal* C277/2, 1976.
18   *Official Journal* C103, 1977.
19   *Official Journal* C13/1, 1974.
20   'Towards European citizenship', *Bulletin of the European Communities*, Supplement 7/75, 1975.
21   *European Parliament Document* 481/75, pp. 39–43.
22   *Official Journal*, C299/26, 1977.
23   Known as the Adonnino report after its chair, and published in *Bulletin of the European Communities*, Supplement, 7/85, 1985.
24   *Official Journal* C246/3, 1988, superseded by discussions within the pre-Maastricht intergovernmental conference on EU citizenship. It was, in fact, Directive 93/109 of 6 December 1993 and Directive 94/80 of 31 December 1994 that extended voting rights for local and European elections to citizens of the EU, as provided for by Article 8 of the Maastricht Treaty.
25   *Europe Document* No. 1653, 2 October 1990.
26   *Gaygusuz v. Austria, European Court of Human Rights. Report of Judgements and Decisions*, 16 September 1996 – IV.
27   The texts of Council of Europe conventions are available from the Council's Website at http://www.coe.fr/index.asp

3

Immigration and asylum policy after the Single European Act

Introduction

The SEA had fundamental effects on free movement, immigration and asylum. Its provisions for the creation of a single market made it clear that free movement had unavoidable immigration and asylum implications, but did not necessarily mean that immigration and asylum would become supranationalised policy competencies with scope for constitutionalisation and institutionalisation and associated new legal and political processes and activity. Far from it, because the post-SEA period demonstrated an intergovernmental brake on integration. It showed the reluctance of member states to cede competencies to supranational institutions for immigration and asylum issues that would open the possibility for the kinds of legal and political effects that have arisen from the establishment of a supranationalised free movement framework. Yet between 1986 and 1993 – from the negotiation of the SEA until Maastricht's ratification – it became clear that it was well nigh impossible to detach the low politics of market-making from the high politics of immigration and asylum. This period of EC history also demonstrated the preference of member states for, on the one hand, intergovernmental *co-operation* on immigration and asylum combined with attempts to slip domestic political and judicial constraints on immigration control, but, on the other, a resistance to immigration and asylum policy *integration* that could impose new constraints on national executive authorities and their agents by empowering supranational institutions.

The significance of the SEA should not be underestimated. It kick-started the EC after years of apparent stagnation during the 1970s when the Community had appeared trapped in the glare of the headlights of the economic recession and by the challenges posed by uncompetitiveness in world markets in key economic sectors. The SEA's centrepiece was the plan for free movement for people, services, goods and capital within a single market, which would see a progressive extension of the common market and within which internal frontiers between member states would

67

be removed. The SEA also made more evident the connections between free movement and immigration and asylum. Intergovernmental co-operation outside of the treaty framework on immigration and asylum policy – not supranational integration – was the preferred form of action. This limited form of co-operation demonstrated the blurred distinction between external and internal security and the connections between free movement and immigration and asylum policy. This blurring arose because of the twin-track emphasis on external frontier controls coupled with burgeoning internal security arrangements. There was also co-operation from 1985 onwards by a smaller group of member states that signed the Schengen Agreement, which sought quicker attainment of free movement for people, with 'compensating' immigration, asylum and internal security measures. Immigration and asylum were constructed as security issues and the priority given to these had a 'crowding-out' effect on the possibilities for an EU debate about migrant inclusion.

The resurgence of European integration

Capax imperii nisi imperasset[1] was the epitaph provided for the EC by *The Economist* in its edition of 20 March 1982. The EC appeared moribund at best, yet within four years a remarkable resurgence in European integration occurred that stemmed from the challenges addressed by the SEA and the view among key member states that deeper European economic and political integration was an essential element of an effective response to these challenges. The SEA placed at the core of European integration the plan to create a single market within which people, services, goods and capital would be able to move freely. Once attained, the single market would contribute to an economic renaissance and help close the gap that had emerged between EC economies and their principal rivals, or so it was claimed (Cecchini, 1988).

Free movement for EC nationals within the single market brought with it pressure for closer co-operation on immigration and asylum. Questions of external frontier control were transplanted to those member states on the edge of the single market. There was, however, no explicit treaty competence for immigration and asylum policy areas; there was in fact a marked reluctance on the part of the British, Danish and Greek governments in particular to extend the remit of supranational institutions into these areas. Informal internal security co-operation had occurred since the late 1960s, although immigration and asylum were largely beyond the remit of these nascent structures. The foundations were being laid for future co-operation on immigration and asylum within this internal security framework.

Despite the reluctance on the part of some member states to counten-ance immigration and asylum policy integration, there was evidence of integrative intent among a smaller group of member states that resolved to move more quickly towards a frontier-free Europe within which people could move freely. In 1985 five EC governments (Belgium, France, Germany, the Netherlands and Luxembourg) signed the Schengen Agreement in the eponymous Luxembourg town. Even though this was outside of the EC treaty framework, it embodied a resolution by the signatories to move more quickly towards the abolition of border controls so as to secure free movement for people between participating states.

The SEA also reaffirmed the distinction between free movement for EC citizens and TCNs. Free movement for EC nationals was a supranationalised competence with Commission and ECJ competencies. The SEA provided new impetus to the free movement framework and put in place decision-making processes – principally qualified majority voting (QMV) – that aimed at speeding implementation of many single market issues, although not free movement of people, which remained subject to unanimity. In comparison, immigration and asylum policies remained outside the treaty framework. They were dealt with by *ad hoc* intergovernmental co-operation. The Commission was only loosely associated with this work, while the ECJ and EP were excluded. Executive authority was strengthened while judicial and legislative authority were weak.

Free movement in the SEA

The SEA arose, as do all revisions of the Treaty of Rome, from an intergovernmental conference (IGC) of member states' governments convened in this instance by the summit meeting of the European Council held in Milan in June 1985. Within the IGC, decisions upon substantive change had to be agreed unanimously. The distinction between negative and positive integration is apposite: the legal basis as well as the economic, political and ideological impetus behind the market-making project and associated removal of obstacles to trade was far stronger than pressure for the kinds of positive integration necessary to develop new immigration and asylum policy structures at supranational level (Sandholtz and Zysman, 1989; Fligstein and Mara-Drita, 1996).

The need for unanimity raised particular problems because of the general reluctance of the British, Danish and Greek governments, all of which had even opposed the convening of the IGC in the first place. The basic divergence was not so much about the desirability of the single market programme (the British, for instance, were keen advocates because it chimed with domestic policy preferences and were prepared to see use of QMV in the Council), but about the level and the extent of supranationalisation that would be associated with it. More enthusiastic member states raised the possibility – probably as a bargaining device –

that a 'two-speed' Europe could emerge, within which the reluctant member states would find themselves in a marginalised 'slow lane'.

Once again, while delving into the specificities of the SEA, it is important to bear in mind both the links between free movement, immigration and asylum and the continued exclusion of TCNs from EC provisions. The SEA defined a single market in Article 8a as: 'an area without internal frontiers in which the free movement of goods, persons, services and capital is ensured within the provisions of this Treaty'. The SEA gave a decisive boost to the free movement impulse put in place by the Treaty of Rome, and consolidated by the creation of the common market in 1968. Moreover, it established a deadline of 31 December 1992 for attainment of these targets. Although the deadline had debatable legal standing and was not wholly met, it imparted a degree of urgency and gave the Commission a stick with which to beat member states if they tried to block proposals. Equally importantly, the introduction of QMV for key aspects of the single market programme – but not free movement of people – reduced the ability of individual member states to block Commission initiatives.

The Commission's White Paper presented to the Milan summit in June 1985 had contained nearly 300 legislative proposals for the creation of a single market. It included proposed measures on refugee, asylum and visa policies and the status of TCNs, but these were not included in the final legislation (CEC, 1985a; Callovi, 1992). Rather ambitiously, the Commission had envisaged EC action on immigration and asylum policy – not intergovernmental co-operation – because the single market was viewed as analogous to existing national markets. The Commission's view was that the free movement provisions and the abolition of internal controls applied to all people, regardless of their nationality. This seemed both logical and practical, as it would be impossible for states to dismantle controls on movement by nationals of EC member states and retain them for TCNs. The White Paper's plans for the co-ordination of national rules on residence, entry and employment of TCNs, an EC policy on visas, and the fixing of common rules on extradition were all seen as necessary if checks at internal frontiers were to be abolished. The integrative 'logic' expounded by the Commission was not politically feasible, however, because there was not the will among member states to cede competence for immigration and asylum policies to the EC.

As well as questions relating to external frontier control, the SEA also raised internal security issues. The removal of internal frontier controls at borders between member states shifted the emphasis to immigration controls at the external frontiers of the member states on the edge of the single market and to internal security measures within the member states. The nascent EC immigration policy framework sought to combine co-operation on measures at the external frontier with the quest for exercise of controls within those frontiers. The importance of southern member states' immigration policies increased although, as noted in chapter 1, a shift to tighter external frontier controls was likely to be difficult to implement even if formal policies of restriction were put in place.

Member states' resistance to the Commission-driven 'spillover' of the White Paper's plans for immigration and asylum integration illustrate one of the difficulties with mechanistic neo-functionalism. The ability of member states to resist integration into areas of high politics was evident in their negative response to Commission immigration and asylum policy proposals. Such integration required unanimity and some member states were not prepared to countenance measures impinging upon national immigration and asylum policies. Member states were though prepared to seek closer co-operation on immigration and asylum policy.

The negative response from member states to immigration and asylum policy also meant a negative answer to a central question posed by the SEA. Would free movement for people become a generalised right applying to all people permanently resident in the EU? Article 8a of the SEA – as Article 48 of the Treaty of Rome had done before it – left scope for an expansive interpretation because it did not specify that free movement was a right to be restricted to nationals of EC member states. O'Keeffe (1992: 16–17) wrote that: 'If the Community is to have an area without internal frontiers, it becomes progressively absurd that non-Community nationals established in the Community should not be afforded the protection of Community law'. The key issue with regard to the rights of legally resident TCNs was neither entry nor residence nor movement, but equal treatment, which was already a principle of Community law with regard to gender.[2] Member states, however, sustained a less expansive interpretation of the SEA's provisions and the distinction was maintained between EC nationals and TCNs. Unequal treatment persisted and was sanctioned by EC law.

The decision-making procedures put in place by the SEA facilitated attainment of ambitious single market objectives in an EC that had grown from to nine to twelve member states between 1981 and 1986.[3] The SEA added a new Article 100a to the Treaty of Rome to give institutional backing to the policy objectives by shifting towards QMV for issues related to the single market. Importantly, Article 100a did not apply to free movement of persons, which continued to depend on unanimity. This did not mean that the EC lacked competence to act for free movement of people, rather that it derived competence from different Treaty articles than the new Article 100a. The Treaty articles that were particularly relevant for free movement of people were Articles 100 and 235 of the Treaty of Rome, both of which required unanimity.

The member states rejected immigration and asylum policy integration and, as shown below, preferred forms of intergovernmental co-operation outside of the Treaty framework. This presented the Commission with a dilemma. Its preference outlined in the 1985 White Paper was for a supranational policy, but this was infeasible. What stance should the Commission adopt in response to forms of co-operation on immigration and asylum that related to key aspects of Community competence for free movement but that were not governed by the EC's institutions? The Commission adopted a pragmatic stance: it was prepared to forswear the moral high ground of opposition to informal co-operation and participate when able in forms of co-operation between member states that occurred outside of the Treaty framework. The Commission moderated its stance to secure a seat at the intergovernmental bargaining table when immigration and asylum policy co-operation was undertaken (Monar, 1994). It was seen as better to observe and thereby attempt to exert some influence on co-operation rather than shun nascent co-operation because it fell short of more ambitious targets. The Commission adopted a similar stance on Schengen.

A paradox of liberalisation?

Freer movement for some has brought with it attempts to establish tighter controls on movement by TCNs. Liberalisation within the single market was bounded by the prior possession of the nationality of a member state. It was not free movement for all – it was essentially a glorified plan for a functional right of free movement for workers. The single market brought with it closer co-operation on external frontier controls and internal security in an attempt to restrict entry to the single market and to police movement within it. Consequently, freer movement for privileged EC nationals prompted new internal security controls and attempts to impose tighter restrictions on entry, residence and movement by TCNs. Those subject to these controls or not covered by treaty provisions could view this bounded liberalisation as paradoxical in that market-making and free movement actually led to efforts to put in place tighter controls on population movement. Yet if this is a paradox of liberalisation, then it only replicates those that already exist within EU member states, which have combined free movement within their own national markets with attempts to control entry, movement and residence by non-nationals by policing their own territory. The EU adds a supranational component with its own institutional configuration to internal and external securitisation. 'Control' issues have other dimensions. The creation of national welfare states led to the consolidation of nation states *qua* national welfare states, with the borders of those states serving as institutionalised thresholds of inequality and reinforcing pressures for immigration restriction (Bommes, 1998).

The ceding of policy competencies coupled with the establishment of patterns of co-operation for free movement, immigration and asylum demonstrates how the EU has assumed some of the policy responsibilities previously located at national level (Richardson, 1996a). The regulation of the movement of people via immigration policies has been viewed as a legitimate public policy aspiration in EU member states, irrespective of some of the ethical arguments that have been advanced (Barry and Goodin, 1992). Responsibilities relating to movement of people and control of population that had previously been exercised by member states had, by the 1980s, acquired a European dimension.

In practical terms, the maintenance of free movement as a functional right related to attainment of labour market purposes meant that free movement was not free for all. Moreover, plans to abolish border controls between participating states in a single market would not mean un-impeded or unmonitored movement, because internal security checks became more important. It was never the corollary for those member states that were prepared to remove their external frontiers that free movement was a route to abolition of controls on population. Rather, co-operation between member states was a way of attempting to reinforce existing national controls while also raising the possibility of pan-European controls exercised through co-operation between national agencies and emergent European-level institutions. Aspects of these internal security arrangements – such as the form that identity checks at the internal frontiers of the single market could take – fell within the ECJ's juris-diction. To be in accord with the principles of Community law, the ECJ decided that controls needed to be sporadic and unsystematic and not 'systematic, arbitrary or unnecessarily restrictive'.[4] Also, only identity controls were to be allowed. Questioning that went beyond attempts to ascertain identity breached Community law. More detailed questions could be asked only when non-nationals sought the right of residence.[5]

Ad hoc co-operation

Despite opposition to the immigration and asylum policy proposals of the Commission's 1985 White Paper laying out plans for the single market, the member states realised that the supranationalisation of free movement within a single market raised immigration and asylum issues. The chosen form of action was *ad hoc* and intergovernmental in character. In a political declaration attached to the SEA, the member states noted that in order to promote free movement of persons, they were to co-operate without prejudice to the powers of the Community, in particular as regards entry, movement and residence of TCNs. At the same time, the member states also declared that nothing contained within the SEA affected the rights of member states to introduce measures they saw as necessary to control immigration from third countries. The SEA was a recipe for blurred competence.

In its 1988 communication on the abolition of border controls, the Commission illustrated its pragmatic stance, which reflected its desire to keep a seat at the intergovernmental negotiating table (CEC, 1988b). Once again, the link between removal of internal frontier controls and European competence for external controls was stressed, but the Commission directed attention towards practical effectiveness rather than legal doctrine. Free movement was a fundamental EC aspiration, but it gave birth to forms of co-operation that excluded supranational institutions. Immigration and asylum policy were connected with the integrative impetus imparted to free movement by the SEA, but the institutional form chosen to secure co-operation maintained a distance between itself and the Community. Ultimately, the rigidity of this demarcation was to be questioned by both the Maastricht and Amsterdam Treaties.

Co-operation on internal security policy did not just emerge in response to the SEA – it built on previous patterns of co-operation. Before the SEA, EC member states had already put in place some mechanisms for co-operation on internal security issues. The 1967 Naples Convention dealt with mutual co-operation between the customs authorities of the six EC member states. Judicial co-operation occurred within the framework of European political co-operation (EPC), established in 1970. This co-operation was outside the treaty framework, unencumbered by the jurisdiction of supranational institutions, and almost impossible to subject to political or judicial scrutiny at either national or European level. Democracy and accountability fell through the net of intergovernmental internal security co-operation between EC member states, although these policy areas could hardly be characterised as being particularly open or accountable at national level either.

Interior policy co-operation took a stronger organisational form following a European Council meeting in Rome in 1975 that set up a special working group called Trevi, which operated within the framework of EPC and had particular responsibility for dealing with problems posed by terrorist groups. Trevi met twice a year under the chair of the minister for home affairs from the country holding the EC presidency. In practice, its management mimicked that of the Council and it was presided over by a troika comprising the country holding the EC presidency and the two countries that had either just held or were about to assume the presidency. These ministerial meetings were supported by the work of national officials. Trevi's working groups, composed of national officials, dealt with terrorism, equipment, public order, training, drugs, serious crime and, later on in its existence, the internal security implications of '1992'. Trevi helped instigate a 'wining and dining' culture of co-operation among interior ministry officials, which was strengthened during the 1980s and 1990s (den Boer, 1996). European integration was beginning to have an impact on policy areas, such as interior policy, that had hitherto been quintessentially national.

As noted in the previous chapter, Commission attempts during the 1970s to bring aspects of immigration and asylum policy under EC control – such as action against clandestine migration – had been firmly rebuffed by the Council. The Commission took further tentative steps towards the establishment of EC competence in 1985, when it proposed *Guidelines for a Community Policy on Migration* (CEC, 1985b). This document stressed the importance of free movement for EC nationals while also emphasising the importance of 'equality of treatment in living and working conditions for all migrants, whatever their origin' (p. 8). With regards to TCNs, the *Guidelines* used terms such as consultation, experimentation and information rather than legislation (Handoll, 1995: 355). In July 1985, on the basis of its *Guidelines*, the Commission proposed a decision establishing prior consultation and communication procedures on migration policy aimed at 'achieving progress towards a harmonisation of national legislation on foreigners'.[6] The decision required member states to give advance notice of measures they intended to take that affected TCNs and their families. Denmark, France, Germany, the Netherlands and Britain challenged the use of Article 118 of the Treaty of Rome for such a decision and argued that it exceeded Commission competence. In July 1987, the ECJ annulled certain aspects of the decision,[7] but a consultation procedure was established and the ECJ ruling did not completely block the Commission's first tentative steps towards institutionalisation of an extra-EC migration policy context (Papademetriou, 1996: 21). Even so, there was no evidence that the guidelines were ever operationalised (EP, 1991).

Nothing was so likely to arouse the ire of the British government as proposals for EC immigration and asylum policy competencies. The British Conservative government was a champion of informal, inter-governmental co-operation and during the British Council presidency tenure of the second six months of 1986 the *Ad Hoc* Group on Immigration was established, following a meeting of immigration ministers of the member states and the Commission Vice-President, Martin Bangemann. The *Ad Hoc* Group on Immigration was composed of high-level immigration policy officials from the member states and was divided into six subgroups dealing with asylum, external frontiers, forged papers, admissions, deportations and information exchange. The Commission was represented on the Group when EC powers were involved, but had no power of initiative. Bureaucratic support for the *Ad Hoc* Group was provided by the Council Secretariat. This meant a loose association between *ad hoc* intergovernmental co-operation and the Commission, but no room for involvement by the ECJ or EP.

The member states still faced the problem of trying to ensure co-ordination between the free movement objectives of the single market programme and the internal security issues raised by its creation. The heads of government meeting in the European Council at Rhodes in December 1988 established a Group of Co-ordinators charged with seeking the co-ordination of activities occurring within and outside of the treaty framework. The groups it sought to co-ordinate included Trevi and the *Ad Hoc* Group on Immigration. The Group of Co-ordinators was composed of representatives of the member states and reported regularly to the European Council on progress, or lack of it. The Rhodes Council also grandly declared that: 'The internal market will not close in on itself. 1992 Europe will be a partner and not a "fortress Europe"' (quoted in Handoll, 1995: 357).

Within six months the 'Palma document' was presented to the European Council at its meeting in Madrid in June 1989 (Statewatch, 1997: 12–16). A senior Commission official (Fortescue, 1995) viewed the Palma document as a realistic attempt to plot a politically manageable course through the thorny issues associated with free movement by dividing them between those seen as 'essential' and those deemed 'desirable'. Deemed 'essential' were the harmonisation of external frontier controls, a common visa policy and the right of TCNs residing in a member state to move without a visa to another member state.

> The result was a comprehensive and responsible programme which, if completed on schedule, should make it possible to confront governments with this stark but essential question: since the programme you agreed to be necessary is now complete, how can you any longer justify the maintenance of controls at the frontiers between you? (Fortescue, 1995: 30)

But such developments still relied to a large extent on unanimity among member states within informal structures for co-operation that were outside the treaty framework. Co-operation also exacerbated the 'democratic deficit', because of the increased powers in the hands of largely unaccountable government officials. There was also an 'information deficit', marked by confusion about whether the Palma document was confidential or could be made public. This reflected a more general confusion about the new internal security mechanisms that were being created. The Palma document entered the public domain when scrutinised by the British House of Lords in July 1989, but when the Dutch government distributed it to MPs, some of them treated it as confidential. As well as these difficulties, the Group of Co-ordinators also faced practical problems justifying its title because of the diverse forums within which the issues it was concerned with were discussed.

Asylum and external frontiers

As a result of the Madrid Council's acceptance in 1989 of the Palma document, the *Ad Hoc* Group on Immigration turned its attention to two of the most pressing issues: asylum policy and external frontier control. The tail end of these discussions occurred during a period when asylum issues increased greatly in salience following the end of the Cold War and large increases in intra-European movement as a result of the conflict in Yugoslavia. The German government, in particular, pressed for a Europeanised response to what it saw as a European problem. Other member states were less willing to embrace this conceptualisation of a European problem if it meant sharing responsibility for migration with Germany. However, during the 1980s and 1990s, it was noticeable that European level co-operation allowed EC member states to circumvent domestic legal and political constraints and elaborate a European policy framework that emphasised restriction (Lavenex, 1998a). Lip service may be paid to international legal standards, but aspects of European asylum policy can bear dubious relation to these standards.

The asylum efforts of the member states came to fruition at Dublin on 15 June 1990, when the member states (except for Denmark, which signed on 13 June 1991) signed the Convention Determining the State Responsible for Examining Applications for Asylum Lodged in one of the Member States of the European Communities, or the Dublin Convention as it was rather more conveniently known (Handoll, 1995: 419–25; Statewatch, 1997: 49–54). The Convention sought to remove the possibility in a frontier-free Europe of asylum-seekers making applications in more than one member state, so-called 'asylum shopping'. The Convention did not attempt to harmonise the rules for examining applications; rather it aimed to ensure that in a frontier-free Europe only one member state would be responsible for judging any one particular asylum application. The principle underpinning the Convention was that an application for asylum would be made in the member state that the applicant had arrived in, unless he or she was joining a spouse or dependant in another member state. This meant that not all asylum applications would be investigated, because if the applicant had arrived from another EC member state then he or she would be returned to that member state. The Convention also effectively pushed the problems of asylum to member states bordering third countries or those with large air and seaports. The Dublin Convention also off-loaded responsibility for asylum to non-EC 'third countries' deemed 'safe' in relation to their compliance with the Geneva Convention. Guild and Niessen (1996: 120) note that:

> The Dublin system began as a logical development of the internal market. The difficulty is that what might have been a solution providing some security to asylum applicants in an integrated Europe is now being used to move asylum-seekers out of the Union altogether.

Evidence for this is contained in the readmission agreements signed with third countries deemed 'safe'. These agreements reduce the administrative and financial burdens of asylum-seeking on EU member states and off-load substantial costs on to 'safe' countries in central and eastern Europe that are less likely to be able to meet them, with obvious deleterious effects on the standards of treatment received by asylum-seekers (Hockenos, 1993). The complex web of readmission agreements that were signed between EU member states and central and eastern European countries then formed part of the context for incorporation of these countries into the EU's migration control framework during their pre-accession process (Lavenex, 1998b). These aspiring member states have thus been obliged to participate in the EU's restrictive immigration and asylum policies.

Other asylum-related developments were linked to the Dublin Convention. A meeting of immigration ministers held in London between 30 November and 1 December 1992 adopted a resolution on 'manifestly unfounded applications for asylum'.[8] An application was to be deemed manifestly unfounded if it raised no issues under the terms of either the Geneva Convention or New York Protocol. This could be because there was no fear of persecution in the applicant's own country, or because the claim was based on deception or an abuse of procedures. Applications suspected of being manifestly unfounded would be fast-tracked, leading to speedier resolution and more often than not rejection. Paragraph 1(a) of the resolution on manifestly unfounded applications made reference to countries where there was deemed to be no serious risk of persecution. A set of conclusions drafted by the immigration ministers at their London meeting explained the criteria by which countries were to be deemed safe:

> This concept means that it is a country which can be clearly shown, in an objective and verifiable way, normally not to generate refugees, or where it can be clearly shown, in objective and verifiable way, that circumstances which might in the past have justified recourse to the 1951 Geneva Convention have ceased to exist. (Quoted in Statewatch, 1997: 66)

There was an outcry from human rights groups when a draft version of the criteria judged states by the human rights standards they had signed rather than by whether or not they actually respected them. The final version went some way to assuage these concerns when it referred to both criteria. The basic purpose of the procedures as a mechanism to reduce the numbers of asylum seekers was noted by Guild and Niessen (1996: 181), who wrote that they were 'clearly designed to fit a numbers game' because 'an assessment of a state will only be relevant where substantial numbers of people from that state apply for asylum in the member states. Therefore the assessment of a country is a tool for the rapid refusal of asylum applications.' If a country was deemed to meet the criteria for being 'safe', then all applications from that country could be assumed to be unfounded, unless individuals could overcome massive odds and prove otherwise in their own particular case. The elaboration of an asylum policy framework within the EU was giving its member states – not the EU, because it does not possess the power to expel – increased powers to expel those deemed to be abusing the asylum system.

A resolution on a harmonised approach to questions concerning host third countries was also agreed at the London meeting. Its preamble outlined the intention to return refugees and asylum-seekers to third countries deemed safe if they had unlawfully left those countries. With a degree of understatement, Guild and Niessen (1996: 168) refer to this as a 'somewhat unreal document' because: 'It is somewhat irregular in international law that one state or group of states should seek to impose obligations unilaterally or through an agreement *inter alia* on other states which have not participated in or accepted the obligation'. An information clearing house, the Centre for Information, Discussion and Exchange on Asylum (which in French produces the acronym CIREA) was established by a meeting of immigration ministers in Lisbon in June 1992 for the deposit and exchange of information to assist member states in their harmonisation of asylum determination procedures. Sharing the same staff was an immigration information clearing house called the Centre for Information, Discussion and Exchange on the Crossing of Borders and Immigration (in French, CIREFI).

The intention to exert tight controls on asylum-seekers was evident in the European Data Archive Convention (EURODAC), which sought to give effect to Article 15 of the Dublin Convention. The draft EURODAC proposed the compulsory fingerprinting of asylum-seekers over fourteen years of age. The Austrian and German governments have pressed for its extension to illegal immigrants. Once the member states had taken the fingerprints, then the images were to be promptly transmitted to the EURODAC database. Former British Home Secretary Michael Howard illustrated the motivations for this kind of action designed to speed up assessment of asylum applications. He hoped it would:

> Serve to identify asylum applications made on entry at UK ports to which the UK was not obliged to give substantive consideration and which offered the possibility of effecting a swift return to the Member State having responsibility. There would in any such instance, be potential savings in benefit. (Quoted in *Statewatch*, July–August 1996: 1)

In 1990, two reports on immigration policy were submitted to the Rome meeting of the European Council. The first was prepared by a group of independent experts and discussed 'immigrant integration' (CEC, 1990). The report made the connection between immigration control and immigrant integration and argued for legal residence, equal opportunities in jobs, education, vocational training and housing, and easier access to naturalisation for TCNs. The experts' report also called for tolerance between communities, especially as a result of the establishment of 'structures for dialogue'. The Commission's basic problem was that whether or not it agreed with these objectives, it did not possess the capacity to act in these areas. Competence for such measures did not exist in the Treaty of Rome, nor was there the political will among member states to put it in place.

The second report was prepared by the *Ad Hoc* Group on Immigration and paid particular attention to migration from southern, central and eastern Europe. The report advocated a 'root causes' approach to try to stem migration pressures by, for instance, aid programmes designed to stimulate economic development. The report noted that control of immigration was an important component of any policy that sought to integrate settled migrants (Papademetriou, 1996: 45). A problem with root causes approaches is that the dislocation caused by attempts to promote economic and social development in emigration countries may actually prompt increased short-term migration. A 'root causes' approach is a policy for the medium- to long-term (Martin, 1993).

The attempt to elaborate an external frontiers policy was also a key task for the *Ad Hoc* Group. The immediate outcome in June 1991 was the draft External Frontiers Convention (EFC). The EFC's travails illustrate both the difficulties associated with co-operation between member states with disparate histories and policies on immigration issues and the limitations of the chosen form of intergovernmental co-operation, which relied on enacting conventions in international law. Such conventions needed to be signed by all member states and then ratified at national level. The path towards ratification for the Dublin Convention was tortuous: ratification in all the member states was not achieved until September 1997. The EFC has yet to attain the necessary signatures. The draft EFC was concerned with the conditions for access to the territory of EC member states by TCNs. In June 1991 agreement was secured on the general principles with regard to the crossing of external frontiers, and surveillance and the nature of the controls at these frontiers, as well as surveillance at airports. The EFC was left high and dry (and remained so in 1999) because of a dispute between the Spanish and British about the status of Gibraltar that dated back to the 1713 Treaty of Utrecht, which ended the Spanish War of Succession. The EFC could not come into effect if it was not signed by all member states. Also, the remit for its introduction changed after the Maastricht Treaty came into force. This led to a revised version of the EFC being introduced under Article K3 of the Maastricht Treaty, but this also remained unsigned.

Schengen

Alongside the development of *ad hoc* co-operation between EC member states on immigration and asylum policy, five pro-integration member states (Belgium, France, Germany, Luxembourg and the Netherlands) resolved to move more quickly towards free movement for people and the abolition of internal border controls between their own territories. Schengen's importance to the development of EU immigration and asylum policy should not be underestimated. It has been seen as serving as a 'testing ground for the Community, from the standpoint of completion of the internal market, and as a driving force for those member states which are not signatories to the Schengen Agreements'.[9] This became even clearer when the 1997 Amsterdam Treaty moved the Schengen *acquis* into the EU, although with a strong intergovernmental basis.

A 'mini-Schengen' had been established among the Benelux countries as far back as 1970, but the more immediate impetus behind the Schengen Agreement arose from protests in 1984 by lorry drivers angered by delays at the Franco-German border. This prompted an intergovernmental agreement between the two countries signed at Saarbrucken on 13 July 1984. The Schengen Agreement of 14 June 1985 brought the Benelux countries on board and constituted a more far-reaching attempt to abolish border controls. At this stage, Schengen was an agreement among signatory states and the hard work putting the agreement into effect remained to be done. A convention to implement this agreement was not signed until June 1990. The removal of internal frontier controls between participating states then took a further six years.

The Schengen Agreement foreshadowed the free movement objectives of Article 8a of the SEA. It allowed the signatories to maintain tight control over development of 'Schengenland's' free movement framework. They could exclude EC institutions from involvement, although the Commission viewed Schengen positively and was an observer at meetings. Creation of the Schengen – as opposed to a pan-EC – framework also obviated potential difficulties from EC member states that might be hostile or not well equipped in terms of their own national policies to take part in such an arrangement. For instance, the British government was hostile and never joined, while pro-European Italian governments were rather upset that they were excluded from the original group of members and had to observe from the sidelines. Other Schengen states doubted Italy's capacity to implement Schengen, although Italy has since become a full participating member.

Schengen's immigration and asylum implications are clear. The removal of internal frontiers between participating states meant the introduction of 'compensating' immigration and asylum policies, including harmonisation of visa policies and conditions for entry, and improved co-operation and harmonisation of asylum laws. Schengen's work was to be supported by the Schengen Information System (SIS), a computerised resource shared by participating states to support their activities. The Agreement would not enter into effect until the conditions for its attainment had been met in each signatory state. This caused delay and the Schengen Convention was not signed until 19 June 1990. One reason for the delay was German reunification, which meant that Schengen's provisions needed to be extended to cover the ex-German Democratic Republic so that East Germans would be exempt from visa requirements when entering the territory of the other signatories.

Key points with regard to Schengen are: first, its relation to securitisation of immigration and asylum; second, its contribution to the democratic deficit; and third, the absence of scope for judicial scrutiny. Articles 2–38 of the 1990 implementing Convention provide for the removal of checks at the crossing of internal frontiers, the crossing of external borders, visas for short- and long-term visits, the movement of aliens, the residence and reporting of people not to be permitted entry, carrier liability and asylum policy. Schengen's ambitious goals are evident in Article 17 of the 1985 Agreement, which stated that:

> In regard to the free movement of persons, the Parties shall endeavour to abolish the controls at the common frontiers and transfer them to their external frontiers. To that end they shall first endeavour to harmonise, where necessary, the laws and administrative provisions concerning prohibitions and restrictions which form the basis for the controls and to take complementary measures to safeguard security and combat illegal immigration by nationals of States that are not members of the European Communities.

Articles 131–133 established the Schengen Executive Committee, composed of national officials whose responsibility it was to secure implementation of the Convention. When the Schengen *acquis* was incorporated into the EU by the Amsterdam Treaty, the decisions of these unelected officials were also incorporated, with some becoming part of Community law (see chapter 5).

In terms of scope for democratic and judicial oversight, Schengen was, to put it mildly, rather underdeveloped. This becomes important when bearing in mind arguments about rights-based politics and the role of courts in opening social and political spaces for migrants. The scope for judicial control of the Schengen arrangements was very weak. Article 135 did state that the Convention was subject to the provisions of the 1951 Geneva Convention and the 1967 New York Protocol on refugees. But it would have been more of a surprise if these ritual declarations had not been made and even more surprising if judicial authorities had been given the teeth to interpret Schengen arrangements in the light of these international standards. There was no judicial body able to interpret the Convention or adjudicate if disputes arose. The relationship of Schengen with EC law was outlined in Article 134 of the 1990 Convention. This stated that the Convention's articles were to apply only insofar as they were compatible with Community law. The Commission tended to see the

Schengen arrangements as necessary for eventual attainment of Article 8a
of the SEA on free movement within the single market. Therefore, it
sought to ensure via its role as an observer at Schengen meetings that
there was neither discrimination between nationals of Schengen member
states and nationals of other EC member states nor that Schengen
jeopardised attainment of Article 8a.

Article 2 of the 1990 Convention had established the principle that
internal borders could be crossed without checks on persons, although
there is the derogation from this principle that member states may carry
out checks for a limited period for public policy or national security
reasons. The Schengen Agreement had been supposed to come into
operation on 26 March 1995. Passport controls were dropped, but on 1
July 1995, when it was intended to drop checks at land border controls,
the French government insisted on maintaining them after a series of
bombs went off and they invoked the 'safeguard clause' (Article 2(2)). At
the Schengen Executive Committee meeting of 18 April 1996, the French
government announced that it would maintain controls on the borders
with Belgium and Luxembourg, because they were seen as being transit
countries for drugs leaving the Netherlands. France also promoted a
Council of Europe resolution that sought prohibition of the production
of, and trading in, all drugs. The Dutch refuted the suggestion that they
were 'soft' on drugs, and noted that Schengen made no mention of a
harmonised drugs policy. The French stance was perceived as an oppor-
tunistic move by the right-wing government to offset opposition to
immigration and European integration. Thus the French government had
initially reinstated border controls to combat terrorist attacks and when
these had ended had maintained controls because they said they were
needed because of the problems caused by Dutch drugs policy (*Statewatch*, May–June 1996).

Even though it rested on intergovernmental foundations, Schengen was
not the product of intergovernmentalism as a defence of the nation state.
It facilitated the attainment of participating states' objectives with regard
to control of population in a frontier-free Europe, but also put in place
policies and decision-making structures that demonstrated both the integrative intent of key EC member states and their willingness to embrace
more 'flexible' forms of co-operation and integration if these would allow
them to reach their ambitious objectives. In his famous statement of the
neo-realist position, Hoffmann (1966: 882) argued that states would shy
away from integration in areas of high politics because 'Russian roulette
is fine only as long as the gun is filled with blanks'. The functional
method of integration with its spillover dynamics would, it was argued,
be confounded by the opposition to political union because 'Functional
integration's gamble could be won only if the method had sufficient
potency to promise an excess of gains over losses, and of hopes over

frustrations. Theoretically, this may be true of economic integration. It is not true of political integration.' The spillover effects of the SEA blurred this distinction between political and economic integration: economic purposes underpinned free movement but drew into the remit of integration the political questions of immigration and asylum policy. Rather than embarking on some kind of death pact, the Schengen signatories were developing forms of co-operation intended to lead to deeper integration in key areas of state sovereignty. Market-making and population control could not be separated once the single market programme was fully operationalised. The Schengen signatories were pursuing fundamental EC objectives, albeit beyond the 'constraints' imposed by the EC's legal and political order, as well as excluding those member states that were opposed to supranationalisation of these policy areas or unable to fulfil external and internal security requirements.

Conclusion

The SEA marked a key moment in the development of co-operation at EC level on immigration and asylum policy and the establishment of connections between institutionalised free movement and nascent immigration and asylum co-operation. EC member states elaborated a policy of control with few countervailing measures for protection of migrants' rights. The post-SEA period also demonstrates intergovernmental limitations on the constitutionalisation and institutionalisation of a supranational immigration and asylum policy context capable of imposing constraints upon action. The low politics of economic interdependence could not easily be separated from the high politics of state sovereignty because the economics of the free market and free movement became more closely connected at EC level with the politics and policy of immigration, asylum and internal security. The post-SEA preference for intergovernmental decision-making outside of the formal treaty framework, with a limited role for the Commission, ECJ and EP, allowed member states to seek attainment of restrictive policy targets in a secretive and largely unaccountable policy framework. There was a lack of concerted political will among member states to seek integration into EC decision-making of free movement coupled with extra-EC migration policy. The Schengen arrangements saw some of the more pro-integration member states push ahead towards attainment of ambitious targets, once again without the 'constraints' of judicial or democratic oversight.

The post-SEA period demonstrates intergovernmental constraints on supranational action. Ambitious plans for closer integration have often foundered when faced with the scepticism of more reluctant member states which, although they do not constitute a majority, can block 'history-making decisions' (Peterson, 1995) because of the reliance on unanimity. An implication of this for immigration and asylum co-operation was that 'lowest common denominator policies' emphasising intergovern- mentalism and restrictive policies emerged. This was not necessarily because these policies accurately reflected the preferences of member states. Rather, they show how opposition from a small group of member states in an institutional environment within which unanimity is the precondition for 'positive integration' can have a decisive and limiting effect on the range of policy outcomes. Immigration and asylum policy co-operation became skewed in the direction of restriction, which was the most basic issue upon which member states could agree. The direction of future policy development had been established.

Notes

1   It seemed capable of power until it tried to wield it.
2   Council Directive 76/207/EEC of 9 February 1976 concerning equality between men and women.
3   With the accession of Greece in 1981 and Portugal and Spain in 1986.
4   *Commission* v. *Belgium*, Case 321/87 [1989] ECR 997.
5   *Commission* v. *Netherlands*, Case C-68/89 [1991] ECR I-2637.
6   *Official Journal*, L217/25, 1985.
7   Joined cases 281, 283–5, 287/87, *Germany, France, Netherlands, Denmark and UK* v. *the Commission* [1987] ECR 3245.
8   Council press release 10518/92.
9   Commission answer to Written Parliamentary Question 3044/90. *Official Journal* C214/12, 1991.
10 Council press release 10518/92.
11 Commission answer to Written Parliamentary Question 3044/90. *Official Journal* C214/12, 1991.

4

Maastricht's justice and home affairs pillar

Introduction

The Treaty on European Union, or Maastricht Treaty as it is more commonly known, formalised, but did not supranationalise, co-operation on immigration and asylum policy by drawing co-operation that had been outside of the Treaty into an intergovernmental 'pillar' of the newly created EU. Aside from its immigration and asylum policy implications, if the famous – or perhaps infamous – Maastricht Treaty had but one virtue, it was that it drew debates about European integration from the realm of élite discussion, where they had tended to dwell, and placed them more squarely in the spotlight of broader public debate in the member states. This is not to suggest that the minutiae of inter-state negotiations and the riveting detail of Treaty articles transfixed the peoples of Europe: it was probably only the lawyers who truly rubbed their hands with glee. Rather, the deals and compromises struck by national governments, as well as their implications, were subject to more critical scrutiny than had previously been the case. The discussion of the implications of the creation of the EU by the Maastricht Treaty even caused 'Euroscepticism' – conflated with domestic political factors such as the unpopularity of national governments – to advance beyond its traditional territorial confines in 'awkward partners' such as Denmark and Britain, as the French people's *petit oui* in their September 1992 referendum on Maastricht ratification demonstrated.

The movement from post-SEA *ad hoc* co-operation outside a treaty framework to more formal intergovernmental co-operation covered by provisions of the Maastricht Treaty could be construed as indicative of a creeping supranationalisation, because immigration and asylum moved closer to being subject to integration. A weakness of this line of argument is that it contributes to the notion of integrative inevitability derived from teleological perspectives on European integration while neglecting state motivations underpinning co-operation. It can be argued that member states sought release from domestic (national) judicial and political

86

constraints on policy development and that, therefore, they would be reluctant to allow scope for supranational constitutionalisation and in-stitutionalisation of immigration and asylum competencies, preferring instead intergovernmental co-operation. In the Maastricht negotiations, the more sceptical national governments, such as the British and Danish, were able to put a brake on ambitious plans for the development of EU immigration and asylum policy. Maastricht did, however, demonstrate some tentative movement towards policy co-operation within the legal and political structures of the EU, albeit with the member states main-taining their position as the main reference point.

The negotiations

The perceived inadequacies of post-SEA *ad hoc* intergovernmental co-operation on immigration and asylum policy, coupled with a desire on the part of some member states to seek deeper political integration, prompted Maastricht's re-evaluation of immigration and asylum policy co-operation. This was for three reasons. First, decision-making procedures were viewed as inadequate, as evidenced by the difficulties experienced by the Dublin Convention and the EFC. Second, *ad hoc* co-operation exacerbated the 'democratic deficit'. Third, there existed an at best tenuous relationship between, on the one side, internal security policy co-operation and, on the other, civil liberties, human rights and accountability. In its 1991 communication on immigration policy, the Commission noted that the intergovernmental method had failed to produce any meaningful results. The Commission was prepared to be pragmatic because of the difficulties of securing more ambitious forms of immigration and asylum policy integration. It emphasised the importance of dialogue between the EC member states through the General Affairs Council and through meetings of immigration ministers (CEC, 1991). It sought to participate in the development of a restrictive immigration and asylum policy framework while also seeking involvement in policies affecting the chances for inclusion of migrants and their descendants. The EP felt marginalised by the Commission's pragmatic stance. It adopted a highly critical tone, condemned *ad hoc* intergovernmentalism and urged that immigration and asylum policies be brought within the EC framework and that action be taken at Community level to tackle racism and xenophobia.[1]

Despite the views of supranational institutions, it was the policy preferences of the member states that mattered. Ultimately, the Maastricht Treaty was to give legal effect to a messy compromise between integrative 'maximalists', who favoured deeper integration, and 'minimalists', who were opposed. As is often the case, maximalists outnumbered minimalists, but negotiations proceeded on the basis of unanimity, with the effect that the preferences of more reluctant member states had a decisive and limiting impact on the range of possible outcomes. This did not mean that the outcome mirrored the policy preferences of the minimalists, but that they were able to put a brake on more ambitious integrative objectives by limiting the range of outcomes. Effectively precluded from the outset was communitarisation of immigration and asylum policy.

The immigration and asylum policy compromise between maximalists and minimalists was reflected in the creation of the 'third pillar' of the Maastricht Treaty that dealt with justice and home affairs (JHA) policy. The JHA pillar made a clear connection between immigration and asylum and other internal security issues. It seemed that the immigration issue was boiled down to a rather undernourished conceptualisation of a problem of numbers, with little scope for countervailing measures aimed at migrant inclusion. A trade-off at member state level between control and migrant inclusion was decisively shifted in the direction of control at EU level. This did not necessarily occur because the member states were not prepared to countenance supranational action for migrant inclusion. Rather it was a tangible manifestation of the difficulties associated with securing agreement on the content of such a policy, given the widely divergent policy paradigms in member states and the need for unanimity if an EU context were to be established. There was, however, far less divergence on the need for tight immigration controls and there was a detectable intergovernmental preference convergence on this issue. This provided all the necessary ingredients for a 'lowest common denominator' immigration and asylum policy, emphasising tighter restriction. It also laid the foundations for blurred competence, derived from the cautious ceding of competencies that left question marks concerning competence, discretion and the location of capacity to act.

The intention of Maastricht's drafters was for the JHA pillar to stand alongside the 'first pillar' (the Community pillar) and the 'second pillar' (dealing with a common foreign and security policy, CFSP). Co-operation on CFSP had occurred outside the framework of the Treaty of Rome since 1970, when EPC had been established (see chapter 3). Inter-state dynamics during the Maastricht negotiations and the political sensitivity of immigration and asylum issues precluded supranational integration, despite the hopes of integrative maximalists, such as the Dutch government, which drafted the Maastricht Treaty. The Maastricht negotiations, the Treaty itself and its aftermath also illustrate the articulation between the single market's liberalisation and the development of an interior policy with a security focus including immigration and asylum. Freer movement for EU citizens prompted closer co-operation on entry, residence and movement of TCNs, but did not dictate that these areas had to be supranationalised.

The Dublin meeting of the European Council in June 1990 had agreed to convene two IGCs composed of national ministers to consider treaty reform. One dealt with EMU, the other with political union. The two

IGCs were formally opened at the Rome summit in December 1990. The EMU IGC was rather more straightforward, because the groundwork for the discussion had been laid in the Delors report, which had investigated the prospects for EMU and suggested a plan of action (Delors *et al.*, 1989). The agenda for the political union IGC was far less certain and there was greater scope for conflict between member states over object-ives. Immigration and asylum aroused particular controversy within the discussions. There was a basic measure of agreement that the *ad hoc* structures put in place after the SEA were problematic for a number of reasons, including democratic scrutiny, accountability and decision-making efficiency. Two basic questions configured discussion of future policy development. Would immigration and asylum be incorporated within the existing EC structure, with the implication of a significant degree of supranationalisation? Or, would new structures be established which would place immigration and asylum in a separate intergovernmental pillar? The former option would mark a significant encroachment of supranational authority into policy areas strongly associated with state sovereignty. The latter would bring immigration and asylum within the structure of the EU, but restrict the extent of communitarisation of the policy because of the reliance on intergovernmental co-operation.

The Luxembourg government took responsibility for management of the IGC process when it assumed the Council presidency for the six months between January and June 1991. In January 1991 it made four immigration and asylum policy suggestions, between which member states were invited to express a preference: first, the maintenance of existing *ad hoc* arrangements; second, that a reference be made in the Maastricht Treaty to co-operation but that the Council be left to sort out the details; third, that more elaborate Treaty provisions be made, outlining areas of co-operation; fourth, and most ambitiously, that immigration and asylum policies be fully incorporated into the Treaty framework and use the EC method of decision-making. Opinions among member states were divided. The Danish government favoured the first option. The British, Irish and Greek governments preferred the second. France, Germany and Portugal expressed a preference for the third option (for the French and German governments as a short-term measure before full communitarisation). The Netherlands, Belgium, Italy and Spain favoured the fourth option. The majority of member states leaned towards closer integration but there was a requirement to proceed by unanimity. The balance of intergovernmental preferences meant that option four was unattainable. The range of possible alternatives suggested some kind of compromise secured through maintenance of intergovernmentalism, but with a closer association with the legal framework of the Treaty and EC institutions.

In April 1991 the Luxembourg government produced a 'non-paper' containing draft Treaty amendments. This proposed creation of a EU within which would be created separate CFSP and JHA pillars. Because of their long-standing preference for intergovernmentalism, the British Conservative government led by Prime Minister Major favoured this pillared approach. The French, Germans, Belgians and Spanish saw it as too minimalist in its ambitions. The Commission and EP also reacted unfavourably to what they saw as a consolidation of intergovernmentalism that would minimise their role in policy development and decision-making. Despite the satisfaction of the British government, the Luxembourg presidency's suggestions were not *in toto* an intergovernmentalists' charter, because they contained other ambitious proposals for deeper integration, such as plans to extend local and European election voting rights to permanently resident non-EC nationals (ultimately, not to be realised). It was, though, the Luxembourg proposals that were to be the basis of the Maastricht deal, because they were acceptable to the minimalists while they were also seen as opening the possibility for communitarisation in the future.

On immigration and asylum policy integration the German, Belgian, Italian, Greek, Dutch, Spanish and Irish governments, plus the Commission, could broadly be classed as maximalists. All preferred that immigration and asylum be placed within EC decision-making procedures. The Danish and British governments wanted a separate intergovernmental pillar. Luxembourg and France suggested a compromise: the creation of a pillar but with the presumption of temporariness and the likelihood of closer integration in the future. The German government strongly favoured Europeanisation of asylum policy because of the salience of the asylum issue in German politics. The German government thought that a common European effort might help alleviate some of the German responsibility. The prospect of sharing responsibility (i.e. a more equal distribution of asylum-seekers) was one reason why other member states were decidedly less enthusiastic than the Germans about Europeanisation of asylum policy.

On 1 July 1991 the Dutch government assumed the Council presidency. It faced the difficult task of reconciling divergent views within the political union IGC. The Dutch also held their own long-standing preference for deeper economic and political integration, embodying some kind of explicitly stated 'federal vocation'. There were also other pressing issues for the Dutch presidency to deal with, particularly the civil war in Yugoslavia, which dominated the political agenda. The Dutch government took a maximalist approach and sought a statement in the Treaty expressing support for federal objectives. This was reflected in proposals that resulted in a black day for Dutch diplomacy, 30 September 1991, when an ambitious draft Treaty proposed among other things communitarisation of immigration and asylum. The Dutch proposals likened the EU to a tree, with immigration and asylum as one of its branches, subject to the Community method of decision-making. Only the Belgian government and the Commission rallied to the Dutch proposals. Other member states strongly criticised the Dutch draft, refused to negotiate on the basis of it, and expressed a clear preference for the Luxembourg version (with its plan for a pillared structure). The Dutch government had to swallow its pride and the eventual basis for negotiation at the Maastricht summit was far closer to the Luxembourg proposals than the more overtly federalist Dutch plans.

In October 1991, as part of its contribution to the IGC process, the Commission issued a communication covering immigration and asylum (CEC, 1991). The document called not only for the control of migration to become an integral element of EC policy, but also for the strengthening of European-level measures aimed at the integration of settled migrants and their descendants. The Commission contended that European-level co-operation was skewed in the direction of control, with few countervailing measures designed to promote migrant integration. The non-binding Social Charter of 1989 had indicated some of the problems that were faced when its outline of a strengthened EC social dimension made no commitment to the fundamental social rights of TCNs. As had become very clear when the free movement policy was enacted, the rights of TCNs who were not dependants of an EC national or covered by an Association Agreement were matters for the member states, not the EC. The EP criticised the Commission's communications for being compliant with the restrictionist drift of policy.[2] The communication maintained the Commission's pragmatic stance towards policy development while reflecting the constraints imposed by the limited legal basis for EC action. It did, however, also propose laying the foundations for a comprehensive EC migration policy, encompassing a threefold strategy combining immigration control with immigrant integration and measures to tackle the root causes of migration.

The work of national ministers responsible for immigration and asylum continued in the run-up to Maastricht and fed into the IGC process. The immigration ministers presented a report to the Maastricht European Council that set out an immigration and asylum work programme.[3] This concentrated on the harmonisation of admission policies for family reunion, work, study or humanitarian reasons. It also sought the development of a common approach to illegal immigration, labour migration policies and the status of TCNs, including labour market access. The work programme also spelt out priorities for asylum policy related to the implementation of the Dublin Convention. Asylum policy harmonisation would include attempts to define the principle of first host country as well as a common interpretation of the definition of a refugee. The report outlining the work programme expressed no opinion on the institutional structures within which the work should be conducted, because this would have been too controversial. It did, though, express a commitment to policy development based on social justice and human rights, with implications for refugee policy and family reunion, as well as for anti-discrimination and migrant integration policies. This work programme formed the basis for the subsequent co-operation within the JHA pillar discussed later in this chapter.

Maastricht's pillars

The Maastricht Treaty was negotiated on 9–10 December 1991 and signed in Lisbon in February 1992, but then hobbled through a ratification process that was not completed until November 1993, when the German articles of ratification were deposited following the defeat of challenges made in the German constitutional court. The Treaty created a pillared structure incorporating JHA and CFSP into the framework of the EU, but maintaining intergovernmental co-operation for decision-making and a severely constrained role for supranational institutions in these two areas. This led to the Treaty structure being likened to a Greek temple, the roof of which was supported by three pillars. The central and largest pillar was the 'Community', with significant supranationalisation across a range of policy sectors. Within these sectors, the core elements of a supranational community were evident: EC law had direct effect, the ECJ held jurisdiction, QMV applied to more policy areas, the Commission was closely associated with policy development and the EP was, to varying degrees, involved in policy development. The second and third pillars were intergovernmental: the CFSP pillar built on EPC structures put in place in 1970, while the JHA pillar formalised prior patterns of *ad hoc* co-operation. Free movement was supranationalised, while immigration and asylum remained intergovernmental.

How appropriate was this temple analogy? Handoll (1995: 32) suggests that it was not particularly useful because the pillared structure did not create 'classical harmony', but an unbalanced and lopsided structure that was part of a process by which the two new intergovernmental elements would be gradually subsumed by the Community element (the central pillar). As well as the absence of architectural symmetry, the rather strange constitutional design of the pillared structure – the product of compromise, not of clear intent – also raised the issue of the legal foundations of the EU. What legal status did the pillars possess? Clearly, they were not EC laws as typically understood, because they were neither supreme nor possessed of direct effect. Müller-Graff (1994) described the Maastricht framework as 'legal sandstone' not 'legal granite'; the pillars were not amendments to the Treaty and so were not part of EC law, but were likely to be eroded as a consequence of gradual encroachment by the Community pillar. This meant that the legal foundations of the Treaty were public international law. Snyder (1994: 89) agreed that the JHA pillar was not EC law as usually understood, but argued that the connections were close because the third pillar was an integral part of the EU and subject to its single institutional structure: 'The European Community and the European Union are thus distinct but intimately related'.

These intimate relations stemmed from procedural, institutional and functional connections between the third and first pillars (Müller-Graff 1994: 24–30). Procedural connections derived from the incorporation of interior policy within the EU's single institutional framework. Institutional connections arose from the fact that even though they relied on unanimity, EU institutions were empowered to act upon immigration and asylum issues (with significant limitations). Functional connections derived from links between the attainment of single market objectives and interior policy issues drawn into the realm of EU competence, which included immigration and asylum. It was not possible, for instance, to demarcate clearly between free movement ('communitarised') and immigration and asylum ('intergovernmental') and deal with them entirely separately: functional connections meant that the issues were linked. This is a key point and an important factor underpinning pressure for supranationalisation of immigration and asylum policies. Legal and institutional connections created a web of linkages between intra- and extra-EU migration policy and meant that the two could not be treated as though they were wholly distinct. The economic logic of market-making had political consequences that drew issues of high politics into the EU's remit. Free movement had become communitarised, while immigration and asylum remained largely beyond the remit of national and supranational institutions. Indeed, immigration and asylum policy saw the development of patterns of co-operation that emphasised control and security dimensions of policy rather than in areas relating to migrant inclusion.

The JHA pillar

Title VI of the Maastricht Treaty dealt with JHA co-operation. Article K1 listed the issues that were to be regarded as matters of 'common interest', that is, not 'common policies'. The distinction is important. Indeed, for the British Conservative government, the JHA pillar was a diplomatic triumph, or 'game, set and match' as John Major put it when speaking to the press outside the Maastricht negotiating rooms (perhaps unwisely in the light of the calamities that would befall his government as a result of the European issue). Major stated that:

> At Maastricht we developed a new way, and one much more amenable to the institutions of this country – co-operation by agreement between governments, but not under the Treaty of Rome. It covers interior and justice

matters, foreign affairs and security, and the option is available for it to
cover wider matters in the future. (Quoted in Duff, 1994: 20)

Was Major right? Was this a new way of co-operating on immigration
and asylum issues that could be sustained in the long term and, perhaps,
broadened to cover other policy areas? Major was mistaken. Other
member states did not share his vision of enlarging spheres of intergovernmental co-operation. Indeed, even a cursory analysis of the negotiations
preceding the Maastricht summit would show that most member states
saw the pillars as a compromise and not as a model for future development – as 'sandstone' not 'granite'. For maximalists, the pillared structure
was also part of what they saw as a slow and incremental movement
towards immigration and asylum policy integration. The JHA pillar was
likely to set the ground rules for debate about further extension of EU
competence for immigration and asylum in the future. Bieber (1994: 38)
noted of the third pillar arrangements that: 'their intrinsic evolutionary
and provisional quality is framed by the first pillar, which hence establishes the long-term centre of gravity of this complex system'.

From this perspective, Maastricht's JHA pillar was a compromise, but
a 'bridge' existed between the third and first pillar which could lead to
greater supranationalisation of immigration and asylum issues in the
future. This bridge was provided for by Article K9, which created a
procedure for a *passerelle* from the JHA pillar to the Community pillar;
albeit this was a procedure that lawyers liked to analyse, but member
states preferred not to follow (Bieber, 1994). To restate a by now familiar
point about the difficulties of positive integration: crossing the bridge
from the third pillar to the first required unanimity among member states,
which was unlikely to be forthcoming. Even when the free movement,
immigration and asylum provisions of the Amsterdam Treaty did cross a
bridge to the Community pillar, the member states took with them the
reassuring paraphernalia of intergovernmental decision-making.

The new JHA pillar also had a clear security emphasis, which accompanied single market liberalisation, and helped blur the distinction
between internal and external security in a frontier-free Europe. This
emphasis on security has been discussed in terms of a reorientation of
security activity from 'national' to 'societal' security, with the additional
implication that the construction of immigration as a threat involved both
an external and an internal dimension derived from the supposed threat
to national borders as well as to internal security (Wæver *et al.*, 1993).
Immigration was constructed as an external challenge and an internal
threat to societal stability and cohesion. In a detailed analysis of the
practices of security agencies in the post-Cold War period, Bigo (1996)
discussed a move from control of territory to control of population in a
frontier-free Europe, where distinctions between external and internal
security become blurred. The emphasis is on the development of new

technologies for population control and the ways in which migration becomes subsumed within the practices, processes and discourses of securitisation.

As well as their strong security emphasis, Maastricht's JHA provisions were also seen as widening the 'democratic deficit' (Geddes, 1995). Patterns of democratic control and accountability at national and supranational level were weak. This widening of the democratic deficit arose as a consequence of the intergovernmental bargaining process rather than necessarily being a distinct preference of most member states. Indeed, the preference of most member states was for some form of supranationalisation of immigration and asylum policy with an extended role for the Commission, ECJ and EP. The democratic deficit was not necessarily widened because of a malevolent disregard for democracy exacerbated by European integration (the conspiracy theory of European integration) but because of difficulties securing agreement between maximalist and minimalist states during intergovernmental negotiations (the problems of positive integration). The majority of member states would have preferred more 'democracy', as measured by increased power for the EP, albeit within a more secretive institutional framework than for other integrated policy areas. However, an insufficient number of member states preferred this option and, in a system reliant on unanimity, the minimalists were able to hold sway. Britain and Denmark, in particular, were reluctant to see communitarisation of immigration and asylum issues, with increased power for the EP, Commission and ECJ, despite other member states being prepared to see these issues brought within the framework of the EU. The point is not that the preferences of Denmark and Britain prevailed exactly (they had to make some concessions on these and other issues), but that they decisively affected the possible outcomes in a negotiating environment reliant on unanimity. If supranationalisation rather than intergovernmentalism had been the chosen path, then the problems of democratic accountability might not have been so marked; but this route was patently unacceptable to a minority of member states, which were able to decisively influence the Treaty outcome.

JHA provisions

In terms of Maastricht's nitty-gritty, the following areas were recognised by the Treaty as being of 'common interest':

- asylum policy;
- rules governing the crossing by persons of the external borders of the member states and the exercise of controls thereon;
- immigration policy and policy regarding TCNs –
  - (a) their conditions of entry to and movement within the territory of member states;

(b) their conditions of residence on the territory of member states, including family reunion and access to employment;

(c) combating their unauthorised immigration, residence and work on the territory of member states.

Article K1 also listed other issues that were to be covered by intergovernmental co-operation, such as combating drug trafficking and addiction, international fraud, terrorism, police co-operation (via Europol) and judicial co-operation in civil and criminal matters. Immigration and asylum were placed alongside internal security issues. Countervailing immigrant integration measures were limited and did not possess a sure footing in the Treaty. A declaration added to the Treaty at the instigation of the German government did, however, declare that co-operation on asylum policy would be a priority.

Article K2 stated that these matters of common interest would be dealt with in compliance with the ECHR and the Geneva Convention. This was an easy declaration to make, but more difficult to enforce because the provision was not justiciable by the ECJ. Third pillar issues would be subject to ECJ review in the light of international obligations only if arrangements were made to extend ECJ jurisdiction to cover these matters. This indicated superficial regard for the symbolic importance of these international obligations, but scant regard for ensuring effective compliance. Twomey (1994: 56–63) points out that states cannot ignore their international obligations by simply stating that breaches of them are due to the creation of the third pillar and that this somehow excuses the breach. Declarations by EU member states of their collective respect for international law may not tally with practices. For instance, the assumption by non-state agents of responsibility for aspects of migration control, such as airlines, can compromise the very standards that the member states have pledged to uphold. The result of the imposition of carrier sanctions on airlines carrying undocumented migrants has been that inadequately trained airline personnel have to deal with complex immigration questions while knowing that the threat of large fines hangs over the heads of their employers if the 'wrong' people are allowed to travel (Lahav, 1998). Restriction is incentivised.

Article K3 of the Maastricht Treaty confirmed unanimity in the Council of Ministers as the basis for decision-making. Except for the visa provisions of Article 100c of the Community pillar (see below), there was to be no provision for QMV. The Commission's powers were also watered down because it would have to share its right of initiative with the member states. Indeed, the Commission proved to be so sensitive about national policy preferences in the third pillar that most initiatives actually came from the member states. The ECJ was deprived of jurisdiction unless it was specifically allocated under the terms of an international convention.

Moreover, the legal basis of the JHA pillar was also weakened because the issuance of regulations or directives – the mainstays of the Community legal system – were not options. Instead, three far less substantive courses of action were available to the member states:

- *joint positions*, which did not have binding effect;
- *joint actions*, which could have binding effects in relation to the kinds of action agreed upon and could be implemented by use of QMV, if member states agreed unanimously to do so (the unanimity problem again);
- adoption of *conventions* in international law, which would need to be ratified at national level and could be interpreted by national courts in accordance with the characteristics of national systems (but remember the travails of the Dublin Convention, which took seven years to enter into effect, and the EFC, which in 1999 had still not even been signed by all the member states).

There were also the tasks associated with bureaucratic support for the operation of Council of Ministers dealing with JHA issues. This role was assumed by the 'K4 Committee' (the name was derived from the Treaty article), composed of senior officials, which assumed the responsibilities previously performed within groups such as Trevi and the *Ad Hoc* Group on Immigration. The K4 Committee preferred similar levels of secrecy and helped propagate an information deficit arising from the absence of publicly available documentation on its activities. Article K5 committed the member states to defending common positions adopted under the third pillar provisions.

The Commission and, particularly, the EP and ECJ were marginal to decision-making. There was a precedent within the framework of EPC (on foreign policy) which developed during the 1970s for exclusion of the Commission and EP (Monar, 1994). It was difficult to justify exclusion of supranational institutions from immigration and asylum policy issues that related so strongly to the fundamental objectives of the EU associated with attainment of the single market's free movement objectives. The *passerelle* clause, Article K9, established a potential bridge from the JHA pillar to the EU. It provided that the Council, acting unanimously on the initiative of the Commission or a member state, could decide to apply Article 100c of the Treaty to areas covered by Articles K1–6 and determine the relevant voting conditions, that is unanimity or QMV. In theory this could have prompted the supranationalisation of immigration and asylum issues, but in reality it did not. The declaration on asylum attached to the final act of the Maastricht Treaty required the Council to consider, by the end of 1993, the possibility of applying Article K9 to asylum policy. Such a move would involve amendment of the Treaty, so there was also the requirement that any decision to use the *passerelle* would need to be ratified by member states in accordance with their respective constitutional requirements. A November 1993 Commission report on the possibility of applying Article K9 to asylum policy identified certain advantages, but argued that it was too soon to take such a step (CEC, 1994a). This was a realistic assessment of the position by the Commission, because there was little prospect that the member states would all agree.

A revised draft of the EFC was drawn up to take account of Maastricht's JHA pillar. The proposal was for a Council Decision based on Article K3 of the Maastricht Treaty (CEC, 1993; O'Keeffe, 1994). The reformulated proposal sought to maintain the political consensus that had existed on the previous draft EFC brought forward within the post-SEA *ad hoc* procedures. The disagreement between the Spanish and British governments about the status of Gibraltar continued to prevent agreement being reached on the draft EFC. In the absence of such agreement, the Commission pushed ahead in July 1997 with proposals for practical co-operation between national immigration officials and the EU through the 'Odysseus' programme, which would provide fourteen million ECU between 1997 and 2001 (CEC, 1997b).

The Maastricht Treaty also contained social policy provisions in its Social Chapter that have some effect on the rights of TCNs. The Social Chapter, signed by eleven member states, with Britain opting out (and opting back in after the election of a Labour government in May 1997), includes among the objectives of EU social policy: improved living and working conditions, proper social protection and the combating of exclusion. It has been noted that 'All these objectives naturally concern the position of all workers, irrespective of nationality (and arguably residence status)' (Handoll, 1995: 392) and thus apply to TCNs. The Social Chapter has been utilised by pro-migrant lobby groups as they have pressed for a 'Resident's Charter' to extend to permanently settled TCNs many of the rights held by EU citizens (see chapters 6 and 7 for more details). The social dimension is particularly important in this respect: migrants who are legally resident in EU member states acquire social entitlements as a result of residence, but at EU level social entitlements derive from prior possession of the nationality of a member state.

To examine the scope for supranational constitutionalisation and institutionalisation, we need to assess the competence of supranational institutions and their ability to shape policy outcomes. For JHA issues, this was essentially non-existent. The JHA provisions stated that the Commission was to be 'fully associated' with JHA issues. The Commission did not hold the same power in the third pillar that it was able to exercise in communitarised areas. For instance, Articles 155 and 163 of the EC Treaty, which allowed Commission monitoring of compliance with Treaty obligations by member states and other actors, did not apply in the JHA pillar. The Commission continued to face the dilemma it had encountered in the aftermath of the SEA. Advocating supranational integration could risk distancing the Commission from day-to-day co-operation between member states on JHA policy that had significant free movement implications. Participation could offend maximalist sensibilities but would offer the practical advantage of allowing the Commission to continue to develop its immigration and asylum policy role in a piecemeal and pragmatic way with communitarisation as the eventual objective. To the chagrin of the EP, which was hostile to intergovernmental co-operation that excluded it from participation, the Commission continued to choose the pragmatic course of action. Even though the Commission's own 1985 White Paper on the single market had staked out an ambitious immigration and asylum policy role for supranational institutions, the Commission was prepared to compromise ambitious objectives to secure a role in discussions about immigration and asylum. The Commission took the view that some member states were not prepared to countenance the kind of deeper integration it had envisaged in 1985. To this end, the free movement Commissioner, Martin Bangemann, stated that: 'where the best prospects for progress lie in going down the road of intergovernmental conventions rather than Community legal instruments, the Commission has opted for making progress rather than fighting time-consuming battles for competence' (quoted in Monar, 1994: 71).

The EP was marginal to the work of the third pillar. It only had the right to be informed after the fact of third pillar developments. In formal terms, the Council presidency and the Commission were obliged to 'regularly inform' the EP of their discussions, 'consult' it on 'principal aspects of activities' and take its views 'into consideration'. The EP was determined to express its opposition to what it saw as the deficiencies of intergovernmental co-operation with regard to its implications for human rights, democracy and accountability. The main vehicle for its attempts to examine third pillar provisions was its Civil Liberties and Internal Affairs Committee, which showed the eagerness of the watchdog, but without the necessary teeth. The effect was that parliamentary scrutiny was rather like being barked at by a puppy. The EP was also hampered by the absence of information on JHA activities. National parliaments were not much better placed to monitor European decisions, which had often been made behind closed doors before they were opened to any form of public scrutiny.[4] The EP did bring forward an ambitious – and at the time unrealistic – draft inter-institutional agreement which formalised EP involvement in JHA issues and gave the EP quite substantial powers of consultation over action taken within the third pillar.[5] For instance, before adopting joint positions, joint actions or conventions, the Council would first have to consult the EP. But the Council was under no compulsion to negotiate on the issues covered by the draft agreement and in February 1994 made it clear that it had no intention of doing so. There was nothing the EP could do about this and it was forced to continue to state its case from the sidelines for closer involvement in immigration and asylum policy and EU action against racist and xenophobic discrimination.

Not all immigration and asylum issues were placed in the JHA pillar. Article 100c of the Community pillar covered visa policies and created a problem of blurred competence (which was also to be a theme within the reflections on the Maastricht Treaty during the IGC leading up to the 1997 Amsterdam Treaty). The German government had favoured more extensive supranationalisation of immigration and asylum policy within the Community framework, not a separate pillar. Article 100c provided that the Council, acting unanimously, would draw up a list of third countries whose nationals needed visas to cross the external borders of the member states. In emergencies, the Council was given power to act by QMV. The Council was also given power, acting by QMV, to draw up a uniform format for visas. The K4 Committee was also to be involved in this work on the visa list and uniform visa format. As well as imparting an element of supranationalisation into immigration and asylum policy, Article 100c added some confusion because visa policy was now to be dealt with by Article 100c in the Community pillar and Articles K1(2), (3) in the third pillar.

Two regulations were introduced based on Article 100c. Regulation 1683/95 established a uniform visa format and Regulation 2317/95 listed the 101 countries whose nationals needed visas to enter the EU. There were some problems of co-ordination, as evidenced by the fact that the separate Schengen visa list named 129 countries, while nationals of a further twenty-eight countries required visas to enter certain EU member states (Baldwin-Edwards, 1997: 499). However, the ECJ annulled Regulation 2317/95 in June 1997 after a challenge from the EP arising from a lack of proper consultation with it.[6] The Commission was forced to bring forward new proposals.

EU citizenship

Another innovation contained within the Maastricht Treaty was the introduction of citizenship of the EU. The problems of the 'democratic deficit' and the creation of a 'people's Europe' began to be cast as problems to which European citizenship was a possible solution. The Spanish government's influential memorandum proposed the establishment of EU citizenship as a complement to national citizenship and as a 'qualitative step' from 'privileged foreigner' to 'European citizens' and, as such, associated with the creation of a political union.[7] EU citizenship was to be a derived right, derived from holding the citizenship of a member state and thereby complementing, not replacing, national citizenship. The effect of it being a derived right was that legally resident TCNs who were not citizens of the member state in which they resided were not entitled to become EU citizens. Although the creation of EU citizenship could be construed as evidence of the deterritorialisation of citizenship, which has been discussed in terms of post-national membership, this view needs to be qualified by the exclusion of TCNs. It also remained a clear principle enunciated in the Treaty (and in international law) that it was for states to determine who could or could not become a national (and, thereby, a citizen of the EU). A Declaration attached to the final act of the Maastricht Treaty stated that: 'the question whether an individual possesses the nationality of a Member State shall be settled solely by reference to the national law of the Member State concerned'.

The creation of citizenship of the EU did, however, draw the nationality criteria of member states into question. For instance, the establishment of EU citizenship could be seen as creating some anomalies arising from, for instance, ease of access to national citizenship in different member states and subsequent entitlement to rights accruing from EU citizenship. For example, descendants of immigrants born in France can relatively straightforwardly acquire French nationality at the age of eighteen and thereby automatically become EU citizens. They can then move freely within the EU and exercise the rights of EU citizens, such as voting and standing in local and European elections. Immigrants and their descendants in Germany, on the other hand, find it far more difficult to acquire citizenship because of the emphasis on blood descent (*jus sanguinis*) in German nationality law (an issue reopened by Schröder's Social Democratic government elected in 1998). Consequently, a French person of immigrant origin who had acquired French nationality at the age of eighteen could move to Germany and stand and vote in local elections, while a person of, say, Turkish origin born in Germany and who had lived there her whole life could not. This situation may appear anomalous, but is the consequence of the transposition of a derived right of EU citizenship on divergent criteria for allocation of nationality (Weil, 1996).

In terms of formal provisions, citizenship of the EU as created by Maastricht has been described as of rather limited value, although others have emphasised its constructive potential (Martiniello, 1994; Wiener, 1997). Article B of the Maastricht Treaty stated that one of the objectives of the EU was 'to strengthen the protection of the rights and interests of the nationals of its member states through the introduction of a citizenship of the Union'. Article 8 provided that every person holding the citizenship of a member state was to be a citizen of the EU. To some extent, the rights associated with EU citizenship actually bundled many pre-existing rights which had been scattered across the framework of the

Treaty of Rome and the SEA. As a result of Maastricht, nationals of member states, as EU citizens, would be entitled to:

- move freely and reside within the EU;
- vote and stand in municipal and European elections;
- acquire rights of diplomatic protection;
- petition the EP and the newly created ombudsman.

In addition to this, newly created EU citizens also possessed entitlements within the Union's social dimension.

Chapters 6 and 7 analyse the institutional context at EU level within which chances for migrant inclusion are mediated. The argument is developed that the scope for inclusion is given meaning by the EU's institutional context, which provides the legal, political and social context through which those making claims for inclusion operationalise their arguments.

The parameters of policy

Following Maastricht's ratification, the member states and EU institutions began to develop an immigration and asylum framework via a morass of non-binding recommendations and declarations that would render weary even the most ardent student of European integration. The limitations of the Treaty framework led to a fragmented system of decision-making without clear ascription of competence at EU level for even those areas where co-operation was deemed desirable. What emerged was a complicated and secretive five-level immigration and asylum policy decision-making structure (box 1), although to characterise it as a decision-making structure could be to exaggerate its effectiveness. At the top was the Council, supported by the Committee of Permanent Representatives, beneath which was the K4 Committee comprising senior interior ministry officials; the work of the K4 Committee was then conducted through steering groups and working parties.

Immigration and asylum in the post-Maastricht period was clearly not supranationalised. The Commission had to share its power of initiative with member states and preferred to state its position by way of communications to the Council and EP. For instance, the Commission's 1994 communication called for: the harmonisation of the legal status of permanently resident TCNs; attention to the residence status of relatives of TCNs; the realisation of the objective of free movement within the EU for legally resident TCNs; the removal of nationality criteria for access to rights or benefits when not objectively justified; the monitoring of agreements between EU member states and third countries; and the ratification of the UN's 1990 International Convention on the Protection of the Rights

Box 1. The JHA pillar's five-level structure

Council of Justice and Home Affairs Ministers

Committee of Permanent Representatives

K4 Committee

Steering group	*Steering group*	*Steering group*
Immigration/asylum	Police/customs co-operation	Judicial co-operation in civil and criminal matters

Working parties	*Working parties*	*Working parties*
Asylum	Terrorism	Extradition
Immigration	Police co-operation	Criminal law
Visas	Fight against	Brussels Convention
External frontiers	organised crime	Transmission of acts
False papers	Europol	Driving bans
EURODAC	Drugs	
	Customs co-operation	

of All Migrant Workers and Members of Their Families. Such plans had little chance of success, because of opposition from more sceptical member states and the requirement for unanimity (CEC, 1994a). Participation by the Commission in policies affecting immigration control (the JHA pillar) and immigrant integration (through the Migrant Integration Unit within the Commission's Social Affairs Directorate, DGV, for instance) is evidence of the potential for 'separate universes of discourse' and 'orders of comprehension' that can develop within administrative organisations (Dunsire, 1978). This reflection within the Commission of the control and integration dimensions of policy should be expected, given that these tensions have been clearly evident in European immigration policy and politics since at least the 1970s. It also counteracts any tendency to view the Commission as a monolith. The intergovernmental co-operation that developed in the post-SEA period showed how this form of European integration has presented opportunities for states to circumvent domestic constraints on immigration and asylum. The Commission has been drawn into these forms of co-operation and integration while also espousing increased EU-level rights for migrants and their descendants.

The difficulties faced by the Commission in developing a JHA role stemmed in part from limitations derived from member states' sensitivities to its activism in these areas. In addition, the Commission's own resources in terms of staff and political leadership were limited. A five-person JHA task force was established within the Commission's General Secretariat, but JHA co-operation was not perceived as a high priority, particularly when compared to the resources devoted to promoting the EU's external political profile through the CFSP. The Commission's caution could be construed as a lack of dynamism, but also indicated how prevailing inter- and intra-institutional dynamics at both national and supranational level tempered ambitious plans for integration.

Between 1993 and 1998 the Council adopted more than seventy immigration and asylum measures. The immigration ministers meeting in the Council preferred to use non-binding recommendations, resolutions and conclusions. This meant that the efficacy of the policy output was questionable, that it was difficult to monitor, because many agreements were not actually published, and that it contributed to a 'competence gap' derived from the absence of clear decision-making responsibilities at EU level. A joint action plan agreed in April 1998 is illustrative of the EU's developing immigration and asylum framework. This was adopted on the basis of Article K3 of the Maastricht Treaty, to provide finance for the 'voluntary repatriation of displaced persons who have found temporary protection in the Member States and asylum seekers' in the EU. A Council press release of 27 April 1998 stated that the joint action plan gave 'a legal and financial basis to the implementation of the Action Plan on the influx of migrants from Iraq and the neighbouring regions'. The General Affairs Council had adopted this forty-six-point action plan on 26 January 1998. Although its title referred to the influx of migrants from Iraq and neighbouring countries, the intentions were broader: 'the initiative is primarily concerned with plugging the gaps in the operation of existing policies (for example, the Dublin Convention and EURODAC) and second, and specifically, to deal with migrants coming through Turkey' (*Statewatch*, May–August 1998: 1). Seven Council working parties – asylum, EURODAC, immigration, visas, Europol, CIREA and CIREFI – were circulated with copies of the Plan and each were assigned tasks. In March 1998 a high-level group of EU officials visited Ankara and Istanbul to seek Turkish co-operation with migrants passing through Turkey from Iraq, Iran, Egypt, Sri Lanka, Pakistan and Bangladesh (*Statewatch*, May–August 1998). The title of a press release issued by the British Refugee Council on 18 May 1998 gave a good indication of the views of pro-migrant NGOs: 'EU Asylum Policy – help Turkey to keep people out'. The Turkish government said that it would create 'reception houses' for which the Commission and presidency offered the prospect of EU expertise and funding. The Turkish government was not interested in seeking readmission agreements with neighbouring states, but did state that it would be content to allow the EU to take the lead and negotiate readmission agreements with Bangladesh and Pakistan on Turkey's behalf.

The action plan marks Turkey's incorporation within the EU's 'buffer zone' created by the complex web of agreements already existing with neighbouring states to the east and south of the Union, and which form part of pre-accession and other agreements.

The action plan also marks a movement towards elaboration of the EU's emphasis on developing schemes for temporary protection. A 1996 Council resolution noted the need for a separation between the problems of temporary protection and the examination of forms of protection for *de facto* refugees and those with humanitarian residence permits.[8] The European Council on Refugees and Exiles (ECRE) argued that 'temporary protection should be implemented in situations of emergency and should extend for a period, between six months and two years only to deal with the consequences of that emergency' (ECRE, 1997a: 1). The ECRE opposed any further extension of such schemes because they would deny security of status to refugees and create the objective risk of a state enforcing an order for premature return without any individual legal remedy. The ECRE broadly welcomed the Commission's 1997 proposals for a joint action on temporary protection but argued that its main failing was that it did not specify a maximum duration for temporary protection schemes after which persons would be allowed to regularise their status (CEC, 1997b; ECRE, 1997b). The suspicions of those who saw temporary protection as a way of reneging on international obligations and seeking to circumvent constraints on immigration control were heightened in July 1998, when the Austrian government presented a strategy paper on migration. The Austrian paper suggested a re-evaluation of EU asylum policy via the development of a system of temporary protection. The Austrian plan contained a critique of the Geneva Convention, which was viewed as both outmoded and encouraging permanent settlement (Travis, 1998; *Statewatch*, October 1998).

It would seem that EU immigration and asylum policy is, to use Lowi's (1972) term, a 'constituent' rather than a 'regulated' policy sector, because the parameters of the policy are still in the process of being negotiated, although control and security are clearly emphasised. The post-Maastricht period allows us to sketch the emergent EU immigration and asylum policy, which is represented diagrammatically in figure 1 by four concentric circles. Figure 1 illustrates that policies are skewed towards control and that restrictive policies are moving 'out' from core EU member states to those on the periphery, as well as to non-state agencies, such as airlines, which have acquired increased responsibility for monitoring the status of people who travel with them. Restrictive policies need not mean attainment of restrictive targets, but the consequence of non-attainment can be a ratcheting up of the rhetoric of immigration control and increased misery and hardship for those people who are the target for controls. Movement through the circles and away from the EU's inner

Circle 1
'Schengenland' (plus the UK and
Ireland)

Policy priorities:
• elaboration of restrictive policies
• incorporation of neighbouring
  states into a regime of control

Circle 2
'Aspirants' in central, eastern and
southern Europe

Policy priorities:
• adoption of restrictive frameworks
  connected to potential Accession/
  Association Agreements with EU

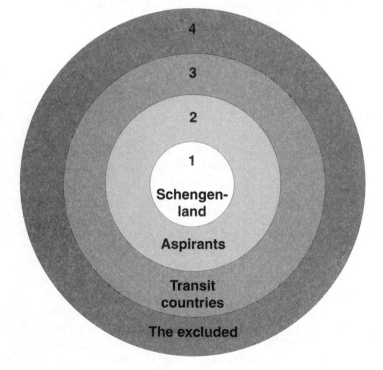

Circle 3
'Transit countries': Turkey and north
African and former Soviet states

Policy priorities:
• transit checks and action against
  illegal immigration
• incorporation within a 'temporary
  protection' system for refugees

Circle 4
'The excluded': China and Middle
Eastern and African states

Policy priorities:
• the 'targets' of the control regime
• vague commitment at the EU level
  to a 'root causes' approach to
  tackling migration

Figure 1. Emergent EU immigration and asylum policy

core sees increased emphasis on restriction while scope for protection of migrants' rights diminishes. A key dilemma for EU member states is that the movement of control to other EU member states and to non-state actors, such as airlines, need not guarantee effective implementation, because of diffuse lines of command, multiple actors and the difficulty of imposing sanctions on non-compliers. The policy also needs to be based on a valid theory of cause and effect. If restriction actually leads to increased migratory pressure (exploited by criminal gangs and unscrupulous employers) then these circles of control can do little else but increase the sum of human misery in states surrounding the EU to which the problems of immigration control are being transplanted.

As figure 1 shows, the EU can be seen as moving towards a differentiated external strategy. The inner core (circle 1) comprises the Schengen states (plus the UK and Ireland), which have well established control and internal security measures. In the second circle are neighbouring states in central, eastern and southern Europe and the Mediterranean area. Many central and eastern European states have been included within a restrictive policy framework as a result of pre-accession agreements with the EU or other bilateral or multilateral arrangements. The intention appears to be to export the restrictive emphasis to this second circle. A third circle, comprising Turkey, some Balkan states and North Africa, will be 'encouraged' (e.g. via linkages between economic aid and migration controls) to establish transit checks and combat networks that support and encourage illegal immigration. In the fourth circle (China and Middle Eastern and African states) the policy focus is on the elimination of 'push' factors, although the political and economic costs of such action would be extremely high and such an objective very difficult to secure.

The eventual trajectory of policy resulting from the anticipated accession of central and eastern European countries suggests an enlarged inner core with free movement and 'compensating' Schengen system/EU measures for internal security; a second circle of southern member states and potential new member states in central Europe, such as Poland, the Czech Republic and Hungary, to which much of the responsibility for external frontier control will shift; and a third circle comprising buffer states and those to be excluded, at which restrictive policies are directed. The EU has assumed increased responsibility for free movement and for the control dimensions of immigration and asylum policy, but its role in shaping the chances for inclusion of resident migrants and their descendants remains underdeveloped. The developing European immigration policy framework – and the underpinning *problematique* – is centred on its control and security dimensions. This reflects lowest common denominator decision-making where national preferences for control are relatively well established and, in distinction to this, diverse responses to immigrant 'integration' which reflect differing traditions of citizenship and nationhood.

Conclusion

The post-Maastricht elaboration of immigration policy co-operation left little room for the kinds of supranational constitutionalisation and institutionalisation that have been significant for free movement. The member states appeared determined to advance co-operation, while at the same time leaving little scope for democratic or judicial oversight of their actions. The aftermath of the Maastricht Treaty also presented the observer with a confused and confusing immigration and asylum policy picture that did little to assuage concerns about the democratic, information and management deficits. The absence of effective structures of supranational scrutiny and accountability allowed for the elaboration of a policy of control with fewer countervailing measures that protect the rights of TCN migrants in areas such as entry, movement, residence and anti-discrimination. The Maastricht Treaty was a significant development in the sense that it marked the formalisation of co-operation on immigration and asylum policy and allows us to sketch the parameters of an emergent EU immigration policy framework.

The Treaty did draw immigration and asylum closer to the EU because of the linkage between the intra-EU free movement framework and the resultant increased salience of external frontier controls and internal security checks. The connection between freer movement for some (EU citizens) and tighter control on movement for others (TCNs) was accompanied by development of a strong security impulse, with internal and external dimensions, and the co-option of neighbouring states into attempted implementation. It was evident that the restructuring and formalisation of immigration and asylum co-operation within the JHA pillar were built on patterns of co-operation that had developed since the 1970s and laid the foundations for further consolidation of the close connection between free movement, immigration, asylum and security issues.

The post-Maastricht policy arrangements suggest a reconfiguration of the politics of immigration in contemporary Europe, derived from the establishment of EU competence, subsequent Council actions (albeit with dubious legal effect in most cases) and development of an immigration policy strategy involving the creation of a buffer zone around the EU targeted particularly at asylum-seekers and undocumented migrants. The basic parameters of an EU immigration and asylum policy were beginning to become clearer, as well as the role that non-EU countries and prospective member states would be expected to play in it. Policy was skewed towards control and security, with few measures dealing with aspects of immigrant integration policy, such as action against discrimination on grounds of ethnic or racial origin. Simultaneously, policy was evolving in secretive, intergovernmental committees mainly composed of officials, while important questions about the scope for future policy development and the feasibility of the establishment of further European-level regulation of immigration and asylum policy remained open. For instance, free movement, immigration and asylum were separated by the 'pillared' institutional architecture. Would future treaty reform bring them closer together and, perhaps, create scope for legal and political processes at supranational level with the potential to expand the rights of migrants? It fell to the drafters of the Amsterdam Treaty to seek clarification of the structure put in place by Maastricht. Amsterdam did indeed draw free movement, immigration and asylum into the main body of the Treaty, but maintained the intergovernmental constraints on policy development that hinders clear definition of competencies and within which there is limited scope for judicial and political oversight.

Notes

1   See, for instance, EP resolutions on the harmonisation of policies on entry to the territories of the member states, *Official Journal*, C72/213, 1991; on the abolition of border controls at internal frontiers and the free movement of persons within the EU, *Official Journal*, C337/211, 1991; on migrant workers from third countries, *Official Journal*, C175/180, 1990; on racism and xenophobia, *Official Journal*, C69/43, 1989; and on European immigration policy, *Official Journal*, C337/94, 1992.

2   See, for instance, the EP's resolutions on the European Council meeting in Luxembourg on 28 and 29 June 1991, *Official Journal*, C240/132, 1991, and on the IGCs, *Official Journal*, C125/81, 1992.

3   *Ad Hoc* Group on Immigration, *Report from the Ministers Responsible for Immigration*, SN 4038/91 (WGI 930). A summary of this report is contained in the 1992 *Report on Community Migration Policy of the House of Lords Select Committee on the European Communities*, Session 1992–93, 10th Report, HL Paper 35.

4   These problems were identified in the Robles Piqeur report, EP Document A3-0215/93.

5   PE Document 207.086.

6   Case C-392/95, 10 June 1997, I-3213.

7   Europe Document 1653, 2 October 1990.

8   Council Resolution Laying Down the Priorities for Co-operation in the Field of Justice and Home Affairs for the Period July 1 1996 to June 30 1998, *Official Journal*, C319/1, 1996.

5

The Amsterdam Treaty

Introduction

Analysis of arrangements put in place following the Maastricht Treaty demonstrates the changing parameters of EU immigration and asylum responsibilities. Even though structures were put in place in the post-Maastricht period, there was still a need for clearer definition of the relationship between free movement, immigration and asylum. These were central components of the discussions leading up to the Amsterdam Treaty, negotiated in June 1997. The key features of the Amsterdam Treaty were the creation of 'an area of freedom, justice and security' covering free movement, immigration and asylum, the incorporation of the Schengen *acquis* into the EU, and the potential for expanded anti-discrimination provisions to cover racial or ethnic discrimination. Immigration and asylum were thus moved from the 'pillar' to the EU, but the member states have taken with them the reassuring paraphernalia of intergovernmentalism. Amsterdam does not constitute supranationalisation and the scope for institutionalisation of immigration and asylum policy remains uncertain, with important implications for migrant inclusion.

When compared with the Maastricht Treaty, Amsterdam appears an unambitious document. Indeed, proponents of European integration, as well as advocates of legal clarity, professed to be horrified. The lawyer Philip Allott made a remark that gives an insight into the grounds for dismay at the lack of legal uniformity: 'The Amsterdam Treaty will mean the coexistence of dozens of different legal and economic sub-systems over the next ten years, a sort of nightmare resurrection of the Holy Roman Empire' (cited in Moravcsik and Nicolaïdis, 1998: 14). Others argued that the outcome was dangerous for the EU because it went against the 'bicycle theory' of European integration – if momentum is lost it can never be regained. Moravcsik and Nicolaïdis (1998: 16–17) dispute this assessment by arguing that:

> The teleological ideal – a United States of Europe characterized by central-ized, uniform, universal and undifferentiated institutions is no longer an

appropriate standard (if it ever was one) by which to judge further steps towards integration.... Governments continue to move forward towards centralized federal institutions in some areas – notably EMU – but seek pragmatic, flexible solutions in areas where the lack of negative externalities renders decentralized policy-making a workable solution.

From within this climate of relative caution came the new Title IV, dealing with free movement, immigration and asylum. This drew immigration and asylum closer to the Community method of decision-making, but was a cautious embrace because of the strong intergovernmental control over the scope and direction of policy within Title IV. Communitarisation it was, but supranationalisation it was not.

To communitarise or to fudge?

The member states faced a similar question when drafting the Amsterdam Treaty to that confronted at Maastricht: should immigration and asylum be supranationalised by being brought within the first pillar? This question had been answered in the negative at Maastricht. At Amsterdam, the member states did bring free movement, immigration and asylum into the first pillar, but brought with them intergovernmental decision-making with an emphasis on unanimity. Moreover, if Amsterdam were to supranationalise immigration and asylum, then a whole series of other questions needed to be addressed. In particular, how could the staunch opposition of the British government be overcome? Would some form of 'flexible integration' be inevitable, with pro-integration member states forming a hard core at the cost of a fragmentation of the legal basis? In addition, by drawing immigration and asylum into the Community pillar, the undernourished conceptualisation of the immigration issue as a question of the numbers of migrants with a strong security emphasis would be drawn into the spotlight. Should the focus of migration policy be broadened by, for instance, extending the Treaty's anti-discrimination provisions to cover racial and ethnic discrimination? Such an extension of the Treaty framework had been a key demand by pro-migrant NGOs seeking EU-level action to combat discrimination.

During the pre-Amsterdam IGC, a core group of member states stated that they favoured supranationalisation of immigration and asylum policy, combined with tougher Treaty articles against racism and xenophobia, the protection of fundamental human rights via accession to the ECHR and incorporation into the EU of the Schengen *acquis*. A smaller group of member states were opposed to such rapid integration, with the British Conservative government once again holding fast to the banner of minimalism and a refusal to countenance loss of external frontier controls (with a future Labour government waiting in the wings that shared these policy preferences). A diverse range of national policy preferences needed to be accommodated during the IGC. On immigration policy there was a broad measure of agreement on the 'control' dimensions of policy, but there was disagreement about the form that EU-level co-operation/integration should take and the extent to which the EU should develop responsibilities affecting the rights of migrants. Bargaining between states reflected relatively well established policy preferences and, thus, did not accord too closely with a 'garbage can' model of decision-making in which national policy preferences are fluid to begin with and become more clearly formulated only during bargaining processes. However, 'state-centric rationalism', which focuses on the policy preferences of member states, is weakened in its application to free movement, immigration and asylum because the proliferation of non-state and transnational actors and diverse structures of bilateral and multilateral co-operation and integration across Europe are reflective of the 'internationalisation of the state' (Cox, 1987). State preferences are key input elements, but the proliferation of non-state and transnational migration policy actors and the sub-national, national and transnational resonance of debates about inclusion and exclusion means that state power in the area of migration policy is not the sole determinant of outcomes but becomes part of what is to be explained (Cox, 1986: 222–3). It is important to explore the policy preferences of member states, but to bear in mind that the ability to determine policy outcomes slips beyond the capacity of individual member states. Discussing what 'Britain' or 'Germany' wants disguises a more complex reality, beneath which lurk a diverse range of policy actors for whom national governmental preferences are not the sole point of reference.

In terms of the laggards in the pre-Amsterdam negotiations, the British and Irish governments were not even members of Schengen, and although Denmark was a Schengen signatory it opposed supranationalisation of immigration and asylum. Britain had long opposed the relaxation of internal frontier controls that would jeopardise its own highly restrictive policy framework developed since 1962. Ireland was tied to Britain through their Common Travel Area. Irish participation in Schengen with Britain outside would raise the politically unpalatable prospect of the border between the Irish Republic and Northern Ireland becoming an external frontier at which Irish citizens would be required to show their passports. France sought to limit any extended jurisdiction of the ECJ to internal security matters. The Dutch government sought limitations on ECJ involvement on asylum applications. The Germans maintained their preference for greater sharing of responsibility for migrants between the member states (Monar, 1998: 138). The 1998 federal elections and a desire to maintain a 'tough' policy stance on immigration and asylum also affected the German stance.

The Amsterdam Treaty was, as were its predecessors, the product of compromises rather than of a design capable of imparting clear structure to the issues of free movement, immigration and asylum. It did, though, make more explicit the close relation between free movement, immigration and asylum policy by moving immigration and asylum issues from the third pillar to a newly created Title IV of the Community pillar. If, however, the Amsterdam Treaty did constitute movement towards supranationalisation – erosion of the 'legal sandstone' of the third pillar – then movement in this direction was rather tentative, because the Council retained the upper hand in decision-making, with unanimity as the decisional *modus operandi*. EU institutions were constrained. The Commission had to continue to share the right of initiative with member states for at least five years after ratification, while the EP and ECJ found their roles limited by the emphasis on intergovernmentalism. Amsterdam also specified a timescale of five years for the adoption of many immigration and asylum measures. This could be difficult to reconcile with the need for unanimity: how could targets be attained if member states opposed them and, what is more, possessed the voting power to give teeth to their opposition? Provisions for closer co-operation removed the more obvious recalcitrance of the British government, which opted out, but drew into the spotlight the intentions of other member states that had previously been able to hide behind British 'awkwardness'.

The negotiations

Article N of the Maastricht Treaty had stated that 'A conference of the representatives of the Member States shall be convened in 1996 to examine those provisions of the Treaty for which revision is provided'. Three general considerations with immigration and asylum implications contextualised these IGC discussions (Moravcsik and Nicolaïdis, 1998: 14). First, the price of the Maastricht compromise had been a pledge to the more federally inclined member states to reconsider political union soon. A key area of unfinished business was the JHA pillar. Second, the problems encountered by the Maastricht Treaty during the ratification process prompted greater attention to be paid to closing the 'democratic deficit' and bringing the EU closer to its citizens. Third, there was pressure on member states to reform the policy-making and institutional structures of the EU in readiness for the accession of central and eastern European countries.

During the pre-Amsterdam IGC, the EU's institutions expressed eagerness to take account of the views of a wide range of NGOs as a way of reducing the potential for the hostile reaction engendered by the Maastricht Treaty. Pro-migrant lobby groups were active in the run-up to the Treaty, but their effect appears to have been marginal and they expressed disappointment with the outcome. In the words of the ECRE, Amsterdam's asylum provisions constituted a technical transfer of competence without the substantive role for the ECJ and Commission that groups such as the ECRE had sought (ECRE, 1997c). For these groups, supranationalisation with attendant EU legal and political effects was viewed as desirable in order to ensure a more democratic and accountable EU immigration and asylum policy.

The IGC was launched at the Corfu European Council in December 1994. A Reflection Group chaired by the Spaniard Carlos Westendorp was established, with one of its purposes being to evaluate the role of the EU in seeking to 'provide a better response to modern demands as regards internal security and the fields of Justice and Home Affairs more generally'. The Reflection Group was composed of one representative from each of the member states, plus Commissioner Marcelino Oreja, and two MEPs, the French Socialist Elisabeth Guigou and German Christian Democrat Elmar Brok. The Group concerned itself with the creation of a 'people's Europe', a 'Union closer to its citizens', while also thinking about the role of the EU's institutions in a 'more democratic and efficient Union' (Reflection Group, 1995).

Much of the agenda for the pre-Amsterdam IGC developed by the Reflection Group and at meetings of EU leaders had direct relevance to migration issues. The Corfu meeting of the European Council in December 1994 listed six issues as priorities for discussion, of which five were especially relevant to immigration and asylum policy. The first priority was to address the new challenges facing the EU, one of which was new sources of migration. Second was a consideration of the JHA pillar and whether it should be 'communitarised' by being moved to the first pillar or whether mainly intergovernmental co-operation should remain in place. Third was the need for greater openness and decision-making efficiency. Immigration and asylum policy decision-making was neither open nor efficient. Fourth was an attempt to build a Europe closer to its citizens, with reinforced human rights, which included discussion of the incorporation of the ECHR into Community law. A fifth priority for discussion was the issue of subsidiarity. Immigration and asylum policy had been nationally based and closely linked to national sovereignty, but supranational action was now deemed appropriate.

The Reflection Group's basic headings for discussion were then boiled down within the IGC to three immigration and asylum policy issues:

• the possible supranationalisation of immigration and asylum policy via incorporation of all or some parts of the JHA pillar provisions into the main body of the Treaty, with a concomitant increase in competence for supranational institutions;

- strengthened Treaty provisions for EU action against racism and xenophobia;
- the possible incorporation of the ECHR into the Treaty.

As the discussions progressed, member states and EU institutions produced documents outlining their positions on the key issues.

As had been the case before the Maastricht Treaty, it was the Dutch government that held the Council presidency and it assumed a leading role in drafting the proposed Treaty changes. The Dutch were keen to avoid the diplomatic calamity that accompanied their draft version of the Maastricht Treaty, which had united virtually all the other member states in opposition to it. The Dutch presidency proposed a strengthened immigration and asylum role for the ECJ, Commission and EP, as well as increased scope for an EU approach to immigration and asylum policy, and incorporation into the EU of the Schengen *acquis*. In February 1997, a Dutch 'non-paper' on the incorporation of Schengen also recognised the possibility of some form of flexible integration because Ireland and Britain were not Schengen members.

The key IGC players were, as usual, the French and German governments. In December 1995, a joint declaration by Chancellor Kohl of Germany and President Chirac of France listed a series of objectives for the IGC. JHA was identified as one of four key priorities for reform. Both governments favoured supranationalisation of immigration and asylum policy, the strengthening of anti-racism and xenophobia provisions and accession to the ECHR. As had been the case during the Maastricht negotiations, Germany seemed keen to ensure supranationalisation and a transfer from the third to the first pillar because of the disproportionately large number of asylum-seekers Germany attracted compared with other EU member states. France also favoured the creation of legal instruments at EU level to combat racism and xenophobia, while Germany favoured police co-operation to counter the cross-border dissemination of racist material and also advocated an EU-wide ban on the offence of holocaust denial. A Franco-German initiative at the 1994 Corfu Council saw the creation of a Consultative Commission on Racism and Xenophobia, chaired by the Frenchman Jean Kahn. The Commission's work was divided between three sub-committees: the first dealt with communication and information; the second with education and training; and the third with policing and justice. In April 1995 the Kahn Committee proposed the creation of a European Observatory on Racism and Xenophobia, which, after some opposition from Britain, was established in 1997 and based in Vienna.[1]

Of particular importance during the IGC were Franco-German positions on 'flexible integration' (Stubb, 1996) that could allow the hard core of pro-integration member states to by-pass the more reluctant member states. The Kohl–Chirac declaration of December 1995 contained the following statement:

> Where one of the partners faces temporary difficulties in keeping up with the pace of progress in the Union, it would be desirable and feasible to introduce a general clause in the Treaties enabling those Member States which have the will and the capacity to do so to develop closer co-operation among themselves within the institutional framework of the Union. (Quoted in Hix and Niessen, 1996: 49)

The key problem was, of course, not so much that partners faced 'temporary difficulties in keeping up', but that the British government was implacably opposed to supranationalisation of immigration and asylum. Moreover, the change of government from Conservative to Labour in May 1997 did not change this stance. Other countries also expressed reservations about flexibility. Greece and Ireland favoured supranationalisation of immigration and asylum policy, but expressed opposition to integrative flexibility that could relegate them to the 'outer core' of the EU.

A further joint declaration by the French and German foreign ministers, de Charette and Kinkel, of 17 October 1996, spoke of 'intensified co-operation in the light of the further deepening of European integration'. It advocated the placing of a new flexibility clause within the Treaty allowing for 'closer co-operation' between more integration-minded member states (quoted in Ehlermann, 1998: 6). The declaration then contained specific proposals for a new article of principle covering all three pillars and three special articles dealing with each of the pillars in more detail. The Dutch presidency took up these proposals and – except for the CFSP provisions, which were omitted – entered the proposed Amsterdam Treaty in Title VII, 'Provisions on Closer Co-operation'. The main target of the Franco-German statement on flexible integration was the British government. In a White Paper in March 1996, revealingly entitled *A Partnership Among Nations*, the British Conservative government stated that co-operation on JHA issues should continue to be dealt with on a 'multinational basis' (Foreign and Commonwealth Office, 1996). This meant continuation within the existing intergovernmental pillar, with unanimity for decision-making and no increased role for the Commission, ECJ or EP. The British government adopted the most minimalist position in the IGC negotiations and argued that the JHA pillar had worked better than either the Commission or EP was prepared to admit. The British government was, though, prepared to accept that what it called 'variable geometry' might be the solution to the impasse between maximalist and minimalist member states. It also opposed the extension of Treaty competence to cover action against racism and xenophobia by arguing that British race relations policy already made adequate provision in these respects and that national action should remain the basis of the response (Hix and Niessen, 1996: 57–8).

The British government was not alone in opposing full supranationalis-ation of immigration and asylum policy. The Danish government admitted that some transfer of competence was 'conceivable', but expressed the opinion that decision-making should remain mainly intergovernmental and based in the Council, with the role of the Commission, ECJ and EP kept to a minimum. The Danes, reflecting the importance of the Common Market Relations Committee in their own parliament, called for a strengthening of the role of national parliaments as the guardians of citizens' rights, but did concede a role for the EU in the fight against racism and xenophobia. The Swedish government also argued that JHA issues were closely linked to national sovereignty and should remain largely the responsibility of national governments, although the role of supranational institutions could be increased if it enhanced the effective-ness of policy co-operation. The Finnish government was quite specific in their proposals when they called for measures that would improve the security of groups of people excluded from the Treaty provisions for free movement and social entitlement, such as TCNs, asylum-seekers and refugees. Of the other member states, the Benelux countries issued a joint memorandum in which they adopted the strongest pro-integration stance and called for the supranationalisation of immigration and asylum policy, the incorporation of Schengen into the Treaty and provisions on the protection of civil, social and political rights regardless of 'racial' origins. Austria, Italy, Portugal and Spain also supported greater supranational-isation, accession to the ECHR and the strengthening of provisions on racism and xenophobia, as did Greece and Ireland, with reservations about flexibility.

The most decisive event during the negotiations was the change in Germany's stance when domestic political considerations led Chancellor Kohl to oppose the extension of QMV to immigration and asylum. This opposition stemmed from the migratory pressures faced by Germany, the involvement of *Länder* competencies for immigration and asylum, and the 1998 federal elections and desire of the centre-right coalition to take a tough line on immigration and asylum policy. German opposition put an end to any lingering hopes that the Amsterdam Treaty could secure fully supranationalised immigration and asylum policy, albeit with provisions for opt-outs for those, such as the British and Danes, who were unwilling to participate.

The main EU institutions also issued position documents before the IGC. The Council presented a report to the Reflection Group that reviewed the operation of existing procedures, but did not contain proposals for reform (Reflection Group, 1995; Hix and Niessen, 1996). The Council expressed the view that JHA provisions were inadequate with regard to use of legal instruments, because in the first eighteen months of operation following ratification in November 1993, only two joint actions were adopted. Ministers preferred non-binding recommendations and resolutions. The Council also expressed dissatisfaction with blurred competence, because of the absence of clear demarcation between what were first pillar matters and what were concerns of the third pillar. It was also noted that many of the provisions of the third pillar, such as the ability to extend jurisdiction to the ECJ or to act by QMV, had not been used. The Council also expressed dissatisfaction with the overly complicated decision-making structures resulting from the five-level framework with the Council, Committee of Permanent Representatives, the K4 Committee, plus various steering groups and working parties (see box 1, p. 103).

The ECJ also prepared a report on possible treaty revisions but did not include concrete proposals for reform because this was not seen as a proper role for the Court (Reflection Group, 1995; Hix and Niessen, 1996). Instead, the ECJ pointed out some difficulties with its role caused by the operation of a third pillar from which it was excluded, while being obliged to protect the rights of individuals affected by EU activities in the first pillar. This was seen as particularly important in relation to JHA activities, because they were likely to impinge quite significantly on citizens' rights. The ECJ stated that:

> Judicial protection ... especially in the context of co-operation in the fields of Justice and Home Affairs, must be guaranteed and structured in such a way as to ensure consistent interpretation and application of both Community law and of the provisions adopted within the framework of such co-operation. (Quoted in Hix and Niessen, 1996: 38)

The ECJ's view was that the EU could not accede to the ECHR because the treaty basis for this (Article 235 of the Treaty of the European Communities) was deemed insufficient. Moreover, there were other complicated questions that would be raised by accession for which there existed little guidance, such as the relation between the ECJ and the European Court of Human Rights. Accession would also involve a fundamental change in the EU's human rights protection regime, by integrating the EU into a different international legal community with associated implications for member states' legal systems. The ECJ's view was that if accession were to occur, then it would require a change to the Treaty which made this an explicit objective and provided a clearer basis for it.

The Commission issued two reports as its contribution to the IGC process. The first, in May 1995, was to the Reflection Group on the operation of the Maastricht Treaty. The second, in February 1996, focused on political union and preparations for enlargement (CEC,

1995a, 1996). In its May 1995 report the Commission strongly criticised the operation of the JHA pillar. It was characterised as ineffectual, because the instruments available were inappropriate and the cumbersome decision-making process and lack of openness compounded problems. As an example of this, the Commission noted that there was disagreement among member states about whether or not common positions or joint actions were mandatory, except in circumstances where they contained explicit obligations. It also criticised the reliance on unanimity, which was portrayed as a brake on decision-making. For instance, the October 1993 meeting of the European Council in Brussels had called for a joint action on minimal procedural guarantees for granting asylum, but member states could then only agree on a far weaker non-binding resolution. For other adopted texts, on family reunification and admission for employment, the Commission noted that 'it was more an exercise of reproducing the existing rights in the member states than of bringing them into line' (*Migration Newsheet*, 147/95-06, June 1995: 1).

The Commission went on to argue that the basic challenges facing the EU were democracy and effectiveness and that deeper European integration was the solution to both. This would involve more QMV, with increased use of co-decision-making to strengthen the role of the EP. The Commission expressed opposition to 'lowest common denominator' decision-making arising from the emphasis on unanimity in the JHA pillar. It also noted that it felt constrained in its own role within the JHA pillar, because of the politically sensitive nature of immigration and asylum policy, and wanted the right of initiative in all JHA matters. The Commission was reluctant to antagonise member states that were sensitive about supranational encroachment into immigration and asylum policy. Most JHA pillar initiatives emanated from the country holding the presidency, with the Commission preferring to state its views via communications, such as those issued on immigration and asylum policy in 1994 (CEC, 1994a).

The Commission referred to the same problems of blurred demarcation between the first and third pillars that had also been addressed by the Council. For instance, the formulation of a list of countries whose nationals required a visa to enter the EU was a first pillar matter, while conditions for issuing a visa were in the JHA pillar. 'Hence in determining whether a policy is adopted under the first or third pillar, the legal provisions of the Treaty are less important than the level of political commitment for common action' (quoted in Hix and Niessen, 1996: 33). The Commission proposed that JHA objectives be summarised into 'main themes'. It also proposed that more effective legal instruments, such as directives, be used and not just non-binding joint actions or common positions. Finally, it was deemed essential that decisions be subject to ECJ review. In short, the Commission proposed supranationalisation of immigration and asylum policy with accession to the ECHR (or a clearer statement on human rights in the Treaty) and the introduction of Treaty provisions against racism and xenophobia.

Not surprisingly, the EP also adopted a maximalist position in its two reports and expressed strong opposition to the JHA arrangements (Hix and Niessen, 1996). It called for supranationalisation and the strengthening of legal instruments, accession to the ECHR and tougher Treaty articles on anti-racism, xenophobia and holocaust denial. It did, though, argue that the transfer of competencies associated with supranationalisation should be achieved 'progressively' and be associated with strengthening of the roles of the Council (via majority voting), the ECJ and the EP.

Amsterdam's provisions[2]

The Amsterdam Treaty added a new objective in its Article 2, which provided for the maintenance and development of the EU as 'an area of freedom, justice and security'. Amsterdam's tentative movement in the direction of supranationalisation was marked by the incorporation of immigration and asylum into the EU pillar via a new Title IV, combined with the maintenance of unanimity in the Council as the basis of decision-making for at least five years after its ratification. The recast third pillar remained, but was slimmed down to deal with judicial co-operation in criminal matters and police co-operation. The new judicial and police co-operation (JPC) pillar is representative of the recurrent securitisation emphasis and the targeting by the member states of security issues as part of the effort to bring the EU closer to its citizens. A big question is the extent to which the movement of immigration and asylum into the new Title IV creates scope for the institutionalisation of a migration policy context and political and judicial effects that help open 'social and political spaces' for migrants at EU level. This is the focus of the next two chapters, which specify more clearly the motivations, calculations and alliance-building strategies of EU-level institutional actors in relation to Europeanised migration issues (free movement, transferable social entitlements, anti-discrimination and asylum).

As in the previous chapters, it is important to outline Treaty specificities while keeping an eye on the bigger picture, particularly the relationship between constitutionalisation, institutionalisation and the scope for migrant inclusion. Title IV, Article 61 specifies that the Council shall adopt within five years of the entry into force of the Treaty measures to ensure the free movement of persons and 'directly related flanking measures' with respect to external frontier controls, asylum and immigration. Even though asylum and immigration were brought into the Community pillar, unanimity in the Council was to remain the basis of decision-making for five years (to 2004). The member states imported the comfort blanket of intergovernmentalism and constrained the scope for supranational institutionalisation. Even after the end of this five-year period there is no guarantee of a move towards QMV, because all member states must agree to such a change. The five-year time limit for most immigration and asylum issues is important because it provides a deadline and, therefore, an impetus for action. It may also create the potential difficulty that the deadline will be frustrated because of the requirement for unanimity. The SEA made provisions for QMV as a way of attempting to guarantee its ambitious targets. Title IV of Amsterdam does not make similar provisions.

With regard to the rights of TCNs, the Amsterdam Treaty proceeded cautiously. Article 62 gave the Council five years to adopt measures in compliance with Article 14 of the Treaty to ensure the absence of any controls on persons, irrespective of whether they are EU citizens or TCNs, when crossing internal borders. Article 62 is the only article in the whole of Title IV that confers rights on TCNs. All persons, be they EU citizens or TCNs, will be able to rely on it to defeat any attempt to impose national discretion over controls once legislation has been adopted.

On external frontiers, the Council is, within the same five-year period, given responsibility to adopt measures setting standards and procedures to be followed by member states when carrying out checks on persons. The Council is also required to adopt rules on visas for stays of less than three months. This includes a list of third countries whose nationals need a visa when crossing the EU's external frontiers, the procedures and conditions for issuing visas by member states, and rules on a uniform visa format. A regulation on a common visa list provided for by the Maastricht Treaty was annulled by the ECJ in June 1997 following a challenge from the EP about inadequate consultation (see chapter 4).

Title IV also contains provisions on asylum. Article 63 states that EU asylum policy must be in accord with the Geneva Convention and the New York Protocol. The extent to which systems of temporary protection are in accord with these agreements – or may indeed subvert them – are important questions. Article 63.1 covers the criteria and mechanisms for determining which member state is responsible for considering an asylum application. This is the subject matter of the Dublin Convention (see chapter 3). Article 63 also provides for minimum standards on the reception of asylum-seekers, with respect to the qualification of TCNs as refugees, and on procedures in member states for granting or withdrawing refugee status. Although the creation of minimum standards may provide a basis upon which applicants denied these standards can challenge decisions, there are no thresholds established in the Treaty below which minimum standards must not fall.

Article 63.2 deals with measures on refugees and displaced persons and covers minimum standards for giving temporary protection to displaced persons and 'promoting a balance of effort', but this is not covered by the five-year period. In May 1997, the Commission proposed a convention on temporary protection (CEC, 1997c; see chapter 4 for more details).

Article 63.3 specifies immigration policy measures relating to conditions of entry and residence and standards on procedures for the issue of long-term visas and residence permits, including those for family reunion, but these are also not covered by the five-year period. Guild (1998: 617) noted that all these issues were dealt with intergovernmentally within the third pillar arrangements and 'are characterised by a lack of clarity, uniformity or consistency'. This article also brings within the five-year framework the adoption of measures on illegal immigration and illegal residence, including repatriation of illegal residents.

Also outside of the five-year deadline are the adoption of measures defining the rights and conditions under which TCNs who are legally resident in a member state may reside in another member state. In July 1997 the Commission used the *extant* JHA provisions to propose a convention giving a limited right of free movement for economic purposes to TCNs. This is considered in more detail in chapter 6, when pro-migrant lobbying, and the responsiveness of EU institutions to it, is considered in more detail (CEC, 1997d).

A protocol was also added to the Amsterdam Treaty that covered asylum for nationals of EU member states. This forbids the making of an asylum application by an EU citizen in another EU member state. Belgium reserved the right to judge all applications on their merits. The protocol arose as a result of Spanish pressure derived from the domestic problems with ETA and Basque separatism. The assumption underpinning the protocol is that all EU member states respect human rights and are, therefore, assumed to be safe. It has been argued that the protocol could place the EU in contravention of the Geneva Convention. Dennis McNamara, the Director of the Division of International Protection at the Office of the UN High Commissioner for Refugees (UNHCR), stated that the protocol 'in our considered view (supported by the Office of the Legal Counsel in New York) violates the object and purposes and some of the basic provisions of the Refugee Convention' (ECRE, 1997d: 8; see also Bank, 1998).

Other provisions relate to emergency situations, judicial co-operation and decision-making procedures. Article 64 states that Title IV measures shall not affect the ability of member states to maintain law and order and safeguard internal security. However, in the event of an emergency, such as a sudden inflow of TCNs, then the Council can act by QMV, on a proposal from the Commission, to adopt measures lasting no longer than six months for the benefit of the member state(s) concerned. Articles 65 and 66 cover judicial co-operation in civil matters. Article 67 specifies that the five-year period is 'transitional' and that during this time the

Council shall act unanimously on a proposal from the Commission or on the initiative of a member state (the shared right of initiative was a feature of the JHA pillar). At the end of the five-year period, the Council, acting unanimously but after consulting the EP, can determine that all or some of the areas covered by Title IV are to be covered by QMV. There is, though, no guarantee that, at the end of the five-year period, a shift to QMV will occur.

The extent to which democratic and judicial oversight at EU level is established directly impinges on the potential for the opening of social and political spaces for migrants. The ECJ is given only limited jurisdiction over Title IV issues by Article 68, which covers both the interpretation of Title IV and rulings on the validity or interpretation of acts of the institutions of the EU when a case is raised before a court of final instance (against whose decision there is no remedy in that member state). These national courts or tribunals can then request a ruling from the ECJ. This differs from the powers of the ECJ in other areas where any court or tribunal is able to ask the ECJ to clarify Community law and courts of final instance are required to do so if there is ambiguity. 'Therefore coherence will be much slower dependent first on the adoption of measures which will regulate TCNs in the Community and it will take much longer for interpretative questions to reach the Luxembourg Court' (Guild, 1998: 619). The Amsterdam Treaty also excluded measures regarding controls on persons at internal frontiers from the ECJ's jurisdiction if these relate to the 'maintenance of law and order and the safeguarding of internal security', as well as excluding judgements of national courts that have become *res adjudicata* from the application of the ECJ's rulings (Monar, 1998: 141).

Amsterdam also formalised the possibility of a two-speed EU with laggards like Britain in the slow lane. The flexibility provisions of the Treaty were particularly important with regard to the free movement, immigration and asylum provisions. A key feature of the Treaty was its provision for 'closer co-operation'. Ehlermann (1998: 1) noted that:

> For the first time, the Amsterdam Treaty regulates in general terms the objectives, procedures and legal consequences bound up with closer co-operation of one group of member states within the EC/EU institutional framework and with its instruments. It thus goes far beyond what was hitherto possible as regards differentiation and flexibility in EC/EU law.

Various protocols added to the Treaty sought to accommodate national policy preferences. The British and Irish governments opted out of Title IV completely. Britain affirmed the right to exercise its own external frontier controls with other member states, while the British and Irish governments secured the right to maintain the Common Travel Area between the two countries. Denmark was granted a similar opt-out from

Title IV to the British and Irish, but because Denmark is a Schengen member it was given six months to decide whether it would implement any Council decision that is binding on the Schengen *acquis* (Monar, 1998: 142).

The balance of the Amsterdam Treaty was towards consolidation of the restrictive emphasis, with limited EU competence for issues affecting the rights of migrants and their descendants (whether they be citizens of EU member states facing racial or ethnic discrimination or TCNs unable to move freely irrespective of permanent residence in a member state). Amsterdam did strengthen the EU's anti-discrimination provisions with a new Article 13 added to the Treaty that empowered the Council to take action against discrimination based on racial or ethnic origin. The new anti-discrimination provisions were not as strong as those forbidding discrimination on the grounds of nationality. Rather, they conferred on the Commission the power to bring forward proposals seeking to counter discrimination based on race, ethnic origin, religion, sexual orientation or religion. These proposals would then have to be agreed unanimously by the Council. The next chapter analyses in some detail the background to this debate and the opportunities and constraints facing pro-migrant organisations seeking to broaden the EU policy focus from the 'control' dimension of policy to areas impinging upon 'immigrant integration'.

Following post-Amsterdam consultations, the Commission's 1998–2000 SAP envisaged three areas of action in relation to Article 13:

- a 'horizontal' directive covering direct and indirect discrimination in employment and occupation and applying to all the forms of discrimination mentioned in Article 13;
- a 'vertical' directive dealing with direct and indirect discrimination on grounds of race or ethnic origin – this would lay down minimum standards enabling member states to introduce provisions more favourable to the protection of the principle of equal treatment and, as in the case of equal treatment, would permit positive action to overcome existing inequalities;
- an action programme to support and complement these proposals.

Amsterdam changed the decision-making procedures. Free movement, immigration and asylum were made subject to standard EU legislative devices. In what post-Amsterdam has become the JPC pillar (the JHA pillar after the removal of immigration and asylum policy), the scope for joint actions was removed and two new decision-making instruments were introduced:

- *framework decisions* seek approximation of laws and are binding on member states with regard to the purposes to be achieved but leave the method of implementation to the member states;

- binding *decisions* are used for other purposes.

It was also decided to make it easier for conventions in international law to come into effect by providing for ratification procedures to begin within a time limit specified by the Council and for a convention to enter into force when at least half the member states had adopted it.

The Amsterdam Treaty was seen as doing little to satisfy the requirement for what in EU-speak is known as greater 'transparency'. Like the Maastricht Treaty, it was almost incomprehensible to anyone not well versed in the particularities of EU-speak. Also, 'the proliferation of protocols and declarations at the end of the Treaty stamp it indelibly with a bazaar-like bargaining character' (Crossick *et al.*, 1997: 3). If we view the policy competencies of the EU as being located along a scale ranging from supranationalisation to intergovernmentalism, immigration and asylum remain at the intergovernmental end, with limitations on supranational action. It has been written that: 'communitarisation hardly merits the term, and Amsterdam has clearly set a highly questionable precedent for the import of intergovernmental procedures into the Community framework' (Monar, 1998: 139). That said, the connections with the free movement framework have become more clearly established. Much of the disappointment with the outcome of the Treaty is linked to the desire for clarity, but is also grounded in a normative supposition implying some kind of teleological perspective on European integration. Amsterdam, in fact, demonstrates – as previous Treaty revisions did too – the contingent nature of European integration and the difficulties of securing positive integration.

Incorporation of Schengen

A key element of Amsterdam is its incorporation of the Schengen *acquis* into the EU. This included the Schengen Agreement and Implementing Accord of 1985 and 1990, the various accession protocols and agreements with member states, and the decisions and declarations adopted by the Schengen Executive Committee. The flexibility/opt-out protocols that were added to the Amsterdam Treaty covered the positions of Ireland and Britain, which were not members of Schengen. They also covered Denmark, which was a member but did not want to participate in the supranationalised free movement, immigration and asylum policy provisions of Title IV. A major task post-Amsterdam for interior ministers and officials was the incorporation of around 3,000 pages of the *acquis* into either the new Title IV or into the JPC pillar. The Danish government released the full list of documents comprising the *acquis* in September 1996 and the Norwegian government, which had non-member 'observer' status, followed suit a couple of weeks later. The list of documents itself was eighteen pages long and contained 172 documents covering all aspects of the 142 articles of the Agreement.

An important effect of the incorporation of the Schengen *acquis* was that decisions made by Schengen's secretive and largely unaccountable Executive Committee would immediately after Amsterdam's ratification become Community law if included within the free movement, immigration and asylum provisions of Title IV. The Council was given responsibility, acting by unanimity, to determine the location of the Schengen *acquis*, that is, whether measures would be placed within the new Title IV or placed in the recast JPC pillar. The ECJ was declared competent to act according to the provisions of the treaties (i.e. whether provisions were to be located in the first or third pillars). The EP was to be consulted about measures included in Title IV. Analysis in *Statewatch* (May–June 1997: 15) identified the provisions in the Schengen Implementing Convention and the related decisions in the Schengen *acquis* and suggested whether they would then be placed in the JPC pillar or included in the new Title IV on free movement, immigration and asylum (box 2).

Article 2 of Amsterdam's protocol incorporating the Schengen *acquis* states that, from the date of entry into force of the Amsterdam Treaty, the Schengen *acquis* would immediately apply to the thirteen signatories of the Schengen agreement. Article 4 allows Britain and Ireland to opt into measures of which they approve, though this is dependent upon unanimity among the other thirteen member states. Article 8 stated that the Schengen *acquis* and associated measures must be accepted in full by all new member states. This is unprecedented, because neither of the other areas of closer co-operation – monetary and social policy – contained such provisions for new members (Ehlermann, 1998: 22). This means that prospective member states in central, eastern and southern Europe are expected to be wholehearted participants in the EU's internal security arrangements and to translate the restrictionist emphasis of migration policies in older member states into their own national systems. Whether they possess the intent or ability to do this is an altogether different question.

The Commission's action plan

The key issue for the Commission was, of course, going to be how it planned to give legal effect to these new arrangements by exercising its powers of proposal and staking a role for itself as a migration policy player in the post-Amsterdam EU. The European Council, meeting in Cardiff in June 1998, called on the Commission, with the Council, to submit an action plan to the forthcoming Vienna Council meeting in December 1998 on how best to implement Title IV provisions. The heads

---

Box 2. The incorporation of the Schengen *acquis* into Title IV and the JPC pillar

Title II: Articles 2–38
Abolition of checks at internal borders and the movement of persons (likely to be placed in Title IV)
   3 decisions on internal borders
  22 decisions on external borders
   4 decisions on readmission
  23 decisions on visas
   4 decisions on asylum

Title III: Articles 39–91
Police and security (JPC pillar)
   5 decisions on police co-operation
  11 decisions on judicial co-operation
   3 decisions on extradition
  10 decisions on drugs

Title IV: Articles 92–119
The Schengen Information System (Title IV and JPC pillar)
  31 decisions on the Schegnen Information System
  16 decisions on SIRENE
   4 decisions on the joint supervisory body

Title V: Articles 120–125
Transport and movement of goods (Title IV)
   2 decisions on transport and movement of goods

Source: *Statewatch* (May–June 1997: 15).

---

of government demonstrated how seriously they took these issues by agreeing to hold a special European Council meeting in Tampere, Finland, in October 1999 (Action Group on Immigration, 2000).

In December 1998 the Council and Commission presented an 'action plan' on implementation of the area of freedom, justice and security.[3] The plan contained a critique of the 'soft law' of the post-Maastricht period, where non-binding recommendations and resolutions had characterised policy development, with inadequate monitoring arrangements. The key feature of the Amsterdam provisions was the amendment to Article 2 of the Maastricht Treaty, which stated general policy objectives. These were extended to state that: 'the Union shall set itself the objective to maintain and develop an area of freedom, justice and security in which the free movement of persons is assured in conjunction with appropriate measures with respect to external borders, asylum, immigration and the prevention and combating of crime'.

The action plan identified measures to be implemented or adopted within two years of Amsterdam's ratification (i.e. by summer 2001) and then within five years (i.e. by summer 2004).

Within two years of Amsterdam's ratification (by 2001)
Asylum and immigration measures:
• the development of an integrated approach for assessment of countries of origin.

Asylum measures:
• monitoring of the effectiveness of the Dublin Convention and consideration of its inclusion within the Treaty provisions;
• the implementation of the EURODAC system;
• adoption of minimum standards for granting or withdrawing refugee status;
• limits on 'secondary movements' by asylum-seekers;
• definition of minimum standards for reception of asylum-seekers;
• a study to assess the merits of a single European asylum procedure. In March 1999 Commissioner Anita Gradin announced the Commission's intention to propose an EC law on asylum procedures once the Amsterdam Treaty had been ratified. In the meantime, a Commission working document highlighted issues needing particular consideration: standards of proof; the 'safe country of origin' principle; refugee status; speeding up procedures; and vulnerable groups.

Immigration measures:
• an instrument on the lawful status of legal immigrants;
• an EU policy on readmission and return;
• combating illegal immigration through information campaigns in transit countries and countries of origin;
• measures concerning external borders and free movement of persons;
• visa procedures, covering resources, guarantees of repatriation and accident and health cover, as well as a list of countries whose nationals are subject to an airport transit visa requirement;
• rules on a uniform visa;
• a regulation on countries whose nationals are exempt from visa requirements and those whose nationals are subject to visa requirements;
• harmonisation of carrier liability laws;

- minimum standards covering temporary protection of displaced persons;
- promoting a balance of effort between EU member states (a long-standing German government concern).

Within five years of Amsterdam's ratification (by 2004)
Asylum measures:
- minimum standards for the subsidiary protection of persons in need of international protection.

Immigration measures:
- measures on the removal of persons denied the right to stay;
- preparation of rules on conditions of entry and residence, and standards on procedures for the issue by member states of long-term visa and residence permits, including those for family reunion;
- determination of the rights and conditions under which TCNs who are legally resident in one member state may reside in another member state.

The Council and Commission have set ambitious targets for themselves as they seek to provide a more coherent structure to the immigration and asylum policy measures already adopted and adapt to the Schengen arrangements. The capacity to act will, of course, depend upon the ability of member states to agree unanimously on measures that are brought forward. The measures also reveal continued emphasis on the control and security dimensions of immigration. The rights of movement and residence for TCNs are not identified as a priority within the action plan and it in fact includes fewer proposals for the expanded rights for TCNs than a Commission-proposed convention introduced in 1997.

Conclusion

To say whether the Amsterdam Treaty was a success or failure depends on the yardstick employed. If judged in terms of the supranationalisation of immigration and asylum policy then it largely failed, because even though the new Title IV has brought immigration and asylum into the EU pillar there remain significant constraints on action by EU institutions. If the Treaty is evaluated in relation to what has gone before – the muddled and confusing transfer of some policy competencies and the narrow focus on restriction – then Amsterdam can be squarely located in the tradition of immigration and asylum policy development in the EU. In this sense, the continued absence of judicial and democratic control demonstrates continued autonomy for member states when developing EU-level immigration control policies, with weaker scope for democratic and judicial oversight than at national level. This could lead us to suppose that the weak role for the ECJ and EP will diminish the scope for 'social and political spaces' for migrants at EU level. The Amsterdam Treaty did not communitarise immigration and asylum policy, nor was this likely, given the impediments imposed by unsympathetic national policy preferences in key member states. British objections could be managed through provisions for flexibility, but opposition from the German government to QMV severely constrained the scope for supranationalisation.

Amsterdam continued the process instigated by the SEA of drawing into clearer focus the connection between free movement, immigration and asylum. Amsterdam also marked the three-stage transition from informal intergovernmental co-operation (post-SEA) to formal intergovernmental co-operation (Maastricht's JHA pillar) and then to incorporation within the Community pillar. The price for this incorporation was high: intergovernmentalism was imported into the Community and the flexibility provisions fragmented the legal basis of the Union. Relatively stable policy preferences – largely centred around convergence on the perceived necessity for control of the numbers of immigrants – are likely to continue to shape EU policy for the foreseeable future (as they have done in the post-Maastricht period). Amsterdam demonstrates that EU-level immigration and asylum policies are narrowly focused on control of the numbers of immigrants, particularly those from less economically developed parts of the world. In the next two chapters we examine attempts to broaden this policy focus by groups seeking to represent the interests of migrants and push for tougher anti-discrimination legislation at EU level, free movement for legally resident TCNs and 'fair' asylum standards as adjudged by correspondence with international standards. This broadening of the focus of the analysis constitutes a push for a broader conceptualisation of the migration issue than is currently evident at EU level. The focus turns towards the chances for inclusion of TCNs at supranational level. This relates strongly to the institutional context established for the management of migration issues and the extent to which the EU serves as a new arena in which tensions between inclusion and exclusion are mediated within a migration policy context embodying both free movement provisions and immigration and asylum policy co-operation/integration.

Notes

1   Council Regulation 1035/97, 2 June 1997, *Official Journal* L151, 1997.
2   I refer to the consolidated version of the Treaty available from the Council's Website: http://ue.eu.int/AG/SUMM2/HTM
3   Available from the Council Website: http://ue.eu.int/jai/

6

Representing migrants' interests

Introduction

The preceding chapters have mapped the policy context established for the management of migration issues at EU level and contributed to a 'top-down' analysis focused on formal legal and political structures and the scope for institutionalisation. The 'objects' of policy – migrants and their descendants – faded from view and became a 'problem' to be managed rather than potential actors in the political process with some ability to shape and negotiate their own chances for inclusion. The key concern of this chapter is their chances for inclusion at EU level in relation to the economic, political and social roles of the EU. It is important to pay attention to the sources of legal, political and social power that give meaning to inclusion and participation at EU level. These mainly arise from the economic, market-making purposes of European integration. The social and political roles of the EU have tended to stem from its economic role and the associated legal, political and institutional framework that structures the meaning of inclusion at EU level.

Institutional channelling

At the most basic level, it is possible to question the extent to which the EU is even relevant to debates about the inclusion of migrants and their descendants, which are far more likely to have sub-national, national and transnational resonance than a supranational EU dimension. The EU is detached from many of these debates about inclusion and a strong subsidiarity argument can be advanced that the EU is not well placed to intervene in these day-to-day issues. In other ways, however, the EU has become relevant because of the Europeanisation of aspects of migration policy, with particular consequences for free movement, social entitlements, anti-discrimination and asylum procedures. Debates about inclusion and participation at EU level are closely related to the EU's core market-making purposes, which are bolstered by a supranationalised legal and

political context. It is the institutional context established at supranational level for aspects of migration policy that structures the debate
about inclusion and provides opportunities for and constraints upon
groups seeking to represent migrants' interests in EU decision-making. As
with most things to do with the EU, this participatory context is quite
detached from the day-to-day lives of migrants, but what this chapter
demonstrates is how participation and inclusion have acquired some
resonance at EU level that is configured by the institutional context
established for policy management. Can a supranational 'political opportunity structure' be identified that is shaped by the institutional context
for policy management that mediates the chances for migrant inclusion
and, indeed, gives meaning to inclusion and participation by turning these
issues into 'problems of European integration'?

   To do this, the chapter develops a discussion of migrant interest
representation that assesses the chances for inclusion of migrants' interests
within the developing EU migration policy context. These chances are
mediated by the institutional context established for migration policy,
within which significant supranational regulatory competence for free
movement policy stands in contrast with the largely intergovernmental
immigration and asylum policy context. The structures of political opportunity for groups seeking to represent migrants' interests in EU
decision-making will relate to both the free movement and the immigration and asylum policy contexts. Pro-migrant lobbyists have sought to
build coalitions at EU level that reflect and articulate the concerns of pro-
migrant organisations in the member states (Joint Council for the Welfare
of Immigrants/European Research Centre on Migration and Ethnic Relations,
1996). The 'umbrella groups' that have emerged seek to provide expert
input into policy development and to build alliances with EU and other
relevant institutions. The close relation between the institutional context
at EU level and the structure of political opportunity means that this
chapter's focus is not on 'ethnic mobilisation' (Rex and Drury, 1994).
Attention is directed towards the formulation of an EU-level migrant
interest agenda in response to the emerging political/institutional responsibilities of the EU for migration policy. The institutional context is
specified as the independent variable structuring chances for inclusion and
participation within which élite patterns of European integration have
tended to produce élite patterns of interest representation. If EU-level pro-
migrant political activity does emphasise ethnic or cultural identities of
migrants, then such activity will draw from the 'institutional repertoire'
created by an emergent EU dimension wherein capacity for management
of some key migration-related issues has been vested. An institutionalist
perspective challenges the view that political mobilisation by ethnic
minority groups takes place along lines conditioned by ethnic or cultural
identities. Mobilisations often do occur within ethnic groups, but the

resources provided by the institutional setting and its impact on strategic calculations about the chances of success structure the possibilities for mobilisation. It has been argued that 'patterns of [immigrant] incorporation can be associated empirically with the institutionalised modes and the organisational logic of membership in particular polities' (Soysal, 1994: 5). These resultant 'institutional repertoires' and the opportunities or constraints they place on political activity structure the opportunities for political action, rather than ethnic or cultural identities. Mobilisations can have an ethnic dimension, but this is 'channelled' (Ireland, 1994) through an EU policy context that has stimulated transnational pro-migrant political activity but closely structured the opportunities and constraints faced by these groups.

Refocused politics?

The institutionalisation of an EU migration policy context involves the establishment of both formal legal rules and decisional capacity; this then creates expectations regarding EU capacity to act and increases the relevance of EU institutions. Clearly, the capacity of the EU to act differs markedly between free movement and immigration and asylum, but the basic point about institutionalisation is an important one for two reasons: first, because of the connections between free movement and immigration and asylum policy, which became very evident after the SEA; second, because the establishment of institutional competencies at EU level brings with it political activity that takes the EU as a frame of reference. The latter is a more general observation about European integration, but does also have applicability to migration policy. As EU migration policy responsibilities have developed, then so too has activity by groups seeking to represent the interests of migrants at EU level. Groups such as Amnesty International, Caritas, the ECRE, the Starting Line Group (SLG) and the EU Migrants' Forum (EUMF) all seek to influence the migration policy agenda and to cultivate alliances where possible with supranational institutions.[1] The components of this pro-migrant agenda are strongly related to the institutional context established for the management of migration-related issues. Whether this context hinders the prospects for effective pro-migrant lobbying is a key question. Indeed, the initial prognosis would seem to be gloomy, because of the oft-analysed problems of the democratic deficit. Despite these difficulties, pro-migrant lobby groups seek to broaden the migration policy focus by promoting a greater emphasis on anti-discrimination, action against racism and xenophobia, enhanced rights for TCNs and 'fair' treatment for asylum-seekers as judged by accordance with the standards laid down in international law. These groups follow a basic axiom of political analysis, of going where power goes. Moreover, there is the possibility that refocused activity can contribute to pressure for further institutionalisation of EU policy by leading to pressure for deeper European integration. This is an important point in relation to pro-migrant lobbying because, although these groups advance a critique of EU migration policy as currently constituted, the answer to the problem tends to be more not less 'Europe'. This indicates the possibility for élite-level pro-integration alliances and the importance of addressing the motivations, calculations and alliance-building strategies of EU-level actors.

As already noted, because of the 'democratic deficit' it would seem that we are venturing onto unpromising terrain. At national level, migrants and their descendants and TCNs often experience social and political marginalisation arising from racial discrimination and/or exclusion from national citizenship. Moreover, the emphasis on nationality as the basis for access to EU rights and the absence of EU legislation to combat discrimination on grounds of race or ethnicity serve to reinforce rather than weaken the importance of national citizenship. To complete the gloomy prognosis, EU migration policy co-operation has focused on efforts by member states to transplant restrictive policies from national to EU level. Policies have been characterised by a concern about controlling the numbers of migrants rather than measures promoting the integration of settled migrants and their descendants, which could encompass EU anti-discrimination measures and expanded rights for TCNs. However, free movement within the single market means that the issues are connected and that there is an EU agenda. The components of this agenda require examination before the possible 'avenues to influence' can be specified and assessed. To begin with, however, it is useful to pay some attention to the more general context for lobbying at EU level in order to see the predominantly élite-based characteristics of this activity.

Lobbying the EU

There is a well developed strand within the literature on European integration that analyses interest group activity. Attention has mainly been directed to areas in which interests are well established at national level and then agglomerated by EU-level 'umbrella groups', such as the Union of European Industrialists, the European Trades Unions Confederation and the Confederation of Agricultural Producers (Mazey and Richardson, 1993). More recent work has attempted to draw in broader perspectives on social movement mobilisation and what has been called the 'Europeanisation of conflict' (Marks and McAdam, 1996; Tarrow, 1998). That these analyses have not explored the representation of migrant interests is hardly surprising. Immigration and asylum are relatively new areas of EU activity. Moreover, migrant interest groups tend not to be entrenched or powerful at national level. There is also the problem of formulating a 'migrant interests' agenda that exhibits some coherence, given the sheer diversity of migrant and migrant-origin communities living in EU member states. The focus of this chapter is not so much on grassroots mobilisation seeking to influence EU decision-makers as on top-down structuring of a migration policy context with implications for inclusion and participation of migrants' interests.

The groups that have emerged at EU level tend to act as 'umbrella groups' for national organisations. Groups from those member states with longer-established policy responses to migration have exerted most influence on the arguments put forward by these umbrella groups. There are, however, difficulties melding a common response from diverse national frameworks and, also, some fear from those countries with relatively well developed migrant integration paradigms that European integration will water down national commitments. A potential weakness with such groups acting at EU level is that they rely on horizontal co-ordination, which can be a 'weak substitute for consolidated formal organisation at national level' (Streeck, 1996: 85). However, EU institutions, particularly the Commission, will sponsor and co-opt interest groups – including pro-migrant NGOs – into consultation processes as a way of enhancing the legitimacy of supranational processes and facilitating the consolidation of the Commission's role as a policy actor.

New political opportunities?

Is there a supranational political opportunity structure for pro-migrant organisations? The institutionalisation of an EU migration policy context has meant the formal delineation of responsibility for both intra- and extra-EU migration policy, coupled with processes of issue problematisation that structure 'the immigration problem'. Analyses of political opportunity structures emerged to explain mobilisation by 'new social movements' during the 1970s and 1980s. Political opportunity structures were conceptualised as a set of independent variables with a strong structural and institutional focus that explained social movement mobilisation and the chances of action by 'outsiders' influencing the political process. Four main variables impinge upon the scope for groups to organise and influence the political process: first, the relative openness or closure of the formal political process; second, the stability or instability of political alignments; third, the availability and strategy of potential allies; and finally, the level of political conflict between élites (Tarrow, 1994). When this kind of analysis is extended to EU level, it is very apparent that the political process is relatively closed – the scope for direct participation is limited. Indirect forms of political activity through lobby groups are particularly prevalent and groups with close connections with national governments are more likely to transplant these relations successfully to European level.

The development of transnational patterns of political mobilisation that have the EU as their focus could be defined as involving 'regular interactions across national boundaries when at least one actor is a non-state agent or does not operate on behalf of a national government or an intergovernmental organisation' (Risse-Kappen, 1995: 3). Other analysts place less emphasis on formal state structures, with transnational dynamics characterised in spatial terms as a way of capturing the translation of goods, ideas, discourses and votes and the new transnational configurations that can arise (Amiraux, 1998: 15–16). Transnational mobilisations also raise questions about the strategies, motivations and calculations of migrant organisations. For instance, is lobbying on behalf of migrants indicative of a struggle for inclusion based on 'strategies of resistance' with the use of independent resources, or does it illustrate quiescence and a willingness to abide by the rules of the game? This is an important question because: 'Inclusion may be of more relevance to the stability of the system than to the interests of the included. But inclusion may also open the door to greater leverage in some circumstances' (Cerny, 1990: 39). This is a key dilemma for pro-migrant lobby groups that seek to mobilise at EU level and build alliances with EU institutions. A risk such groups face is that their participation and implicit compliance legitimises policy developments that are more likely to exclude than include the groups whose interests they seek to represent. The rationale for most pro-migrant groups operating at EU level is that deeper European integration is a solution to the problems against which they rail, particularly lowest common denominator Council-based decision-making with limited scope for democratic or judicial checks. By venturing these kinds of arguments they can contribute to the attempts to consolidate an EU migration policy context, rather than questioning the basis for the ceding of policy competencies. Many groups seek to ride two horses at once: to become players in the game while also maintaining a distance centred on a rather fundamental critique of policy development.

Acts of recognition, participation and compliance contribute to the development of a new 'political field' in Europe, with its own forms of culture, capital and habitus within which policy and patterns of political activity become Europeanised (Favell, 1998; Geddes and Favell, 1999; Favell and Geddes, 2000). By operating at EU level, the issues that lobby groups address become *de facto* 'problems of Europe', to which more often than not the solution is closer European integration (particularly if European integration expands democratic and judicial oversight of policy development). If lobby groups advocate 'European' solutions to 'European' problems, then they become potential allies for supranational institutions, particularly the Commission in its quest for closer European integration.

The Commission is a highly relevant actor in any discussion of lobby groups because, for many of them, units within the Commission are one of the first points of call when a case needs to be made in Brussels. Across the range of its activities, the Commission has incorporated lobby groups into consultation processes. In part this stems from the Commission's small size (around 16,000 staff, of whom around half are administrators or translators), which means that it often relies on the kinds of expertise that lobby groups can bring to the policy process. Outside consultation was also seen as a good thing when the Amsterdam Treaty was being negotiated, because of the difficulties experienced by the Maastricht Treaty. Despite these efforts to be receptive, an 'Alternative Summit' was held in Amsterdam, which allowed expression of oppositional views beyond the realm of legitimised EU discourse within the IGC process. An important component of this oppositional discourse was a civil liberties and human rights agenda that railed against 'fortress Europe' and processes of securitisation.

The formulation of an EU-level migrants' interest agenda necessarily involves attempts to ensure that it is representative of the communities on whose behalf it purports to speak. Successful collective action has been connected with organisational capacity, group consciousness and levels of social control (McAdam, 1982). The diverse origins of migrant communities prompts relatively low levels of group consciousness and diverse sub-national, national and transnational settings, while high levels of social control are exerted through external restrictive immigration policies and internal securitisation processes. These factors connect with the coherence of the agenda which, when combined with the representativeness and authoritativeness of those who seek to represent migrant's interests, will affect the success or failure of attempted political mobilisation by pro migrant NGOs when seeking to operate at EU level.

Migrants' interests

The preceding chapters have plotted the development of free movement, immigration and asylum policies. Being more specific about these issue areas allows for clarity when specifying the relation between institutional structures, policy responsibilities and political activity. Without this specificity, analysis of the political opportunity structure can become tautological, in that it explains political mobilisation in terms of the opening of 'political opportunities' without being precise about why, how and when certain institutional contexts produce certain forms of mobilisation. To be more precise in the evaluation of lobbying activity and attempt to put some flesh on the bones of the notion of political opportunity, it is important to specify the relation between policy issues and the institutions with the capacity to act in these policy areas. This chapter now goes on to delineate three potential avenues for representation of migrants' interests. These are labelled 'technocratic' (via the

Commission), 'democratic' (via the EP) and 'interest-based' (via lobby groups). A fourth, judicial, avenue for the protection of migrants' rights is also considered. Taken together these avenues form part of a lobbying strategy for groups seeking to influence EU-level decision-making; there will also, of course, be national and sub-national activity to try to influence national policy preferences.

Pro-migrant groups at EU level make a claim for authoritativeness based on their ability to represent a migrants' interest agenda that has emerged in relation to developing EU policy responsibilities. Even so, the forms of activity are not so much 'bottom-up', grassroots mobilisations as attempts to agglomerate diverse national group preferences into a coherent agenda with respect to the particularities of the EU context. The components of the EU-level pro-migrant interest agenda are derived from EU responsibilities and can be ascertained in two complementary ways: first, by examining the 'revealed preferences' of pro-migrant lobby groups – the areas in which they are active; and second, using an 'added value' test – to see in what areas European integration has affected policy development such that the most appropriate domain for decision-making has become supranational level (Geddes, 1998b).

Analysing the activity of the EU's NGO immigration and asylum policy network prompts identification of three issue areas around which lobbying activity has occurred and which give meaning to inclusion and participation at EU level:

- conditions of entry, residence and movement within the EU for legally resident TCNs, including entry to the labour market, social entitlements and family reunification;
- development of the Amsterdam Treaty's anti-discrimination framework to counter discrimination on grounds of racial or ethnic origin and action against racism and xenophobia, particularly when such activity has a significant transnational dimension, such as the dissemination of racist material across national borders (before the Treaty, discrimination on grounds of nationality was forbidden but racist discrimination was not, and so a broader anti-discrimination framework has been viewed as a practical contribution to a workable free movement framework that offers some protection to TCNs and EU citizens of immigrant and ethnic minority origin);
- the development of asylum policies that are deemed fair, just and humane in relation to the standards set out in international law.

The technocratic route to representation

The Commission plays an important role in European integration because of its powers of proposal and implementation, but its immigration and asylum policy roles have been constrained by limitations imposed by the Amsterdam Treaty, such as the intergovernmental emphasis and obligation to share the power of initiative with member states. It is also important to bear in mind that the Commission is a 'multi-organisation', within which, to a greater or lesser extent, responsibility for free movement, immigration and asylum and social rights all co-exist but need not be prioritised because of leadership and organisational factors. As we have seen, the Commission has been reluctant to encroach into policy areas where member state sensitivities are high because of national sovereignty concerns. Instead, a pragmatic stance has been adopted that has seen the Commission eschew grander integrative ambitions to take a seat at the intergovernmental bargaining table as a way of attempting to secure attainment of free movement objectives. This participation has also led to close association with restrictive immigration and asylum policies.

Given constraints on its migration policy role, can the Commission be an ally of pro-migrant lobby groups? More specifically, can those units within the Commission with responsibility for migration policy seek to build a pro-migrant agenda at EU level? There is, of course, a legitimacy problem, which was brought into particularly stark relief in March 1999, when managerial incompetence and allegations of fraud and corruption provoked the resignation of the entire Commission. The essence of the legitimacy problem is that the unelected Commission is widely perceived as detached from the concerns of EU citizens. Yet this Commission 'weakness' with regard to detachment from democratic processes may in some circumstances actually provide an opportunity for pro-migrant lobbyists, because the Commission may be less susceptible than national politicians to populist pressure for ever tougher immigration policies. Commissioners and Commission officials do not have to bother about election or re-election and do not have to concern themselves with the kinds of things that national politicians may say or do when running for office. In countries where immigration is a salient issue, national politicians may try to secure votes by being 'tough' on immigration. In this respect, the insulation of the Commission from populist pressures may be an advantage. It has been argued that decisions made behind closed doors can be more liberal in character and thereby more accommodating of the interests of migrants than those taken in public decision-making forums, where appeasement of populist anti-immigration sentiment can prompt a tougher line (Guiraudon, 1997). This suggests the potential for Commission progressiveness. However, this needs to be tempered by noting that while the Commission may pursue pro-integration initiatives that expand the rights of migrants and TCNs, it is also likely to seek to build a role for itself in the control and securitised aspects of migration policy. The important point is that pro-migrant Commission activity need not arise because the Commission has a positive view about the rights of migrants (it may or may not), but because it has a positive view about the role of the Commission (it certainly does).

The scope for what has been called Commission 'policy entrepreneurialism' has been identified as significant in key areas of EU activity where regulatory competence has been established (Majone, 1996). Such scope can arise when the costs of Europeanised policy are concentrated and the benefits of policy diffuse, because incentives to organise are strong for the opponents of the policy, who bear the costs, and weak for those who actually benefit from it. In such circumstances, and where the treaty framework permits, the Commission can play an important role as the protector of diffuse and/or poorly organised interests. Where there is 'an important margin of autonomy and capacity to influence outcomes in the political process', the Commission can play an entrepreneurial role (Laffan, 1997: 423) and not only respond 'to opportunities for action', but also facilitate the emergence of these opportunities and thereby to become a 'purposeful opportunist' (Cram, 1994: 199).

Discussion of policy entrepreneurialism could place a positive gloss on the role of the Commission as a potential progressive migrants' champion, but there are circumstances in which the promotion of deeper European integration and the protection of migrants' rights may conflict. An example of this was the Amsterdam Treaty's asylum protocol for nationals of EU member states (see chapter 5). The protocol assumes that all EU member states uphold human rights and are therefore 'safe'. There is a strong federalising logic underpinning this, which the Commission supports, despite the protocol's ambivalent relation to international legal standards on asylum. Amsterdam's immigration and asylum provisions announce their respect for international legal standards, but the problems raised by the asylum protocol illustrate the tensions created by the EU's assumption of state-like responsibilities while it maintains a dubious relation to an international legal order composed of sovereign nation states.

The democratic route to representation

The rhetoric associated with the quest for a 'people's Europe' has been accompanied by attempts to expand the scope for popular participation and the exercise of the rights of citizenship in a democratised European polity. There has also been pressure for increased power for the EP, but the EP remains marginal to the development of immigration and asylum policy. The Amsterdam Treaty gave the EP the right to be consulted on policy development, but this is a far cry from the powers of co-decision that it has acquired in other policy areas. The EP has been a vigorous critic of intergovernmental immigration and asylum policy co-operation reinforcing lowest common denominator policies of restriction and offering inadequate scope for scrutiny of decisions or for decision-makers to be called to account. The EP has called for supranationalisation of immigration and asylum policy, combined with a strengthened commitment to anti-discrimination and the combating of racism and xenophobia. The Commission has echoed the EP's concerns. The 1998 *Action Plan Against Racism* (CEC, 1998: 4) reported the findings of a 1997 *Eurobarometer* opinion poll which, despite the methodological and interpretative difficulties of measuring 'racism', found that 33 per cent of those interviewed described themselves as 'quite racist' or 'very racist'. The survey also found that these 33 per cent were also likely to be those in socially insecure circumstances with heightened fears about unemployment. On a more positive note, the survey also found that 77 per cent of respondents thought that designating 1997 the European Year Against Racism was a good idea and that 84 per cent called for action by European institutions to combat racism.

The EP has been a vigorous critic of the extreme right and an advocate of EU action against racism and xenophobia. In the aftermath of the extreme right's breakthrough at the 1984 European elections – when the *Front National* won ten of the eighty seats available in France – a Committee of Inquiry into the Rise of Fascism and Racism was established. The resulting report (the Evrigenis report; EP, 1985) concluded that patchy national measures needed to be complemented by European-level initiatives. The first step, it was argued in the report, should be a joint declaration by the main EC institutions against racism and xenophobia. In June 1986 the Council, Commission and EP signed the Joint Declaration Against Racism and Xenophobia, which expressed bold sentiment when calling for the prevention of all 'acts or forms of discrimination'. The 1986 Joint Declaration was, however, 'a false dawn' (EP, 1998: 9). In 1989 the EP requested that the Commission bring forward proposals based on the 1986 Declaration, but the Commission responded that it was unable to do so because there was no legal basis for such action in the Treaty of Rome. The Commission suggested a non-binding resolution that would urge member states without existing provisions to introduce anti-discrimination legislation. The final Council resolution was much watered down and signified disagreement among member states about the appropriateness of EC action against racism.

In 1990 the EP set up a second Committee of Inquiry into Racism and Xenophobia. Its report – the Ford report (EP, 1991) – made seventy-seven recommendations for action, of which three had been implemented by 1999. EP suggestions carried little weight because the Commission still found its policy proposal role hindered by the absence of clear competence for action against racism. The Ford report acknowledged the Commission's difficulties and recognised its intent to bring forward measures combating racism and xenophobia, but stated that 'initiatives are either subject to long delays in the Council of Ministers or they are watered down, if not completely abandoned, by the Commission on the grounds of political necessities, believing that unanimous approval will not be obtained' (EP, 1991: 99).

The EP has also worked with the NGO anti-racism lobby. In 1993 and 1994 resolutions were passed that called for the SLG's anti-discrimination proposals to serve as the basis for Commission proposals for an amendment to the Maastricht Treaty that would extend anti-discrimination competencies.[2] The EP's limited competence does, however, mean that if action is to occur then it is more likely to emanate from other EU institutions upon which the EP can seek to exert influence. For instance, since 1991 the conclusions brought forward by the presidency at the end of Council meetings have frequently mentioned the determination to act against racism and xenophobia, but these declarations are costless, need not imply legislation and possess mainly symbolic significance. In 1995 the Council adopted non-binding resolutions on action against racial discrimination in employment and anti-racist education, with a further declaration on the fight against racism in education adopted in 1997. These resolutions and declarations did not compel member states to act.[3]

Concerns about racism and xenophobia prompted a shift in approach discernible at the Corfu summit held in December 1994. A Franco-German initiative led to the establishment of the Consultative Commission on Racism and Xenophobia. The Kahn Commission (named after its chair, Jean Kahn, President of the European Jewish Congress) called for binding legislation to combat racial discrimination. It argued that the EU had already displayed determination to combat discrimination based on gender: 'it is appropriate that it should be given a similar mandate, and that it should adopt similar measures, to combat discrimination on grounds of race, religion or ethnic or national origins' (European Council Consultative Commission on Racism and Xenophobia, 1995: 59). The EP endorsed the Kahn report and called for an amendment to the Maastricht Treaty to deal specifically with racial discrimination. The Commission's 1995 communication on racism, xenophobia and anti-Semitism reinforced this stance with its own call for the anti-discrimination provisions of the Treaty to be strengthened to cover racial discrimination (CEC, 1995b). The Commission's 1998 *Action Plan Against Racism* sought to 'mainstream' anti-racism by seeking integration across all sectors of EU activity. If we look beyond the jargon of 'mainstreaming', the action plan leaves two questions unanswered. First, it does not apply to immigration and asylum policy, which is a rather striking omission. Second, the Commission has experienced difficulties when trying to 'mainstream'. For instance, the Commission's proposals on parental leave and part-time work included specific non-discrimination sections that were then dropped from the final texts.

Article 13 of the Amsterdam Treaty did create the potential for action against discrimination based on sex, racial or ethnic origin, religion or belief, disability, age or sexual orientation. The requirement for unanimity in the Council weakens the provisions. Article 13 does not have direct effect, which means that it cannot be relied upon in national legal proceedings. Action against racism and xenophobia was also included within a revised Article K.1 of the post-Amsterdam JPC pillar. Even before this reference being made in the JPC pillar, the Council had brought forward a joint action to combat racism and xenophobia.

What does all this tell us about the EP's role? Because of the absence of a substantive basis for EP activity, its main role has been as a persuader and cajoler of national governments and a potential ally for supranational institutions and lobby groups in the quest for deeper immigration and asylum policy integration. The EP has been particularly conscious of the growth in support for the extreme right, not least because of the neo-Fascists who are European Parliamentarians. The EP has also called for a broader conceptualisation of the immigration *problematique* that impinges more directly on questions relating to migrant inclusion.

Interest-based representation

Pro-migrant lobby groups operating at EU level do not command the resources of powerful and well entrenched interest groups such as business, trade unions and agriculture. Moreover, for most groups that seek to represent migrants, the relevant lobbying arenas are at sub-national and national level. The EU is literally and metaphorically distant from many of the day-to-day concerns of migrants and their descendants in EU member states (Danese, 1998). This does not mean that the EU is irrelevant, rather that we need to specify areas in which EU competencies are encroaching upon a series of issues that relate to the position of migrants and their descendants without pretending that migrants are *au fait* with these EU-level organisations. Pro-migrant NGOs have focused their activity on countering racism and xenophobia, seeking enactment of broader anti-discrimination legislation, expanding the rights of TCNs and ensuring that EU asylum policy accords with international legal standards.

The Commission has exerted some 'top-down' (albeit limited) influence on pro-migrant groups and organisations at national and sub-national level. It has funded such groups and, by doing so, imparted a supra-national dimension to localised campaigns and mobilisations. Examples of such funding were provided by a 1995 Commission report on the funding of migrant organisations. Between 1991 and 1993, 560 projects were funded, of which the report evaluated 200 in detail. The largest number of projects, 40 per cent, aimed to give migrants better access to facilities such as housing and education. Eighteen per cent were concerned with modifying the self-image of migrants or attempting to change negative public perceptions. Other evaluated projects covered issues such as reception and settlement (10 per cent) and anti-racist and solidarity movements (9 per cent). Sixteen per cent were categorised as migrant-led. The others were led by NGOs, churches and by organisations active in particular areas, such as housing associations. The average level of subsidy for the groups was 17,888 ECU (CEC, 1995c).

Awareness of a European dimension introduces a new strategic element into the operation of these groups. These processes of strategic re-evaluation were consolidated by the designation of 1997 as the European Year Against Racism, which directed 4.7 million ECU towards projects in member states designed to raise awareness of racism and xenophobia (CEC, 1997c). These projects included those at local level as well as larger events, such as a football match involving some of the world's leading players. Even so, there was still an evident mismatch between these declaratory or symbolic events and actual legislative capacity.

Commission funding has also been made available for other projects that seek the social integration of non-national immigrants in member states, to combat racism and xenophobia and to assist refugees. The Commission has sought to stimulate local initiatives through collaboration with local authorities, including the Cities Against Racism (CAR) and Local Integration/Partnership Action (LIA) projects. CAR ran between 1995 and 1997 and brought together local authorities and NGOs from thirty European towns and cities 'to promote the development and implementation of good practice, and to combine this with the European-level exchange of experience and information between grassroots level actors' (CEC, 1998: 8). The LIA involved twenty-three cities developing local action plans to combat racism. To reinforce its multi-organisational dimension, the Commission has also promoted co-operation between immigration control agencies through the Odysseus programme.

Of the EU-level pro-migrant organisations, perhaps the best known is the EUMF, which was established as an umbrella group for migrant organisations in each member state combined with regional ethnic groups composed of migrants of similar ethnic or national origin (Danese, 1998: 719). The EUMF was originally intended to be a broad inter-community forum, encompassing migrant and non-migrant groups, such as trade unions, which would include institutions and associations opposed to racism (EP, 1985). When it was finally established in 1991, the EUMF had a narrower remit than in the original proposal and was more concerned with providing a forum for the expression of migrants' opinions than pursuing broader cross-community strategies against racism. Danese (1998: 718) notes the broader context within which it is important to locate the EUMF: 'The creation of the Forum has to be seen in the light of the wider discourse on "social Europe" led by European institutions'. (The next chapter explores the relation between migration and the EU's social policy context more closely and shows that although the EU speaks the language of 'social inclusion', it continues to exclude TCNs from key aspects of its social dimension.)

The EUMF receives funding from the Commission, which is one of the institutions it seeks to influence. This accords with a fairly standard model of supranational interest co-option pursued by the Commission across a range of policy areas. Such co-option is designed to add a veneer of legitimacy to policy development.

The EUMF has faced a number of difficulties that have hindered its operation. There is the basic definitional question of who is a 'migrant'. There are millions of people of migrant origin in EU member states who are commonly wrongly thought to be migrants when in fact they are citizens of the member state in which they reside and they can resent the imputation of temporariness. There have also been internal divisions within the EUMF. For instance, at the Forum's General Assembly held on 16–17 December 1993, the representatives of fourteen Turkish associations walked out because they felt under-represented on the Executive Board. Turks constituted a third of 'migrants' (this depends on the definition employed) but a move to limit the voting weight of any ethnic group to a maximum of 10 per cent was seen as 'anti-Turkish' (*Migration Newsheet* 133/94). In 1996 the EUMF was thrown into further turmoil after allegations of financial mismanagement. The EUMF reflected the problems mentioned earlier about co-ordination of groups that operate in diverse national settings. Immigrant integration paradigms differ markedly in Britain, France and Germany and these differences were reflected in tensions within the EUMF. The EUMF has also been used by migrant groups to exert influence on governments in their countries of origin as a way of indirectly exerting pressure on the EU member state in which they reside (Kastoryano, 1994).

Attempting to exert influence on national policy preferences has been a key aspect of EUMF activity. In the run-up to the 1996 IGC, the EUMF published its proposals for the revision of the Maastricht Treaty. It emphasised the point made by the Commission in its 1994 White Paper, *European Social Policy*, 'that action in the area of integration policy remains an essential element of the wider need to promote solidarity and integration in the Union' (CEC, 1994b: 29). The White Paper went on to note that to achieve this, integration policies needed to be directed in a meaningful way towards improving the situation of TCNs within the EU by taking steps which will strengthen their rights relative to those of citizens of the member states. The EUMF called for an amendment to Maastricht's Article 8a, which established citizenship of the EU, to extend EU citizenship to TCNs lawfully resident in an EU member state for more than five years. The five-year period corresponded with the residence requirement in many member states before conferral of permanent resident status or eligibility to naturalise and was the period specified in Article 6(1) of Regulation 68/360 regarding the validity of residence permits for migrant EC nationals. To ensure equal access to free movement rights, the EUMF also proposed that Articles 48–66 of the Treaty of Rome be amended so that they applied equally to TCNs (EUMF, 1996).

The EUMF endorsed the SLG's proposals for expanded EU anti-discrimination competence (see below) with the Council given power to issue directives or make regulations setting out measures required to eliminate discrimination against persons or groups of persons, whether citizens of the EU or not, on the grounds of race, colour, religion, or national, social or ethnic origin. The EUMF also called for greater openness and transparency in immigration and asylum policy, with Council debates opened to the public and verbatim reports made available in the *Official Journal*, including details of votes and declarations by member states. It was proposed that a new article be added to the provisions giving EU citizens a right of access to information at the disposal of EU institutions. The EUMF also called for an extension of ECJ competence to the intergovernmental pillars and co-decision-making power for the EP.

At the forefront of pressure for expanded anti-discrimination provisions has been the SLG. It was founded in 1992 by a group of independent experts from six member states with the support of the Churches Commission for Migrants in Europe (CCME), the British Commission for Racial Equality and the Dutch National Office Against Racism. The original intention was to prepare a draft directive outlawing racial discrimination that would be modelled on the 1976 Equal Treatment Directive (76/207 EEC of 9 February 1976) and use the wide-ranging Article 235 as its Treaty base for anti-discrimination legislation with direct effect. The SLG's proposal, known as 'The Starting Line', was endorsed by national lobby groups and by the EP.

After the Amsterdam Treaty was signed in October 1997, the SLG brought forward a proposal for a directive that would put into effect the principle of equal treatment, which is taken to mean that:

> There shall be no discrimination whatsoever, direct or indirect, based on racial or ethnic origin, or religion or belief in particular in the following areas: the exercise of a professional activity, whether salaried or self-employed; access to any job or post, dismissals and other working conditions; social security; health and welfare benefits; education; vocational guidance and vocational training; housing; provision of goods, facilities and services; the exercise of its functions by any public body; participation in political, economic, social, cultural, religious life or any other public field. (Starting Line Group, 1998)

Commission plans for expanded anti-discrimination legislation were contained in the 1998–2000 SAP (see p. 124).

The SLG also brought forward proposals to extend the right of free movement and access to social entitlements for TCNs. These social entitlement proposals will be analysed in chapter 7, which explores the migration/welfare policy context in more detail and links it to the EU's social dimension.

For asylum and refugee policy, the ECRE is an umbrella organisation for member states' refugee councils and similar organisations and seeks to add a European dimension to national lobbying strategies. The ECRE seeks to co-ordinate its activities with other groups with Brussels representation, such as Amnesty, the UNHCR, Caritas, the Migration Policy Group and the EUMF. Like other groups, the ECRE faces difficulties influencing policy development made in a secretive, intergovernmental institutional environment within which the development of a policy framework emphasising tighter restriction on asylum prevails. The ECRE noted with disappointment the difference between its own *Position on the Functioning of the Treaty on European Union in Relation to Asylum Policy* and the contents of the Amsterdam Treaty (ECRE, 1997c, 1997d). The outcome was described as a technical transfer from the third to the first pillar without the kinds of checks at supranational level that it had called for, such as more Commission involvement, more powers for the ECJ and greater involvement for the EP. The ECRE has, though, viewed the supranationalisation of asylum policy as a potentially favourable development, as more progressive and as a positive restraining force on member states' actions, which may at times have tenuous regard for international legal standards. An example of this is that the ECRE congratulated the Commission on its proposals concerning temporary protection of displaced persons, which it saw as an attempt to ensure that a common approach did not undermine existing standards (CEC, 1997c; ECRE 1997a, 1997b).

Amnesty International has also paid special attention to the EU's asylum policy provisions. It argued that the 1996–7 IGC was 'a unique opportunity for the European Union to pay concrete attention to human rights protection' (Amnesty International, 1996: 2). Existing protection for the rights of asylum-seekers were seen as inadequate, particularly in the light of the 'safe third country' and associated provisions put in place by EU member states. Moreover, in its memorandum containing proposals for a strengthened protection of human rights by the EU, Amnesty (1996: 9–10) argued that:

> The downward spiral of the member states' policies towards the minimum common denominator does not afford sufficient protection for those in need. More and more restrictive national measures on asylum have been adopted over the past six years in many member states. Amnesty International opposes this downward spiral which appears to have no bottom.

Amnesty feared that the EU's harmonised visa provisions would prevent genuine asylum-seekers from fleeing persecution and stated that people should not be prevented from applying for asylum because they do not have the appropriate visa or other documents. Amnesty also opposed the 'safe third country' principle, because of the absence of a requirement that 'safe' countries have satisfactory asylum procedures. The EU recommendation of December 1994 concerning a specimen bilateral readmission agreement between the EU and a third country was criticised for not including guarantees for the protection of the rights of asylum-seekers and refugees. It was also argued that the EU's criterion for manifestly unfounded asylum applications was wider than that contained in Conclusion 30 of the Executive Committee of the UNHCR. EU provisions on the harmonised application of the term 'refugee' were also criticised. The EU's definition differed substantially from that contained in the UNHCR's (1992) *Handbook on Procedures and Criteria for Determining Refugee Status*. In particular, the EU's definition did not include people fleeing non-state forms of persecution, such as civil wars or other forms of internal armed conflict. Amnesty also called for minimum standards, including a proper right of appeal for asylum-seekers and for asylum-seekers to be detained only in the most exceptional circumstances. In summary, Amnesty International detected a gap between EU provisions and the standards laid down in international law.

To summarise, there has been a re-focusing of political activity on the EU, which reflects its growing competencies. The possibilities for effective lobbying depend upon the sources of legal, political and social power provided by the treaty framework. Pro-migrant groups have found their activities hindered by the blurred transfer of immigration and asylum policy competencies and the limited role for supranational institutions. These constraints on democratic and judicial oversight (see below) diminish the possibility for EU-level social and political spaces for migrants. Incorporating the voices of pro-migrant NGOs adds legitimacy to decision-making processes, but does not mean that these voices will be listened to and have a substantive effect on policy outcomes. Intergovernmentalism stymies the potential for institutionalisation and refocused political activity.

Judicial protection

When discussing the ECJ's role, it is important to distinguish between its competence to deal with extra-EU migration (immigration and asylum), which has been limited, and its capacity to deal with intra-EU migration (free movement), which is highly developed and for which a body of case law has developed. The creation of an intra-EU migration regime based on the right of free movement has entailed significant supranationalisation, as the ECJ has been active in establishing and maintaining the principles underpinning intra-EU migration. The operationalisation of the free movement provisions during the 1960s and 1970s meant that the right to it was not extended to TCNs, unless they were the dependants of an EU citizen or covered by an agreement between the EU and a third country. This disjunction between intra- and extra-EU migration policy has hindered the role of the ECJ. However, Guild (1998) has argued that the triangular relationship between EU citizens, member states and the EU, which removes member states' discretion to determine who can and who cannot enter their territory, also applies to those covered by EU–third country Association Agreements. These Agreements have direct effect and have established rights of free movement and the transferability of social entitlements for some TCNs, such as those covered by the 1964 Agreement with Turkey. NGOs have therefore argued that if these rights are extended to some TCNs because of relevant Association Agreements, then it is unsustainable for other legally resident TCNs to be excluded. This leads to a free movement dynamic with potential spillover effects. This contrasts with the immigration and asylum framework, where ECJ jurisdiction over the securitised aspects of immigration and asylum policy has been limited. The Maastricht Treaty did allow for ECJ jurisdiction for specific measures, but only after unanimous agreement on this course of action by member states – which was never forthcoming. Amsterdam does allow ECJ jurisdiction over the free movement, immigration and asylum provisions, but only after referral from the highest court in member states and with a national security proviso that could limit the ECJ's competence (although it is for the ECJ to determine any national security arguments that are used and it has not tended to be in the ECJ's nature to limit its own competencies).

The key point with regard to the role of the ECJ appears to be the articulation between an intra-EU free movement framework and the potential for expanded rights for TCNs. The ECJ has, for instance, made rulings that have extended the rights of free movement to TCNs as a result of Association Agreements. These have, though, run up against the substantial hurdle that the need for prior possession of the nationality of a member state prevents expanded rights for all TCNs who are legally resident in an EU member state. This has underpinned the arguments for a 'Resident's Charter' with free movement rights and associated social entitlements for all legally resident TCNs.

Analysis of the role of the ECJ suggests the potential for the opening of EU-level social and political spaces for migrants and their descendants. Moreover, the ways in which legal norms contained within international legal standards have contributed to post-national forms of membership has also been emphasised by analysts who emphasise new patterns of claims-making. The implication of this post-national perspective is that the nation state is no longer the sole frame of reference when claims for social, legal and political entitlements are made (Soysal, 1994; Jacobsen, 1996). How much force do these arguments possess at EU level? The ECJ was granted little in the way of formal jurisdiction until the Amsterdam Treaty gave it power of review over Title IV, and even then with constraints. The ECJ has been able to interpret the terms of the Association Agreements and other agreements that extend labour market rights to TCNs covered by those Agreements, such as Turks, Moroccans and Algerians. For those TCNs not covered by such agreements, acquisition of the nationality of a member state remains the key issue if rights attached to EU citizenship are to be attained.

Conclusion

The institutional context established at EU level for the management of immigration and asylum issues has structured the political opportunities available for the representation of migrants' interests and given meaning to supranational notions of participation and inclusion that are closely associated with élite patterns of European integration. Secretive decision-making processes within the Council and an emphasis on unanimity have prompted lowest common denominator decision-making with an emphasis on security and restriction. Pro-migrant NGOs have pushed for a deeper, more supranationalised response to the immigration and asylum issues confronting member states. This stance has facilitated the development of alliances with the Commission and EP. There has, though, been only limited success when measured by the quest for expanded supranational decisional capacity as a way of opening of gaps in member state control that could then be exploited by EU-level policy entrepreneurialism instigated by the Commission. The Amsterdam Treaty affirmed Council superiority for at least five years after ratification.

   Progress – as measured by attainment of the objectives of pro-migrant NGOs – has been slow. This has been particularly evident for asylum policy, where an increased emphasis on restriction has led to claims that EU member states are reneging upon international legal obligations. The Amsterdam Treaty did extend the anti-discrimination provisions of the Maastricht Treaty and could be construed as a breakthrough. When the SLG began campaigning for anti-discrimination provisions of the Treaty to be broadened, the prospects for success appeared slight. Yet, within four years, provision had been made in the Amsterdam Treaty. This cannot, of course, be attributed solely to the activities of the SLG and other pro-migrant groups, but does indicate that supranational lobbying can chime with national lobbying strategies that seek to influence member states' policy preferences. The limitations of Article 13 have, however, prompted calls for more concerted EU-level action and the SLG has already drafted plans for a directive giving effect to Article 13.

This chapter also pointed to the importance of NGOs building alliances with supranational institutions. The chances for success of these alliances will depend upon the legal resources that are available and the configuration of responsibility at EU level. In supranationalised areas such as free movement, the Commission and the ECJ are relatively powerful actors. Many of the arguments expounded by pro-migrant lobby groups seek to move anti-discrimination, the rights of TCNs and asylum policy towards supranationalised decision-making. The Commission has an interest in sponsoring and co-opting interest groups as a way of adding legitimacy to EU decision-making while also developing pro-European integration coalitions. Thus, it need not be the case that the Commission has a positive view about migrants' rights (it may or may not and, anyway, is subject to intra-organisational tensions because of its various migration policy responsibilities), but that, rather, it has a positive view about its own role. The downside of this so far as pro-migrant NGOs are concerned is that the securitised immigration and asylum framework also contributes to pressure for deeper European integration. These developments should not surprise us, because if national immigration policies are characterised by tensions between restriction and expansion and inclusion and exclusion then what we are seeing is an institutional reflection at EU level of these debates, coupled with a refraction through the lens of the EU's own institutional context. A further key area of activity for pro-migrant NGOs has been the social entitlements of TCNs with direct relevance to social inclusion. The next chapter develops this discussion by examining the connection between migration and welfare.

Notes

1   The NGO network on European Refugee, Asylum and Immigration Policy was composed of Amnesty International, Caritas Europe, the CCME, the ECRE, the EUMF and the SLG. The UNHCR attended meetings as an observer. It received support from other members of the EU's NGO network: the European Citizens Action Service, Fédération Internationale des Droits de l'Homme, Jesuit Refugee Service Europe, Quaker Council for European Affairs and the Red Cross–EU Liaison Office.

2   *Official Journal*, C342/19, 1993; *Official Journal*, C323/154, 1994.

3   Resolution on the Fight Against Racism and Xenophobia in the Fields of Employment and Social Affairs, *Official Journal*, C296/13, 1995; Resolution of the Response of Educational Systems to the Problems of Racism and Xenophobia, *Official Journal*, C312/1, 1995; Declaration by the Council and the Representatives of the Member States Meeting Within the Council of 24 November 1997 on the Fight Against Racism, Xenophobia and Anti-Semitism, *Official Journal*, C368/1, 1997.

7

Migration and welfare in an integrating Europe

Introduction

Welfare states in EU member states constitute key arenas within which issues of inclusion and exclusion are mediated. At national level, legal residence and contribution usually serve as qualifications for welfare entitlements (Guiraudon, 2000). At EU level, however, the portability of social entitlements that is associated with free movement depends upon prior possession of the nationality of a member state. Although the EU does not and is not likely to have a welfare state, it does have a social dimension, from which TCNs are largely excluded. What are the chances for TCN inclusion? This chapter explores the relation between EU-level inclusion and the legal, political and social resources that have become associated with EU market integration. The previous chapter's analysis of pro-migrant lobbying showed the constraints and opportunities facing groups seeking to extend the EU's anti-discrimination framework to cover TCNs. The scope for an analysis of the EU migration/welfare policy context needs to be carefully delimited in order both to facilitate discussion of what the EU can do and to avoid being swept along by the rhetorical flourishes that can accompany the quest for 'social inclusion'. The analytical focus is directed towards the possibility that the framework established for transferable social entitlements can be extended to cover legally resident TCNs. This is the area in which EU capacity to act is more clearly defined and to which the arguments of pro-migrant NGOs have been directed. Attention is, therefore, directed towards the institutional channelling of 'migrant social inclusion' at EU level.

Migration challenges the welfare state

There is a more general context to this analysis of migration and welfare, because debates about welfare provision and challenges faced by welfare states are salient political issues across Europe (Pierson, 1994). Immigration has been construed as one challenge to the welfare state (Freeman,

1986). A European dimension has been added to these debates by the development of EU capacities in the 'social dimension'. Yet when compared with the 'avalanche' (Pierson, 1998: 777) of recent work on the welfare state, the questions raised by migration – by both free movement within the single market and extra-EU migration by TCNs – are infrequently explored. European integration is unlikely to bring with it a European welfare state. Provision is likely to remain nationally based, but the issues associated with migration and welfare provision do prompt a rethinking of relationships between nationality and social entitlement.

Debates about migration and welfare are, of course, nested within more general debates about the future of welfare provision. The welfare state faces pressures from economic globalisation, budgetary deficits, demographic change, as well as the effects of neo-liberal thinking on welfare provision. Immigration and multiculturalism have also been seen as posing some kind of threat or challenge to the welfare state. Kitschelt (1995: 270) asks whether 'the multiculturalization of still by and large homogenous or ethnically stable Western Europe will lead to a decline of the welfare state?' In short, does immigration threaten to erode standards of welfare provision by undermining the position of the domestic workforce in countries of immigration? Freeman (1986: 61) argued that not only was immigration 'a disaster' but that 'It has led to the Americanization of European welfare politics'. This is to exaggerate the erosion of standards of welfare provision to US levels, but when divided into three components it does serve as a useful guide to aspects of the migration/welfare nexus. First, there is an argument about Americanisation resulting from immigration, which will supposedly lead to a lowering of standards of social protection. This was at the core of Freeman's (1986) analysis, but empirical evidence does not lend credence to this argument (Rhodes and van Apeldoorn, 1998). The threats to the levels of welfare provision are real, but welfare states are well entrenched in EU member states and serve as an important source of political legitimacy for national governments (Flora, 1986; Banting, 1995). Second, there may well be more enthusiasm about some form of Americanisation of European labour markets measured in terms of the attainment of US levels of labour mobility. This would likely be viewed as desirable and as imparting an increased degree of labour market 'flexibility' to an EU where, despite the provisions for free movement, the exercise of this right has lagged behind expectations (Muus, 1997). Third, Americanisation could be construed as implying some kind of federal response via the creation of a European welfare state, perhaps as a way of attempting to shore up a European social model in the face of the challenges posed to social protection by economic globalisation. In this sense, a federal response could actually constitute an attempt to develop some form of collective action that aims to maintain levels of social protection. Indeed, since the mid-1980s there has been an extension in the ascription of formal treaty competence to the EU for social policy. Concomitantly, the commitment to – and rhetoric associated with – social inclusion has become an important part of the debate about building a Europe closer to its citizens. It is, however, important not to overstate the significance of the EU dimension while also iterating that welfare provision retains its strong national context.

EU social policy

Social policy integration has lagged behind economic integration and risked being dismissed 'as a pipe dream or as an afterthought to the EU's main project of economic integration' (Pierson and Liebfried, 1995: 4). The multi-level dimension imparted to debates about migration and welfare by European integration needs to be located in the context of a strong horizontal dimension derived from well entrenched national welfare states (George and Taylor-Gooby, 1996). This could be construed as directing attention towards the importance of the acquisition of national citizenship as a vehicle for the integration of immigrants and their descendants. However, to focus on nationality as the basis for social entitlement for migrants and their descendants would be misplaced because inclusion within the provisions of national welfare states has not necessarily depended upon acquisition of the nationality of the country of residence. Entitlements actually arise as a consequence of legal residence and contributions to national welfare states. Social spaces at national level have thereby been opened for immigrants and their descendants. It is also the case that the prospect of future entitlements resulting from further immigration contributes to the emphasis on restrictive immigration policies to protect the nation state *qua* national welfare state. Migratory pressures can also lead to a redefinition of the criteria for entitlement. In Germany, for instance, increased migration has prompted a rethink of the status of the *Aussiedler* (ethnic German). In this context, the national welfare state can be understood as an institutionalised threshold of inequality, with great importance ascribed to the criteria for membership of these national welfare systems (Bommes, 1998).

Despite legal residence being the basis for access to welfare rights at national level, it remains the case that at EU level the possession of the nationality of a member state is the main basis for access to free movement rights and associated social entitlements. This suggests a re-evaluation of the Marshallian notion of sequential progression between legal, political and social rights. The economic impetus underpinning European integration has meant a reordering, because social rights were important to the exercise of free movement, while political rights were not so important and lagged behind. Moreover, institutional blocks derived from EU decision-making procedures impede social policy integration and have prevented the extension of free movement rights and transferable social entitlements to TCNs. If substantive policy integration were to occur, it would require unanimous agreement. Member states have been prepared to cede competence in those areas that relate to attainment of the economic purposes of the single market. Consequently, social entitlements within the EU are linked to the functional right of free movement for workers. Even though access to national welfare systems can arise as a consequence of legal settlement, the possession of the nationality of a member state is the key that opens the door for access to social entitlements associated with free movement within the EU. TCNs may well have acquired social entitlements at national level, but because they do not possess the nationality of a member state, they are not entitled either to move freely or to enjoy the transferable social entitlements associated with European integration.

This basic observation has the effect of delimiting the subject matter for an evaluation of the extra-EU migration/welfare policy context at EU level. Rather than probing the various meanings of 'social inclusion', it can be more helpful to analyse the ways in which the EU's institutional framework for attainment of social policy objectives is configured and the effects this has on debates about inclusion. Once this is done, the institutional configuration's effects on the prospects for expanded rights for TCNs can be examined. In short, it needs to be borne in mind that market-making rather than market-correcting objectives drove the establishment of a supranational framework that sought to guarantee transferable social entitlements. The concern of policy has tended to be with protecting 'the civil right to enter into contracts and not with industrial and social rights relating to their outcome' (Streeck, 1996: 72). This emphasis on securing the conditions for factor and labour mobility within the single market has meant that EU policy has been largely concerned with 'technical matters' rather than with 'social conscience' (Lodge, 1989: 310).

The fact that nationality of the country of residence is not a necessary criterion for entitlement in the member states but is at EU level has led to the argument that a certain illogicality pervades the EU social entitlement provisions and that legally resident TCNs should receive equal treatment. Furthermore, this form of exclusion of TCNs could be seen as resting uneasily with the EU's oft-voiced commitment to 'social inclusion', which forms an important part of an effort by the EU to emphasise that it is not an economic club detached from the aspirations of its citizens. However, the commitment to inclusion can garner its strength only from the treaty framework, which is weak and underdeveloped with regard to the rights of TCNs. The Commission could be as bold, expansive and entrepreneurial as it likes when making claims for the social inclusion of TCNs, but must confront the political reality that it is likely to encounter a sceptical Council asking from where is derived the treaty basis for such action.

European integration and social entitlements

While national welfare states are likely to remain the providers of key aspects of welfare provision such as employment, education and health care, the EU is involved in two ways. First, there is a need to establish transferable social entitlements, to buttress the free movement framework. Second, it is involved in what has been called 'encapsulated federalism' (Streeck, 1996: 76), where member states have been prepared to allow extension of supranational policy competence for areas such as gender equality, workplace consultation and working hours. There have often been strong arguments based on national interests for the extension of competence in these areas derived from fear of so-called social dumping, where member states compete on the basis of lowering standards of social protection.

The Treaty of Rome's provisions for the creation of a common market within which goods, services, workers and capital could move freely required that some attention to be paid to social policy. In general terms, welfare states and social policy were key aspects of national policy and the plans for European integration had clear social policy consequences. This led to some largely rhetorical commitments, such as the placing in the Treaty's preamble of the objective of securing 'economic and social progress of the member states' and 'the constant improvement of the living and working conditions of their peoples'. Article 2 contained a commitment to high employment standards and high levels of social protection. Articles 118–123 contained other social policy provisions relating to, for instance, gender equality (Article 119) and the creation of a European social fund (Article 123).

The connection between free movement and social entitlement was made clear in Article 51, which gave the Council the power to adopt measures for social security provision for migrant workers who were nationals of an EC member state. Measures had to be agreed unanimously by the member states. The provision for unanimity has not been altered by subsequent amendments of the Treaty and was reaffirmed by the Amsterdam Treaty. Article 51 applied to the aggregation and payment of benefits for nationals of one member state residing in another.

As shown in chapter 2, the Treaty of Rome did leave open the possibility that free movement rights could be extended to TCNs, but when the Treaty's provisions were given effect free movement rights were restricted to workers who were nationals of a member state. The early rules covering transferable social entitlements were contained in Regulations 3/58 and 4/58 of 1958,[1] which attempted to ensure co-ordination of entitlement for workers and self-employed people moving between member states. These regulations established the principles of equal treatment for all workers (holding the nationality of a member state) and the aggregation of benefits within the EEC and transferability of social benefits. These regulations also made it clear that the aim of EEC policy was *co-ordination* not *harmonisation*.

In the aftermath of Regulation 1612/68,[2] which provided for free movement for workers, Regulation 1408/71[3] updated provisions with respect to the application of social security schemes. Regulation 1408/71 sought the co-ordination of national social security legislation with a view to guaranteeing to all workers holding the nationality of a member state and their dependants equality of treatment and entitlement to social security benefits, irrespective of their place of employment and residence. Regulation 1408/71 was the basis for the development of a complicated policy framework that has seen it amended no less than twenty-seven times between 1972 and June 1998. Regulation 574/72[4] established detailed rules for the implementation of Regulation 1408/71. To give a further indication of the complexity of the policy framework, Regulation 574/72 was amended on twenty-eight occasions between September 1972 and June 1998.

There has been some scope for inclusion of TCNs within these social entitlement provisions. TCNs who are relatives of migrant workers derive rights under Regulation 1612/68.[5] In *Dzodi* v. *Belgium*, the ECJ allowed for spouses to move with the holder of the right, to remain permanently resident in the host state, to be admitted to that state's education system on the same conditions as the nationals of that member state, to have the right to work and have access to social security benefits in the host state.[6] In the *Kziber* case, the social provisions of the Treaty were for the first time interpreted in such a way as to include a TCN as a result of an Association Agreement with a third country. The ECJ ruled that a Moroccan national covered by the Agreement between the EC and Morocco did have the right to special unemployment benefits for school leavers. Clause 41(1) of the EC–Morocco Association Agreement covering equal treatment in social security was ruled capable of creating direct effects.[7]

The essential significance of the free movement/social entitlement legislation put in place between 1968 and 1972 was that it established a close link between intra-EC migration by EC nationals and social entitlements, with some spillover to dependant TCNs and those covered by Association Agreements. Otherwise, TCNs were largely excluded from the EC's social policies. The Commission, in its first SAP, introduced in 1975, initially did include migrants who were not nationals of an EC member state. The Commission's programme contained an extensive section covering problems encountered by TCNs in relation to living and working conditions, social security, vocational training, social services, housing, the education of children, health, and information and training. The Council did not share the Commission's expansive understanding of the term 'migrant' and focused instead on migrant workers holding the nationality of a member state. Member states argued that there was no treaty basis for a more expansive interpretation of matters that brought TCNs within the remit of the SAP. Questions associated with the social, economic and political inclusion of TCNs were questions for member states, not the EC.

Within the SAP, the Council was not prepared to countenance an ambitious interpretation of the EC's role that was likely to trespass on national sensitivities. Council Resolution 311/76, which did set up an action programme for migrant workers and their families, was less broad in its scope and spoke only of encouragement of equal treatment for TCNs, of consultation on immigration policies and co-operation on illegal immigration. Neither 'encouragement' nor 'co-operation' had legal effect. The Resolution concentrated on measures designed to facilitate social policy necessary for the smoother operation of the common market, ensuring the necessary levels of social protection for EC workers moving between member states.

Other SAP measures had the potential to affect TCNs, but, as it turned out, little real impact. For instance, Council Directive EEC 486/77, on the education of the children of migrant workers, watered down a Commission proposal that had included *all* children (including those of TCNs) within the remit of the proposal.[8] For the Council, the term 'migrant workers' applied to nationals of an EC member state moving within the EC, not TCNs. Article 2 of the Directive required member states, in accordance with their national circumstances and legal systems, to ensure that the children of migrant workers who were EC nationals received free tuition to facilitate their initial reception. This included instruction in the language of the host country. Article 3 made provisions for mother tongue teaching, again in accordance with national circumstances and the legal system in member states. A non-binding declaration attached to the Directive did express the political will of the member states to extend the measures to children who were TCNs, but this was another costless declaration. In addition to the limitation on their coverage, the proposals were characterised as being bedevilled by 'confused thinking and practice' and 'contradictions ... between stated aims and objectives' (Reid and Reich, 1992: 229). A 1984 Commission report criticised patchy implementation of the 1977 Directive (CEC, 1984). Handoll (1995: 256) argued that this was hardly surprising given the loose obligations contained in its Articles 2 and 4 and the Commission's preference, stated in a 1994 report on the education of migrants' children, for 'a gradual approach based on a mixture of persuasion, co-operation and pressure to ensure respect of Community law' (CEC, 1994c).

The tension between the Council and Commission could be construed as evidence of the Commission's 'progressiveness' in that it adopted a more sympathetic attitude to expanded rights for TCNs. As noted in chapter 6, member states may be more prone to the kinds of political pressure that induce a reluctance to be seen as pro-immigration/immigrants, whereas the unelected Commission is more shielded from these kinds of pressures. However, the elision of instrumentalism and idealism offers a more convincing explanation. The Commission may be convinced by the logic and moral force of arguments propounding expanded rights for TCNs while, at the same time, also favouring deeper European integration because of the prospect of an expanded role for the Commission.

The Social Charter and Social Chapter

The SEA gave a fresh impetus to EU social policy, because the freedoms given to capital and business were seen as requiring some countervailing social protection measures. The new treaty framework did not alter the basic fact that nationality of a member state was the key that opened the door to EU-level entitlements. A key event was the Council's adoption of the Community Fundamental Charter on the Basic Social Rights of Workers (better known as the Social Charter) on 30 October 1989.[9] It 'acts as a gloss on the limited legal basis of social policy law' (Nielsen and Szyszcak, 1991: 26). The Charter was a non-binding statement of policy principles that outlined twelve fundamental social rights. It essentially reaffirmed the free movement rights of the Treaty of Rome, although its reference to 'workers of the European Community' with respect to free movement and associated social entitlements did raise the question of whether TCNs were included (Handoll, 1995: 248). The Charter's status as a declaration rendered such questions rather academic because it had effect neither as an international agreement nor as a regulation nor as a directive. No attempt was to append the Charter to the EC's primary legislation. The British Conservative government refused to sign the Social Charter, which meant that it became an agreement between eleven member states. On the back of the Social Charter, the second SAP was launched in 1989. The thrust of previous policy was maintained and attention was directed towards the social rights and entitlements of nationals of member states (Streeck, 1995).

The Commission displayed some determination to exploit the social policy opportunities created for it by the Treaty and by the Social Charter and to consolidate the position of the social dimension and the Commission's role as the promoter of social Europe. The Maastricht Treaty added the Social Chapter between eleven participating member states – again, the British Conservative government refused to sign. The agreement covered issues such as improved living and working conditions, proper social protection and the combating of exclusion, which affect all workers and – importantly – not only those who are nationals of a member state. The protocol allowed for QMV in four policy areas, although social security, social protection and conditions of employment for TCNs required unanimity. This placed a brake on the scope for action, but for the first time the employment rights of TCNs had a treaty basis, albeit at the time as an agreement between eleven member states because of the British government's opt-out (since reversed).

Further consultation on the main objectives of social policy continued through the early 1990s. In 1994 a Commission White Paper attempted to plot a way forward for EU social policy (CEC, 1994b). It served as the basis for the third SAP, launched in 1995. Emphasis was placed on balancing fears about lack of European competitiveness in key economic sectors – as discussed in the Commission's 1993 White Paper *Growth, Competitiveness and Employment* – with maintenance of a 'European social model' which was viewed as providing a buttress for prosperity and stability. In a key section, the 1994 social policy White Paper addressed issues associated with the establishment of a European labour market. It recognised that legally resident TCNs 'suffered multiple disadvantages' because they were not covered by the same provisions as EU citizens. As a first step, the Commission stated that they should be entitled to necessary health care benefits (CEC, 1994b: 28). The White Paper also noted that: 'An internal market without frontiers in which the free movement of persons is ensured logically implies the free movement of all legally resident TCNs for the purpose of engaging in economic activity. This objective should be realised progressively' (CEC, 1994b: 29–30).

Even though the Social Chapter had established a treaty basis for TCNs' employment rights, the Commission adopted a cautious approach. A 1995 Commission proposal aimed to ensure that member states gave priority to TCNs legally resident in another member state when job vacancies could not be filled by nationals of that member state or by legally resident TCNs. In October 1997 the Commission proposed a directive which would extend the personal scope of Regulation 1408/71 to all TCNs affiliated to a national social security scheme. By the end of 1998, the proposal was still under consideration.[10] The Commission also pledged to develop an EU-level strategy to combat racism and xenophobia. This included offering financial support for anti-racism projects and funding organisations whose aims and objectives contained a significant anti-racist element (see chapter 6).

Lobbying for migrants' social rights

During the pre-Amsterdam IGC, pro-migrant NGOs sought extension of the treaty framework so that the rights of free movement and the transferability of social entitlements were extended to legally resident TCNs. The EU-level pro-migrant NGO network brought forward a dossier of proposals that, as was seen in chapter 6, dealt with reforming the 'control' dimensions of immigration and asylum policy, but also included measures relating to the social entitlements of TCNs. The CCME saw unequal treatment as a key issue in urgent need of rectification, because of the demotion of TCNs to the status of 'second class citizens'. This analogy was mistaken, because a key point about TCNs is that they are not national citizens and, therefore, not EU citizens. In essence, pro-migrant groups have called for rights of denizenship acquired by TCNs as a result of residence to serve as the basis for access to EU entitlements (Hammar, 1990).

The case for extended rights of EU citizenship to include TCNs would be a difficult one to argue, because it has been made clear that nationality laws are none of the EU's business. This was clearly stated by the member states in a declaration attached to the Maastricht Treaty. The CCME proposed that EU citizenship be extended to TCNs, with a five-year qualification period. As it noted of its proposal: 'One of its key features is that it complements rather than replaces the individual's existing nationality. Therefore Union citizenship could easily embrace TCNs resident in the Union without requiring them to possess nationality of an individual member state' (CCME, 1996: 2). The EUMF echoed the CCME proposals and proposed amendment of Article 8a of the Maastricht Treaty so that it would read: 'Citizenship of the Union is hereby established. Every person holding a nationality of a member state or who has been lawfully residing in the territory of a member state for five years shall be a citizen of the Union' (EUMF, 1996: 3). The European Citizens' Action Service (1996) proposed the extension of the right of EU citizenship to TCNs legally residing in a member state for five years. As EU citizens, legally resident TCNs would enjoy the same free movement rights and the right to equal treatment as other EU citizens.

Amsterdam fell far short of the aspirations of pro-migrant NGOs. It did not extend the citizenship provisions to cover TCNs. The member states displayed little intention to sanction increases in the entitlements accorded to TCNs. The Treaty empowered the Council to set out conditions under which TCNs would have freedom to travel within the territory of the member states during a period of no more than three months. Implementation will require unanimity and the Treaty articles did not cover work, although Maastricht's Social Chapter does apply to conditions of employment. Amsterdam also gave the Council the power to set out the measures defining the rights and conditions of work of TCNs who are legally resident in a member state and reside in another, but this provision was not covered by the five-year timetable.

Proposals for expanded rights

Before the ink had dried on the Amsterdam Treaty, and long before it would be ratified, the Commission proposed in July 1997 a Convention on the Rules for the Admission of Third Country Nationals to the Member States of the European Union (CEC, 1997d). The Convention was introduced using Maastricht's third pillar provisions and stood no chance of adoption as proposed, but the Commission announced its intention to resubmit a proposal for a directive following ratification of the Amsterdam Treaty. The draft Convention marked an attempt by the Commission to stake a claim for a leading role in shaping post-Amsterdam arrangements for free movement, immigration and asylum policy as a way of attempting to ensure future communitarisation of these policy areas. The proposed Convention chimed with many issues raised by NGOs regarding the rights of TCNs and proposed the creation of what could be called a 'Resident's Charter' that would break the connection between nationality, free movement and the transferability of social entitlements within the EU. If such a development were to occur, then the de-territorialisation of social entitlement would fit more easily with a model of membership and entitlement that transcends the national, albeit with the qualification that entitlements would arise from membership of national welfare states, in which the criteria governing entitlement would still be largely determined.

The British-based Immigration Law Practitioners' Association (1997: 1) called the Commission's proposed Convention 'revolutionary stuff indeed'. This was certainly the case when compared with the previous perception of Commission inactivity in these areas. The Convention proposed enforceable rules on employment, self-employment, study and training. It also proposed the creation of a right to enjoy family life. This right would not be extended to the same degree as for EU citizens and member states would still retain an element of discretion over treatment of TCNs that had long since been ceded to the EU for intra-EU migration. Member states would, however, be obliged to justify any use of national discretion on the admission of family members of TCNs. The draft Convention also contained free movement provisions that created a right for long-term resident TCNs to move to any member state to take up employment. It also listed a series of basic rights that they would take with them. These included equal treatment with EU citizens as regards employment, self-employment, training, trade union rights, the right of association, access to housing, whether in the private or public sector, and schooling.

The SLG used the new anti-discrimination Article 13 of the Amsterdam Treaty to propose a directive outlawing racial and religious discrimination. It also sought to exploit opportunities presented by the Amsterdam

Treaty to propose strengthened social rights for TCNs by way of access to rights of free movement and social entitlements (SLG, 1998). The SLG's proposed directive, published in early 1998, derived the force of its argument from the Association Agreements between the EU and third countries. Turkish citizens in EU member states, for instance, were covered by the 1964 Association Agreement between Turkey and the EEC, which gave Turkish nationals established rights in areas such as employment, the right to residence and social entitlements exceeding those given to other TCNs. The SLG argued that the rights given to Turkish nationals should constitute minimum rights to be accorded to all TCNs. The SLG's proposed directive steered clear of a call for the extension of EU citizenship to TCNs because this would push discussion towards nationality laws and render minimal the prospects for successful attainment of expanded rights. Rather, it was proposed that social security rights acquired as a result of denizenship by legally resident migrants and their descendants become transferable within the EU. The proposal was therefore for a Resident's Charter, under which rights are acquired as a result of legal residence rather than acquisition of nationality.

In terms of its nitty-gritty, the SLG's proposal stipulated that after three years' legal employment in one member state, a TCN would enjoy free access to paid employment or self-employment in any member state. The proposed directive then went on to outline provisions for employment and free movement, the right of establishment, the provision of services and family reunion. The directive mirrored the free movement provisions of Regulation 1612/68 by allowing those TCNs who qualified and who were exercising the right of free movement to be issued with a residence permit for five years, with the possibility of automatic renewal. It was also seen as essential that TCNs exercising the right of free movement be granted equal social treatment to other EU citizens. Provisions were, therefore, made for access to employment and self-employment, vocational guidance and training, trade union rights, the right of association, access to public and private sector housing, social welfare, education, health care, and the provision of goods, facilities and services. These provisions would guarantee equal treatment for TCNs.

Migration and social Europe

We now need to ask what this tells us about the relation between migration and welfare at EU level. A delineation of the EU's policy competencies demonstrates that it is important not to exaggerate social policy capacities and discuss EU social policy in terms of movement towards some kind of European welfare state. Similarly, the political/institutional impediments to expanded social entitlements for TCNs in a single market where nationality continues to play a key role should also be emphasised. This does not mean that integration is impossible, because as has been noted there is a strong case for incorporation of TCNs within the free movement/social entitlement provisions. These arguments derive their force from two main sources. First, TCNs can already be included within the welfare state provisions of the member states. This could be construed as imparting an element of illogicality to the nationality requirement for access to EU free movement/social entitlements. Second, if possession of the nationality of a member state does not serve as the qualification for access to social entitlements at national level – legal residence does – then why should nationality continue to be so important at EU level? These arguments underpin the activities of the pro-migrant lobby that campaigns for expanded rights for TCNs.

The impediments to change derive from the *extant* political/institutional configuration and the EU's limited social policy role. This reinforces the point that we should not over-state the capacities of the EU to act and assume we can write onto a blank canvas our particular visions of an inclusive EU. This kind of teleological progressivist perspective on European integration is likely to mislead, because it provokes judgements about the EU's social dimension that utilise inappropriate yardsticks. They ask what the EU should do rather than what it can do and push enquiry in a normative direction that becomes detached from the institutional context and attendant sources of social and political power. The arguments of pro-migrant lobby groups may have strong normative foundations, but tend to be constructed in terms of the EU's practical legal and political realities. The adoption of a practical approach also highlights a potential weakness with strongly normative work on EU social policy because, as Streeck (1996: 64–5) noted:

> given that the Community's 'really existing' social policy seemed so minimal in comparison to what it was supposed to become, it was discussed much more in terms of what it was not, or not yet, rather than what it was – which largely explains the analytical shallowness and the normative declaratory tone of most of the debate. Overcoming this requires that the basic institutional properties of European Union as we now know them be taken into account, which in turn implies breaking once and for all with the teleological federalism that has informed most of the past debate.

Rather than discussing 'social inclusion', it is more helpful to break down the discussion to analyse the scope for incorporation of TCNs within transferable social entitlement provisions of the free movement framework. This draws attention to the legal, political and institutional structures of existing EU social policy and the emergence of a two-tier European social polity. National welfare states and immigration policies with divergent traditions and differing standards and forms of social protection and immigration regulation impart a strong horizontal dimension. A weaker vertical dimension derives from European integration with its free movement, immigration and asylum policy implications. This two-tier polity and associated interdependence gives rise to complex 'nested games' that proceed simultaneously at national and supranational level in a globalised international economy (which places its own pressures on economic development, growth, competitiveness and employment). The horizontal dimension to debates about migration and welfare is likely to remain stronger than the vertical dimension because of the difficulty of securing positive integration that could lead to some form of European welfare state or a common European immigration policy.

The strength of national policy contexts also renders problematic attempts to build a strong vertical dimension linking member states via the EU as a central harmonising authority. In the Scandinavian countries, for instance, levels of social protection are high. In southern Europe a greater reliance is placed on traditional systems of social support, such as the family and Catholic Church. Levelling up for southern European states is unlikely and, anyway, would be tremendously costly. Concomitantly, the prospects for levelling down and erosion of social standards could be politically untenable in those member states with higher social standards, where provision of welfare services has become a salient political issue. Given the need for unanimity among member states for ambitious positive integration to occur, it appears highly unlikely that the EU will acquire welfare responsibilities anywhere near comparable to those in the member states. To use Hoffmann's (1966: 882) analogy, welfare policy is one area where the member states have exhibited a marked reluctance to play Russian roulette with a key aspect of state sovereignty and an important source of domestic political legitimacy.

The recent history of the EU's social dimension illustrates that EU member states have found market-making via the removal of impediments to cross-border trade easier to achieve than positive integration, which requires unanimity among member states. Even so, the distinction between negative and positive integration and between low and high politics should not be over-stated. The day-to-day politics of European social regulation affects member state competencies and discretion. Yet TCNs remain largely excluded from the rights stemming from European integration. The connections between the creation of a single market, free movement and extra-EU migration policy have underpinned arguments for inclusion of TCNs within the EU's social entitlement provisions. Rather than make a claim based on universalised discourses of human rights or notions of social inclusion, pro-migrant lobby groups have based their claim on the legal resources of the EU free movement framework. These arguments have gathered force at European level and acquired the backing of the Commission in its 1997 proposal for a decision on the rights of TCNs (CEC, 1997d). These proposals do, however, need to secure the unanimous agreement of member states, which illustrates the intergovernmental block that can be placed on integration but without meaning that integration is impossible.

The economic impetus underpinning free movement and transferable social entitlements has drawn into the frame of discussion aspects of the political questions of immigration and asylum policy and the rights of TCNs. The future direction of policy integration remains an open question, contingent upon strong national policy contexts and constrained by relatively weak supranational decision-making structures. The arguments for expanded rights for TCNs derive their force from *extant* legal provisions related to free movement. The case that is made is for equal treatment in the single market and thus indirectly for a form of legal and social inclusion. Europeanised notions of social inclusion can make sense only in the context of sectoral institutional dynamics.

Social exclusion and European integration

The motivations, calculations and alliance-building strategies of EU-level institutional actors are central to a discussion of debates about inclusion/ exclusion. There is the potential for instrumentalist/progressive overlap to prompt Commission activity with migrant inclusion implications. Commission 'purposeful opportunism' is linked to the treaty framework and the scope for action that it provides. The movement of the EU into the social dimension has given the Commission a role to play in the areas of social inclusion/exclusion. Inclusion and exclusion have to some extent become problems of Europe to which possible solutions lie at EU level. Combating exclusion and pursuing inclusion are, however, constrained in the first instance by the strong horizontal dimension derived from national welfare policy contexts. The Commission has pushed for extended social policy competencies that have been portrayed as central to the creation of a people's Europe. The rhetoric of social inclusion and cohesion has also become more resonant at EU level and tied in with political objectives in some member states and with priorities identified by the Commission and the EP. It is, however, less clear what the evasive concept of 'social inclusion' means (Hantrais, 1995). Difficulties with the conceptual underpinnings of the social dimension and notions of inclusion reflect differences at both an intellectual level and in practical policy terms. Social theorists differ about the 'meaning' of inclusion and the resultant divergent perspectives are reflected within national policy frameworks in member states that display significant differences regarding the multifaceted nature of the problems of inclusion and appropriate remedies to phenomena associated with exclusion. To meld divergent national responses into some kind of EU inclusion paradigm is likely to be very difficult. This is particularly evident when discussion turns to migrant inclusion, because of the array of policy responses in EU member states refracted through differing national historical traditions of citizenship and nationhood, which have heavily influenced responses to post-war immigration.

Is this absence of conceptual clarity a bad thing? It need not be if we think about the Commission's motivations. Phenomena associated with social exclusion can provide the Commission with opportunities for activity because the quest for inclusion has become one of its tasks, with an NGO dimension and co-option of academic networks through EU-funded 'targeted social and economic research' programmes. The continued existence of social phenomena that can be classed as indicative of exclusion is likely to sustain Commission activity. If those units of the Commission with social policy responsibilities are conceptualised in instrumental terms, then the Commission can benefit from social exclusion in the sense that 'Europeanised exclusion' contributes to arguments for extended supranational competencies. The effect might be that the quest for inclusion can sustain a legal, political and institutional expansive logic of Europeanisation that is a valuable resource for supranational institutions. Moreover, it is advantageous that the terms 'inclusion' and 'cohesion' are vague and their meanings unclear, because this implies that the quest for social inclusion is likely to be able to sustain itself in the long term, with potential to be institutionalised at European level (Geddes, 1998b).

Nevertheless, despite the EU speaking the language of social inclusion, the problem for TCNs is that they remain largely excluded from this dimension of EU activity. EU activity will always be circumscribed by the ascription of competence. If the Commission approached the Council with ambitious migrant inclusion proposals, then the Council could legitimately ask from where the legal basis for such action was derived. If a legal basis does exist, then it is likely to be found within the free movement/social entitlement nexus that has stimulated EU social provisions. Expanded rights at EU level for TCNs depend on the possibility of securing an expanded notion of social entitlement for TCNs that facilitates access to free movement and associated rights without first having to hold the nationality of a member state. This does not require any great leap in logic, as it would involve translation of national practices whereby residence and contribution generate entitlements. Why not extend these principles to EU level? It is hardly likely to prompt a flood of intra-EU migration by legally resident TCNs, although this fear may lurk at the back of the minds of ministers (Muus, 1997). There is no more potent contemporary myth than the immigrant 'welfare scrounger'. Expanded rights for TCNs would also have clear implications for understandings of national citizenship and the possibilities for some form of post-national membership, although the relatively hard frontier between the EU and neighbouring states does not seem particularly amenable to notions of universal personhood. The EU equates with particularist forms of membership that transcend the national in a more limited way, as part of a regional organisation that appears to be setting its face against the migration consequences of globalisation.

Conclusion

This chapter began by asking about the possibility for inclusion of TCNs within the EU's social provisions. It was necessary to delimit the terms of the enquiry to the social entitlements of TCNs residing in member states. The core issue is the portability of social entitlements linked to a right of free movement for legally resident TCNs. By placing the debate about expanded rights for TCNs in its legal, political and institutional context, the extent of the impediments to expansion can be identified. Chief among these is that nationality of a member state remains the main criterion for access to rights associated with European integration. While this remains the case, citizenship of the EU exacerbates the exclusion of TCNs by reaffirming a connection between nationality and rights. The irony of this situation derives from the fact that even though rights of denizenship for legally resident TCNs break the link between nationality and social entitlement in the member states, European integration re-inforces the connection between nationality and entitlements. An EU social dimension stresses inclusion but actually excludes some of the more marginalised members (or non-members) of EU societies from its pro-visions on the grounds that they do not hold the nationality of a member state. EU institutions such as the Commission and EP advocate expanded competence and inclusion of TCNs within the scope of treaty provisions. Exclusion arises from the creation of free movement/social entitlement framework during the 1960s, when it was not clear that the migrant worker 'guests' had come to stay. The free movement/social entitlement provisions that were put in place between 1968 and 1972 emphasised nationality as the basis for entitlement. Unanimity is required for sub-stantive change in this policy framework. The Commission has adopted an expansive stance in its 1997 draft Convention covering the rights of TCNs, but any scope for entrepreneurialism has been impeded by the weak treaty basis for such action.

Pressure for expanded rights for TCNs has developed and is made manifest in the activities of pro-migrant lobby groups, such as the SLG. These groups point to an illogicality in the social entitlement provisions of the EU, which require nationality when this is not required in the member states. Meanwhile, the EU does extend certain social entitlements to TCNs as a consequence of their dependant status or because of agreements with third countries. The argument is for equal treatment and pressure for some form of Resident's Charter that would break the link at EU level between nationality and entitlements. The legal basis for the argument is Association Agreements between the EU and third countries, which give established rights in EU member states to some TCNs. The effect of such legislation would be the supranationalisation of key aspects of immigration policy relating to entry, residence and conditions of employment for TCNs and their families. There would also be the potential for supranational constitutionalisation and institutionalisation resulting from the empowerment of EU actors, particularly the Commission and ECJ. This would recast a discussion of citizenship, membership and identity in an integrating Europe, but is something the member states have been reluctant to do.

The discussion of the migration–welfare link at EU level in this chapter has deliberately not been couched in terms of the potential for the creation of some kind of European welfare state. This would be a blind alley that would distract from analysis of TCN inclusion. The focus of the analysis has been on inclusion of TCNs within the social policy conse-quences of the EU's market-making. From these practical considerations of legal, political and institutional sources of power, authority, capacity to act and constraints, broader conclusions can be drawn. These conclusions also illustrate the value of an institutionalist perspective that analyses how the policy context at EU level shapes debates about inclusion, configures the range of possible policy outcomes, and structures the motivations, calculations and alliance-building strategies of EU-level institutional actors. First, without inclusion of TCNs in the free movement/social entitlement framework, European integration affirms national membership rather than consolidating a post-national model. Proposals for reform seek to extend forms of membership at national level, which do not depend upon nationality, to EU level. Second, the connections between free movement and immigration and asylum policy suggest that the distinction between low and high politics should not be overdrawn. There are clear difficulties with 'positive integration' (requiring unanimity), but immigration and asylum have moved closer to the EU model of decision-making. The path has been strewn with obstacles – not least the requirement for unanimity – but single market integration and free movement have drawn into the realm of discussion the rights and entitlements of legally resident TCNs. The extension of the right of free movement to TCNs would see significant supranational encroachment on key aspects of member state immigration policy relating to entry, residence and conditions of employ-ment. Third, the Amsterdam Treaty was a cautious nudge in the direction of closer free movement, immigration and asylum policy co-operation (and some integration), but it was only a nudge and pressure continues to build from the Commission and from pro-migrant NGOs for equal treatment for legally resident TCNs and their inclusion within the EU's social dimension. It is not possible to prejudge the outcome. But it is clear that the distinction between the low politics of free movement and high politics of immigration and asylum have become blurred, because of the creation of a political/institutional context at EU level for the management of migration policy. This has clear social policy implications for legally resident TCNs that cannot be avoided and are becoming more salient features of the EU's issue agenda.

Notes

1 *Journal Officiel*, 1958, 561 (Regulation 3/58) and 597 (Regulation 4/58).
2 *Official Journal* L257/4, 1968.
3 *Official Journal* L149/2, 1971.
4 *Official Journal* L74/1, 1972.
5 *Official Journal* L257/13, 1968.
6 Joined cases C-297/88 and C-197/89 [1990] ECR 3783.
7 Case C-18/90 [1991] ECR I-199.
8 *Official Journal* L199/32, 1977.
9 *The Community Charter of Fundamental Social Rights of Workers*, Luxembourg, OOPEC, 1990.
10 In its *Action Plan for Free Movement of Workers*, the Commission stated that 'The extension of Regulation 1408/71 to third country nationals is part of the Commission's long-standing policy to improve the legal status of third country nationals residing in the Community. It is no longer justifiable that a worker who is covered by national social security arrangements should be completely excluded from the protection offered by the Community co-ordination system simply because he or she is not an EU national' (CEC, 1997a: 12).

Conclusion

The reshaping of European migration policy and politics by European integration emphasises migration's centrality to European integration. Free movement has been at the core of market-making and drawn immigration and asylum into the realm of European integration and co-operation. Although this link between free movement and migration does not dictate the substantive form that policy co-operation and policy integration will take, the distinction between low and high politics has been blurred as a result of the EU resonance of market-making, liberalisation and securitisation. Certain forms of migration are deemed to threaten the attainment of an integrated Europe because they are seen as demanding tighter external frontier controls, toughened asylum procedures and more internal security measures. It would, of course, be wrong to construe migration as an external issue and direct attention solely to external frontier controls, because migration has also had important effects on the EU and its member states. Not the least of these is that the EU continues to formally exclude from its free movement and anti-discrimination provisions around eleven and a half million TCNs, many of whom are legally resident in a member state. Moreover, the development of EU asylum provisions bears an uneasy relation to international legal standards, while EU citizens of immigrant or ethnic minority origin cannot yet access EU legislation that protects them from racial or ethnic discrimination when exercising EU entitlements.

Without doubt, EU immigration and asylum co-operation has been skewed in the direction of control and security. Consequently, although a connection between economic liberalisation, the single market and immigration and asylum can be detected, there is no requirement for integration to create a common policy with the empowerment of supranational actors. Rather, what is evident is reluctance among some states to see the transfer of competencies to EU level. In such a situation and where intergovernmental agreement is the basis for action, we can detect:

- co-operation on control and security, which reflects well established national policy preferences;
- a hard core of pro-integration states with a tradition of internal security policies moving more rapidly towards common policies;
- limitations on the development of inclusion measures, arising from diverse national immigrant inclusion frameworks and the difficulties of melding a common response.

The transfer of competencies needs to be analysed in a context that accounts for connections between national and European levels, while also recognising connections between the EU and neighbouring states. Moreover, the undernourished conceptualisation of the immigration problem needs to be addressed with regard to the rights, entitlements and 'inclusion' of migrants and their descendants in EU member states.

These are all 'inclusion' issues that have been Europeanised and become components of the EU-level migration issue. Inclusion has, though, been rather neglected as the member states have sought to elaborate a policy of restriction within a narrowly focused immigration and asylum *problematique* at EU level that is strongly focused on control and security. This securitisation is reflective of relatively well established national policy preferences, as well as of difficulties melding diverse immigration and immigrant policy paradigms at EU level. Moreover, the elaboration of a policy of restriction has involved co-option of neighbouring states in central, eastern and southern Europe, often as a feature of pre-accession agreements, with adoption of the immigration and asylum *acquis* a condition for membership.

This raises the question of whether the EU is moving towards consolidation of a 'fortress' constructed on tight external frontier controls and the exclusion of settled migrants. In fact, EU member states are unlikely to possess the capacity, political will or resources to 'control' external frontiers in the strong sense of the term. The power of the 'fortress' actually derives from governments espousing the creation of a fortress while looking anxiously over their shoulders at the lurking menace of the racist extreme right and from an activist discourse which uses the putative fortress as part of an oppositional stance to this aspect of European integration. Restrictive efforts have been directed at those forms of migration deemed to constitute the greatest 'threat', namely 'bogus' asylum-seekers and undocumented migrant workers. There is a sad irony that, despite the supposed threat these potential migrants pose, they are actually often drawn from among the least powerful sections of the world's population. Meanwhile, freer movement for EU citizens, migration of highly skilled workers and other forms of migration such as family reunification and asylum-seeking mean the continued co-existence of restrictive and expansive tendencies in immigration policies. Diverse patterns of immigrant inclusion/exclusion are played out at sub-national, national and transnational level, and through varying patterns of supra-national integration and inter-state co-operation. In such circumstances, the dispersal of power, authority and capacity to act means that EU member states remain a key reference point. Nonetheless, the changing configuration of contemporary European immigration politics demonstrates that state power is something we need to explain, not something that alone causes these developments. 'National models' retain their political, institutional and conceptual potency, but they are being challenged by a proliferation of actors and agents across levels of government, by the diffusion of power and authority through market mechanisms, and by debates about inclusion that have sub-national, national, supranational and transnational resonance. Yet there are also grounds for scepticism about post-national perspectives on rights derived from universalised personhood. Rights for EU citizens do transcend borders, but non-nationals are largely excluded from these rights. Moreover, the EU's emergent polity is bordered by a hard – albeit not impermeable – shell between it and surrounding states and by processes of internal differenti-ation between EU citizens and TCNs.

The institutionalist perspective developed in this book is well placed to capture these developments. By exploring how actors' motivations, calcu-lations, actions and alliance-building strategies are shaped by and shape their institutional environment, insight can be gleaned into the articu-lation between liberalisation and securitisation and the distinct sources of legal, political and social power created by European integration that also structure the meaning of inclusion. Yet despite constitutionalised and institutionalised free movement, the basis for access to EU entitlements arises from prior possession of the nationality of a member state. This causes the continued exclusion of most TCNs. Arguments for inclusion within EU provisions are actually quite specifically formulated and derive potency from the Europeanised migration issues of free movement, transferable social entitlements and anti-discrimination. The EU is not a social and political colossus poised and ready to seek migrant inclusion and, given its major legitimacy difficulties, perhaps we should be glad that it is not. It does not have the competence to intervene extensively and is unlikely to develop such powers because of the difficulties of securing 'positive' integration in areas where unanimous decision-making con-tinues to apply. However, given that many of these TCNs are legally resident citizens of EU member states, a powerful case for some kind of 'Resident's Charter' can be advanced.

In the Introduction, the following question was raised: if a 'people's Europe' is to be built, then who are the people? The member states have developed the legal and political capacity at EU level to offer an expansive answer to this question that includes TCNs. Whether or not they grasp this nettle is a test of what actually lies beneath the rhetoric of inclusion. The key point is that this debate about inclusion derives from élite processes of European economic integration and the institutional context created thereby, rather than from grassroots ethnic mobilisation. The EU is detached from grassroots mobilisations, but this does not mean that it is irrelevant. Rather, the task is to specify relevance and be very clear about the sources of legal, political and social power that go with it.

The supranationalisation of free movement can be contrasted with the intergovernmental framework for immigration and asylum policy co-operation. Even though the Amsterdam Treaty moves immigration and asylum from the JHA pillar to the EU pillar, the member states have chosen to take the comfort blanket of intergovernmental decision-making with them. They face hard choices and tough decisions in the near future when confronted with key free movement, immigration and asylum issues for which they can no longer hide behind 'British' awkwardness, because the British have opted out, preferring to maintain their own fortress efforts. In these newly communitarised areas of immigration and asylum, limitations on the role of the Commission and ECJ inhibit scope for supranational constitutionalisation and institutionalisation. Co-operation outside and within the treaty framework has allowed member states to slip domestic political and judicial constraints and co-operate on repressive state functions that are viewed as a necessary accompaniment to liberalisation. This gives rise to the oft-analysed democratic deficit, although a management deficit is equally problematic and likely to affect implementation of immigration and asylum policies if and when they are developed within the post-Amsterdam framework.

Recent developments can also lead to a gloomy perspective on the potential for rights-based politics and the opening of social and political spaces. If such spaces are to open, then connections need to be made between the legal structures established for free movement and the newly communitarised immigration and asylum issues. A key issue identified throughout the book has been the potential of the EU's institutional context for the management of some aspects of migration policy, thereby opening the possibility for supranationalisation of intra- and extra-EU migration policy. Pro-migrant groups would see integration as countering Council-based lowest common denominator decision-making. For them it would seem that European integration is part of the solution, not part of the problem. The *extant* legal, political and institutional configuration emphasises security and control, but gives some meaning to notions of inclusion in relation to equal rights to participate in EU market-making. But the power to broaden the EU-level conceptualisation of the migration issue continues to reside with the member states acting by unanimity. Once decisions to integrate are made, then member states lose sole control over policy and share power with other actors. European integration and co-operation mean that there are no national solutions to migrant inclusion within the EU's free movement, anti-discrimination and asylum provisions: the response must be European because these are now European issues. If such a response is made, then it will be a measure of the EU's inclusiveness, which is often spoken of, but still in great measure to be realised.

Bibliography

Primary sources

Action Group on Immigration (2000), *Efficient, Effective and Encompassing Approaches to European Immigration and Asylum Policy*, Amsterdam, AGIT.

Amnesty International (1996), *Amnesty International's Memorandum. Proposals for a Strengthened Protection of Human Rights by the EU in the Context of the Intergovernmental Conference*, Brussels, Amnesty International.

CCME (Churches Commission for Migrants in Europe) (1996), *The Starting Point*, Brussels, CCME.

CEC (Commission of the European Communities) (1977), *Freedom of Movement for Workers Within the Community*, Brussels, Office for the Official Publications of the European Community (OOPEC).

CEC (1984), *Commission Report on the Implementation of Directive 77/486*, COM (84) 54 final.

CEC (1985a), *White Paper on the Completion of the Internal Market*, COM (85) 310 final.

CEC (1985b), *Guidelines for a Community Policy on Migration*, COM (85) 48 final.

CEC (1988a), *Communication on a People's Europe*, COM (88) 331 final.

CEC (1988b), *Communication on the Abolition of Controls of Persons at Intra-Community Borders*, COM (88) 310 final.

CEC (1990), *Policies on Immigration and the Social Integration of Migrants in the EC, Expert's Report Drawn Up on Behalf of the Commission of the European Communities*, SEC (90) 1813.

CEC (1991), *Communication on Immigration*, COM (94) 596 final.

CEC (1993), *Proposal for a Decision Based on Article K3 of the Treaty on European Union Establishing a Convention on the Crossing of the External Frontiers of the Member States*, COM (3) 684 final.

CEC (1994a), *Communication on Immigration and Asylum Policies*, COM (94) 23 final.

CEC (1994b), *European Social Policy: A Way Forward for the Union*, COM (94) 333 final.

CEC (1994c), *Report on the Education of Migrant Workers' Children in the European Union*, COM (94) 80 final.

CEC (1995a), *Commission Report for the Reflection Group*, Luxembourg, OOPEC.

CEC (1995b), *Communication from the Commission on Racism, Xenophobia and Anti-Semitism and Proposal for a Council Decision Designating 1997 as European Year Against Racism*, COM (95) 653 final.

CEC (1995c), *Assistance Given to Migrant Organisations*, Brussels, Directorate General for Employment, Industrial Relations and Social Affairs.

CEC (1996), *Report to the IGC. Commission Opinion*, Luxembourg, OOPEC.

CEC (1997a), *An Action Plan for Free Movement of Workers. Communication from the Commission*, COM (97) 586 final.

CEC (1997b), *Proposal for a Joint Decision on a Joint Action Adopted by the Council Introducing a Programme of Training, Exchanges and Co-operation in the Field of Asylum, Immigration and Crossing of External Borders*, COM (97) 364 final.

CEC (1997c), *Proposal to the Council for a Joint Action Based on Article K.3(2)(b) of the Treaty on European Union Concerning Temporary Protection for Displaced Persons*, COM (97) 93 final.

CEC (1997d), *Proposal for a Decision on Establishing a Convention on Rules for the Admission of Third Country Nationals to the Member States of the European Union*, COM (97) 387 final.

CEC (1998), *Communication from the Commission. An Action Plan Against Racism*, COM (98) 183 final.

ECRE (European Council on Refugees and Exiles) (1997a), *Comments from ECRE on the Proposal of the European Commission Concerning Temporary Protection of Displaced Persons*, Brussels, ECRE.

ECRE (1997b), *Position of ECRE on Temporary Protection in the Context of the Need for a Supplementary Refugee Definition*, Brussels, ECRE.

ECRE (1997c), *Position on the Functioning of the Treaty on European Union in Relation to Asylum Policy*, Brussels, ECRE.

ECRE (1997d), *Analysis of the Treaty of Amsterdam in so far as it Relates to Asylum Policy*, Brussels, ECRE.

EP (European Parliament) (1985), *Report of the Commission of Inquiry into the Rise of Fascism and Racism in Europe*, Brussels, OOPEC.

EP (1991), *Report of the Committee of Inquiry on Racism and Xenophobia*, Brussels, OOPEC.

EP (1998), *EU Anti-Discrimination Policy: From Equal Opportunities Between Men and Women to Combating Racism*, Brussels, European Parliament Directorate General for Research Working Document, Public Liberties Series LIBE 102.

EUMF (European Union Migrants' Forum) (1996), *Proposals for the Revision of the Treaty on European Union at the Intergovernmental Conference 1996*, Brussels, EUMF.

European Citizens' Action Service (1996), *European Citizenship: Giving Substance to Citizen's Europe in a Revised Treaty*, Brussels, ECAS.

European Council Consultative Commission on Racism and Xenophobia (1995), *Final Report*, Ref. 6906/1/95 Rev. 1, Limite RAXEN, Brussels, General Secretariat of the Council of the European Union.

Eurostat (1997), *Migration Statistics*, Luxembourg, Eurostat.

Foreign and Commonwealth Office (1996), *A Partnership Among Nations*, London, FCO.

Joint Council for the Welfare of Immigrants/European Research Centre on Migration and Ethnic Relations (1996), *European Directory of Migrant and Ethnic Minority Organisations*, London/Utrecht, JCWI/ERCOMER.

Reflection Group (1995), *Report of the Reflection Group*, Brussels, Secretariat General of the Council.

SLG (Starting Line Group) (1998), *Proposals for Legislative Measures to Combat Racism and the Promotion of Equal Rights*, Brussels, SLG.

SOPEMI (1995), *Trends in International Migration. Annual Report 1994*, Paris, OECD.

UNHCR (United Nations High Commissioner for Refugees) (1992), *Handbook on Procedures and Criteria for Determining Refugee Status*, Geneva, UNHCR.

Secondary sources

Aghrout, A. and A. Geddes (1996), 'The EU and the Maghreb: from development co-operation to partnership?', *International Politics*, 33:3, 227–43.

Alexander, W. (1992), 'Free movement of non-EC nationals: a review of the case law of the Court of Justice', *European Journal of International Law*, 3:1, 53–64.

Amiraux, V. (1997), 'Turkish Islamic associations in Germany and the issue of European citizenship', in C. Peach and S. Vertovec (eds), *Islam in Europe: The Politics of Religion and Community*, London, Macmillan, pp. 245–59.

Amiraux, V. (1998), 'Turkish Muslims in Germany: transnationalising social space', paper presented to the conference 'Integrating Immigrants in Liberal States', European University Institute, Florence, Italy, 8–9 May.

Anderson, M. and M. Den Boer (eds) (1994), *Policing Across National Boundaries*, London, Pinter.

Anderson, M., *et al.* (1996), *Policing the European Union*, Oxford, Clarendon Press.

Baganha, M. (ed.) (1997), *Immigration in Southern Europe*, Oeiras, Celta Editora.

Baldwin-Edwards, M. (1991), 'The socio-political rights of migrants in the European Community', in G. Room (ed.), *Towards a European Welfare State?*, Bristol, School for Advanced Urban Studies, pp. 189–234.

Baldwin-Edwards, M. (1997), 'The emerging European immigration regime: some reflections on implications for Southern Europe', *Journal of Common Market Studies*, 35:4, 497–520.

Baldwin-Edwards, M. and M. Schain (eds) (1994), *The Politics of Immigration in Western Europe*, London, Frank Cass.

Bank, R. (1998), 'The emergent EU policy on asylum and refugees', paper presented to the European Forum on International Migrations, European University Institute, Florence, 22 January.

Banting, K. (1995), 'The welfare state as statecraft: territorial politics and social policy', in S. Liebfried and P. Pierson (eds), *European Social Policy: Between Integration and Fragmentation*, Washington, DC, Brookings Institution, pp. 269–300.

Bibliography

Barry, B. and R. Goodin (eds) (1992), *Free Movement: Ethical Issues in the Movement of People and Money*, London, Harvester Wheatsheaf.

Bauböck, R. (1994), *Transnational Citizenship. Membership and Rights in International Migration*, Aldershot, Edward Elgar.

Bieber, R. (1994), 'Links between the third pillar (Title VI) and the European Community (Title II) of the Treaty on European Union', in J. Monar and R. Morgan (eds), *The Third Pillar of the European Union*, Brussels, European Interuniversity Press, pp. 37–47.

Bigo, D. (1996), *Polices en réseaux, l'expérience Européene*, Paris, Presses de la Fondation Nationales des Sciences Politiques.

Bigo, D. (1998), 'Immigration at the securitarian crossroads', paper presented to the conference 'Dilemmas of Immigration Control in a Globalizing World', European University Institute, Florence, 11–12 June.

Bigo, D. and R. Leveau (1992), *L'Europe de la sécurité intérieure*, Paris, Institut des Hautes Etudes de Sécurité Intérieure.

Bommes, M. (1998), 'Migration, national welfare state and biography: a theoretical case study', paper presented to the conference 'Migration and the Welfare State in Contemporary Europe', European University Institute, Florence, 21–23 May.

Bommes, M. and A. Geddes (eds) (2000), *Welfare and Immigration: Challenging the Borders of the Welfare State*, London, Routledge.

Bommes, M. and J. Halfmann (1995), 'Migration and ethnicity in the national welfare state', in M. Martiniello (ed.), *Migration, Citizenship and National Identities in the European Union*, Aldershot, Avebury.

Bovenkerk, F., R. Miles and G. Verbunt (1991), 'Comparative studies of migration and exclusion on the grounds of "race" and ethnic background: a critical appraisal', *International Migration Review*, 25:2, 375–91.

Brubaker, R. (1992), *Citizenship and Nationhood in France and Germany*, Cambridge, MA, Harvard University Press.

Brym, R. (1991), 'The emigration potential of Russia and Lithuania: recent survey results', *Innovation*, 3:4, 29–32.

Bulmer, S. (1994), 'The governance of the EU: a new institutionalist approach', *Journal of Public Policy*, 13:4, 351–80.

Burley, A-M. and W. Mattli (1993), 'Europe before the court: a political theory of legal integration', *International Organization*, 47:1, 41–76.

Calavita, K. (1994), 'Italy and the new immigration', in W. Cornelius, P. Martin and J. Hollifield (eds), *Controlling Immigration: A Global Perspective*, Stanford, CA, Stanford University Press, pp. 303–26.

Callovi, G. (1992), 'Regulation of immigration in 1993: pieces of the European Community jig-saw puzzle', *International Migration Review*, 26:2.

Cammack, P. (1992), 'The new institutionalism: predatory rule, institutional persistence, and macro social change', *Economy and Society*, 21:4, 397–429.

Caporaso, J. (1996), 'The European Union and forms of state: Westphalian, regulatory or post-modern?', *Journal of Common Market Studies*, 34:1, 29–52.

Castells, M. (1975), 'Immigrant workers and class struggles in advanced capitalism: the Western European experience', *Politics and Society*, 5:1, 33–66.

Castles, S., H. Booth and T. Wallace (1984), *Here for Good: Western Europe's New Ethnic Minorities*, London, Pluto Press.

Castles, S. and G. Kosack (1973), *Immigrant Workers and Class Structure in Western Europe*, Oxford, Oxford University Press.

Castles, S. and M. Miller (1998), *The Age of Migration*, second edition, London, Macmillan.

Cecchini, P. (1988), *The European Challenge 1992: The Benefits of a Single Market*, Aldershot, Wildwood House.

Cerny, P. (1990), *The Changing Architecture of Politics: Structure, Agency and the Future of the State*, London, Sage.

Closa, C. (1995), 'Citizenship of the Union and nationality of the member states', *Common Market Law Review*, 32:2, 487–518.

Codagnone, C. (1998), 'The new migration in Russia in the 1990s', in K. Koser and H. Lutz (eds), *The New Migration in Europe: Social Constructions and Social Realities*, London, Macmillan, pp. 38–59.

Collinson, S. (1993), *Europe and International Migration*, London, Pinter.

Coombes, D. (1970), *Politics and Bureaucracy in the European Community: A Portrait of the European Commission*, London, George Allen and Unwin.

Cornelius, W. (1994), 'Spain: the uneasy transition from labor exporter to labor importer', in W. Cornelius, P. Martin and J. Hollifield (eds), *Controlling Immigration: A Global Perspective*, Stanford, CA, Stanford University Press, pp. 331–69.

Cornelius, W., P. Martin and J. Hollifield (1994), 'Introduction: the ambivalent quest for immigration control', in W. Cornelius, P. Martin and J. Hollifield (eds), *Controlling Immigration: A Global Perspective*, Stanford, CA, Stanford University Press, pp. 3–41.

Cowles, M. (1995), 'Setting the agenda for a new Europe: the ERT and EC 1992', *Journal of Common Market Studies*, 33:4, 501–26.

Cox, R. (1986), 'Social forces, states and world orders: beyond international relations theory', in R. Keohane (ed.), *Neo-Realism and its Critics*, New York, Columbia University Press, pp. 204–54.

Cox, R. (1987), *Production, Power and World Order: Social Forces in the Making of History*, New York, Columbia University Press.

Cram, L. (1994), 'The European Commission as a multi-organization: social policy and IT policy in the EU', *Journal of European Public Policy*, 1:2, 195–217.

Crossick, S., M. Kohnstamm and J. Pinder (1997), 'The Treaty of Amsterdam', in *Challenge Europe: Making Sense of the Amsterdam Treaty*, Brussels, European Policy Centre, pp. 1–4.

Danese, G. (1998), 'Transnational collective action in Europe: the case of migrants in Italy and Spain', *Journal of Ethnic and Migration Studies*, 24:4, 715–34.

Delors, J., *et al.* (Committee for the Study of Economic and Monetary Union) (1989), *Report on Economic and Monetary Union in the EC*, Luxembourg, OOPEC.

den Boer, M. (1996), 'Justice and home affairs: co-operation without integration', in H. Wallace and W. Wallace (eds), *Policy-Making in the European Union*, Oxford, Oxford University Press, pp. 389–409.

Duff, A. (1994), 'The main reforms', in A. Duff, J. Pinder and R. Pryce (eds), *Maastricht and Beyond: Building the European Union*, London, Routledge, pp. 19–35.

Dunsire, A. (1978), *Implementation in a Bureaucracy*, Oxford, Martin Robertson.

Edwards, G. and D. Spence (1994), *The European Commission*, London, Longman.

Ehlermann, H-D. (1998), *Differentiation, Flexibility, Closer Co-operation: The New Provisions of the Amsterdam Treaty*, Working Papers of the Robert Schuman Centre, Florence, European University Institute.

Eichenhofer, E. (ed.) (1997), *Social Security of Migrants in the European Union of Tomorrow*, Osnabrück, Universitätsverslag.

Entzinger, H. (1985), 'The Netherlands', in T. Hammar (ed.), *European Immigration Policy: A Comparative Study*, Cambridge, Cambridge University Press.

Evans, P., D. Rueschemeyer and T. Skocpol (eds) (1985), *Bringing the State Back In*, Cambridge, Cambridge University Press.

Fakiolas, R. (1997), 'Current migration trends in Greece', in M. Baganha (ed.), *Immigration in Southern Europe*, Oeiras, Celta Editora.

Favell, A. (1998), *The European Citizenship Agenda: Emergence, Transformation and Effects of a New Political Field*, paper presented at the 11th Conference of Europeanists, Baltimore, MA, 26 February–1 March.

Favell, A. and A. Geddes (2000), 'Immigration and European integration: new opportunities for transnational mobilisation', in P. Statham and R. Koopmans (eds), *Challenging and Defending the Fortress: Political Mobilisation over Ethnic Difference in Comparative and Transnational Perspective*, Oxford, Oxford University Press, forthcoming.

Fligstein, N. and I. Mara-Drita (1996), 'How to make a market: reflections on the European Union's single market programme', *American Journal of Sociology*, 102:1, 1–33.

Flora, P. (1986), 'Introduction', in P. Flora (ed.), *Growth to Limits: The Western European Welfare States Since World War Two. Volume I, Sweden, Norway, Finland and Denmark*, Berlin, De Gruyter, pp. vii–xxxvi.

Fortescue, A. (1995), 'Opening statement', in S. Perrakis (ed.), *Immigration and European Union: Building on a Comprehensive Approach*, Athens, Sakkoulas, pp. 7–9.

Foucault, M. (1979), *Discipline and Punish: The Birth of the Prison*, New York, Vintage Books.

Freeman, G. (1986), 'Migration and the political economy of the welfare state', *Annals of the American Academy of Social and Political Sciences*, 485:1, 51–63.

Freeman, G. (1995), 'Modes of immigration politics in liberal democratic states', *International Migration Review*, 29:4, 881–902.

Garrett, G. and G. Tsebelis (1996), 'An institutional critique of intergovernmentalism', *International Organization*, 50:2, 269–99.

Geddes, A. (1995), 'Immigrant and ethnic minorities and the EU's "democratic deficit"', *Journal of Common Market Studies*, 33:2, 197–217.

Geddes, A. (1998a), 'Race related political participation and representation in the UK', *Revue Européene des Migrations Internationales*, 14:2, 33–48.

Geddes, A. (1998b), 'The representation of "migrants' interests" in the European Union', *Journal of Ethnic and Migration Studies*, 24:4, 695–714.

Geddes, A. (1998c), 'Migration and welfare: the institutionalisation of a

European Union policy context', paper presented to the conference 'Migration and the Welfare State in Contemporary Europe', European University Institute, Florence, 21–23 May.

Geddes, A. and A. Favell (eds) (1999), *The Politics of Belonging: Migrants and Minorities in Contemporary Europe*, Aldershot, Ashgate.

George, V. and P. Taylor-Gooby (eds) (1996), *European Welfare Policy: Squaring the Welfare Circle*, Basingstoke, Macmillan.

Giddens, A. (1979), *Central Problems of Social Theory: Action, Structure and Contradiction in Social Analysis*, London, Macmillan.

Gill, S. (1992), 'The emerging world order and European change: the political economy of European union', in R. Miliband and L. Panitch (eds), *Socialist Register 1992*, London, Merlin Press, pp. 157–95.

Gilpin, R. (1987), *The Political Economy of International Relations*, Princeton, NJ, Princeton University Press.

Golini, A., C. Bonifazi and A. Righi (1993), 'A general framework for the European migration system in the 1990s', in R. King (ed.), *The New Geography of European Migrations*, London, Belhaven Press, pp. 67–82

Goodwin-Gill, G. (1996), *The Refugee in International Law*, second edition, Oxford, Oxford University Press.

Grant, C. (1995), *Delors: Inside the House that Jacques Built*, London, Brealey.

Grendstad, G. and P. Selle (1995), 'Cultural theory and the new institutionalism', *Journal of Theoretical Politics*, 7:1, 5–27.

Guild, E. (1992), *Protecting Migrants' Rights: Application of EC Agreements with Third Countries*, Briefing Paper No. 10, Brussels, Churches Commission for Migrants in Europe.

Guild, E. (1998), 'Competence, discretion and third country nationals: the European Union's legal struggle with migration', *Journal of Ethnic and Migration Studies*, 24:4, 613–26.

Guild, E. and J. Niessen (1996), *The Developing Immigration and Asylum Policies of the European Union: Adopted Conventions, Resolutions, Recommendations and Conclusions*, Den Haag, Kluwer Law International.

Guiraudon, V. (1997), *Policy Change Behind Gilded Doors: Explaining the Evolution of Aliens' Rights in France, Germany and the Netherlands, 1974–94*, Harvard University, PhD thesis.

Guiraudon, V. (1998), *International Human Rights Norms and Their Incorporation: The Protection of Aliens in Europe*, Working Paper No. 98/4, Florence, European University Institute.

Guiraudon, V. (1999), 'The proliferation of transnational state and non-state actors in migration control: causes and consequences', paper presented to the International Studies Association, Washington, DC, 16–20 February.

Guiraudon, V. (2000), 'The Marshallian triptych reordered: the role of courts and bureaucracies in furthering migrant social rights', in M. Bommes and A. Geddes (eds), *Welfare and Migration: Challenging the Borders of the Welfare State*, London, Routledge, forthcoming.

Gunn, L. (1984), 'Why is implementation so difficult?' *Management Services in Government*, 33, 169–76.

Haas, E. (1960), 'International integration: the European and the universal process', *International Organization*, 15:4, 366–92.

Haas, E. (1964), *Beyond the Nation State: Functionalism and International Organization*, Stanford, CA, Stanford University Press.

Habermas, J. (1992), 'Citizenship and national identity: some reflections on the future of Europe', *Praxis International*, 12:1, 1–19.

Hall, P. and R. Taylor (1996), 'Political science and the three new institutionalisms', *Political Studies*, 44:4, 936–57.

Hammar, T. (ed.) (1985), *European Immigration Policy: A Comparative Study*, Cambridge, Cambridge University Press.

Hammar, T. (1990), *Democracy and the Nation State: Aliens, Denizens and Citizens in a World of International Migration*, Aldershot, Avebury.

Hammar, T., G. Brochmann, K. Tamas and T. Faist (eds) (1997), *International Migration, Immobility and Development. Multidisciplinary Perspectives*, Oxford, Berg.

Handoll, A. (1995), *Free Movement of Persons in the EU*, Chichester, Wiley.

Hantrais, L. (1995), *Social Policy in the European Union*, Basingstoke, Macmillan.

Hargreaves, A. (1995), *Immigration, 'Race' and Ethnicity in Contemporary France*, London, Routledge.

Hartley, T. (1978), 'The internal scope of the EEC immigration provisions', *European Law Review*, 3:2, 191–207.

Heitman, S. (1991), 'Soviet emigration in 1990: a new fourth wave?', *Innovation*, 3:4, 1–15.

Hix, S. (1994), 'The study of the EC: the challenge to comparative politics', *West European Politics*, 17:1, 1–30.

Hix, S. (1998), 'The study of the European Union II: the "new governance agenda" and its rival', *Journal of European Public Policy*, 5:1, 38–65.

Hix, S. and J. Niessen (1996), *Reconsidering European Migration Policies: The 1996 Intergovernmental Conference and the Reform of the Maastricht Treaty*, Brussels, Churches Committee for Migrants in Europe.

Hockenos, P. (1993), *Free to Hate: The Rise of the Right in Post-Communist Eastern Europe*, London, Routledge.

Hoffmann, S. (1966), 'Obstinate or obsolete? The fate of the nation state and the case of Western Europe', *Daedalus*, 95, 892–908.

Hoffmann, S. (1982), 'Reflections on the nation state in Western Europe today', *Journal of Common Market Studies*, 21:1, 21–38.

Hoffmann-Nowotny, H-J. (1985), 'Switzerland', in T. Hammar (ed.), *European Immigration Policy: A Comparative Study*, Cambridge, Cambridge University Press.

Holland, M. (1993), *European Community Integration*, London, Pinter.

Hollifield, J. (1992), *Immigrants, Markets and States: The Political Economy of Post-War Europe*, Cambridge, MA, Cambridge University Press.

Holmes, C. (1988), *John Bull's Island: Immigration and British Society 1871–1971*, London, Macmillan.

Howe, P. (1995), 'A community of Europeans: the requisite underpinnings', *Journal of Common Market Studies*, 33:1, 27–46.

Hune, S. (1994), 'The UN Convention on the Protection of Migrant Workers and Their Families', in J. Cator and J. Niessen (eds), *The Use of International Conventions to Protect the Rights of Migrants and Ethnic Minorities*, Strasbourg, Churches Commission for Migrants in Europe/Commission of the European Communities.

Hunger, U. (2000), 'Temporary transnational labour migration in an integrating Europe: the challenge to the German welfare state', in M. Bommes and A. Geddes (eds), *Welfare and Migration: Challenging the Borders of the Welfare State*, London, Routledge, forthcoming.

Huysmans, J. (1995), 'Migrants as a security problem: dangers of "securitizing" social issues', in R. Miles and D. Thränhardt (eds), *Migration and European Integration: The Dynamics of Inclusion and Exclusion*, London, Pinter, pp. 53–72.

Immigration Law Practitioners' Association (1997), *European Update*, London, ILPA.

Ireland, P. (1994), *The Policy Challenge of Ethnic Diversity: Immigrant Politics in France and Switzerland*, Cambridge, MA, Harvard University Press.

Ireland, P. (1995), 'Migration, free movement and immigrant integration in the EU: a bifurcated policy response', in S. Liebfried and P. Pierson (eds), *European Social Policy: Between Integration and Fragmentation*, Washington, DC, Brookings Institution, pp. 231–66.

Jacobsen, D. (1996), *Rights Across Borders: Immigration and the Decline of Citizenship*, Baltimore, MA, Johns Hopkins University Press.

Jahtenfuchs, M. (1995), 'Theoretical perspectives on European governance', *European Law Journal*, 1:2, 115–33.

Joppke, C. (1996), 'Multiculturalism and immigration: a comparison of the United States, Germany and Great Britain', *Theory and Society*, 25:4, 449–500.

Joppke, C. (1997), 'Asylum and state sovereignty: a comparison of the United States, Germany and Britain', *Comparative Political Studies*, 30:3, 259–98.

Joppke, C. (ed.) (1998), *Challenge to the Nation State: Immigration in Western Europe and the United States*, Oxford, Oxford University Press.

Kaiser, K. (1971), 'Transnational relations as a threat to the democratic process', in R. Keohane and J. Nye (eds), *Power and Interdependence*, Boston, MA, Little, Brown, pp. 356–70.

Kastoryano, R. (1994), 'Mobilisation des migrants en Europe: du national et transnational', *Revue Européene des Migrations Internationales*, 10:1, 127–44.

Katznelson, I. (1973), *Black Men, White Cities: Race Relations and Migration in the United States 1900–1930 and Britain 1948–1968*, London, Oxford University Press for the Institute of Race Relations.

Kaye, R. (1998), 'Redefining the refugee: the UK media portrayal of asylum-seekers', in K. Koser and H. Lutz (eds), *The New Migration in Europe: Social Constructions and Social Realities*, London, Macmillan, pp. 163–82.

Keohane, R. (1989), 'International institutions: two approaches', in R. Keohane (ed.), *International Institutions and State Power: Essays in International Relations Theory*, Boulder, CO, Westview, pp. 158–79.

Kindleberger, C. (1967), *Europe's Post-war Growth: The Role of Labour Supply* Cambridge, MA, Harvard University Press.

King, R. (1993), 'Why do people migrate?', in R. King (ed.), *The New Geography of European Migrations*, London, Belhaven Press, pp. 17–46.

King, R., J. Connell and P. White (1995), *Writing Across Worlds: Literature and Migration*, London, Routledge.

Kitschelt, H. (1995), *The Radical Right in Western Europe: A Comparative Analysis*, Ann Arbor, MI, University of Michigan Press.

Kooiman, J. (ed.) (1993), *Modern Governance: New Government–Society Interactions*, London, Sage.

Koopmans, R. and P. Statham (2000), *Challenging and Defending the Fortress: Political Mobilisation over Ethnic Difference in Comparative and Transnational Perspective*, Oxford, Oxford University Press.

Koopmans, T. (1992), 'Federalism: the wrong debate. Guest editorial', *Common Market Law Review*, 29:6, 1047–52.

Koslowski, R. (1998), 'EU migration regimes: established and emergent', in C. Joppke (ed.), *Challenge to the Nation State: Immigration in Western Europe and the United States*, Oxford, Oxford University Press.

Kostakopoulou, T. (1997), 'Why a "community of Europeans" could be a community of exclusion', *Journal of Common Market Studies*, 35:2, 301–8.

Kostakopoulou, T. (1998), 'European Union citizenship as a model of citizenship beyond the nation state: limits and possibilities', in A. Weale and M. Nentwich (eds), *Political Theory and the European Union: Legitimacy, Constitutional Choice and Citizenship*, London, Routledge, pp. 158–71.

Krasner, S. (1988), 'Sovereignty: an institutional perspective', *Comparative Political Studies*, 21:1, 66–94.

Laffan, B. (1997), 'From policy entrepreneur to policy manager: the challenge facing the European Commission', *Journal of European Public Policy*, 4:3, 422–38.

Lahav, G. (1998), 'Immigration and the state: the devolution and privatisation of immigration control in the EU', *Journal of Ethnic and Migration Studies*, 24:4, 675–94.

Lavenex, S. (1998a), 'Ironic integration: the Europeanization of asylum policies in France and Germany', paper presented to the European Forum on International Migrations, European University Institute, Florence, Italy, paper MIG/9.

Lavenex, S. (1998b), 'Transgressing borders: the emergent European refugee regime and "safe third countries"', in A. Cafruny and P. Peters (eds), *The Union and the World*, Den Haag, Kluwer, pp. 113–32.

Layton-Henry, Z. (ed.) (1990), *The Political Rights of Migrant Workers in Western Europe*, London, Sage.

Layton-Henry, Z. (1992), *The Politics of Immigration*, Blackwell, Oxford.

Lindberg, L. and S. Scheingold (1970), *Europe's Would-Be Polity: Patterns of Change in the European Community*, Englewood Cliffs, NJ, Prentice Hall.

Livi-Bacci, M. (1993), 'South–north migration: a comparative approach to North American and European experiences', in *The Changing Course of International Migration*, Paris, OECD, pp. 37–46.

Lodge, J. (1989), 'Social Europe: fostering a people's Europe?', in J. Lodge (ed.), *The European Community and the Challenge of the Future*, London, Pinter.

Lowi, T. (1972), 'Four systems of politics, policy and choice', *Public Administration Review*, 32:4, 298–310.

Lumsdaine, D. (1993), *Moral Vision in International Politics: The Foreign Aid Regime, 1949–89*, Princeton, NJ, Princeton University Press.

Majone, G. (1996), *Regulating Europe*, London, Routledge.

March, J. and J. Olsen (1989), *Rediscovering Institutions: The Organizational Basis of Politics*, New York, Free Press.

Marks, G., L. Hooghe and K. Blank (1996), 'European integration since the 1980s: state-centric v. multi-level governance', *Journal of Common Market Studies*, 34:3, 341–78.

Marks, G. and D. McAdam (1996), 'Social movements and the changing structure of political opportunity in the European Union', in G. Marks, F. Scharpf, P. Schmitter and W. Streeck (eds), *Governance in the European Union*, London, Sage, pp. 95–120.

Marshall, T. H. (1964), 'Citizenship and social class', in *Class, Citizenship and Social Development: Essays by T. H. Marshall*, New York, Anchor Books.

Martin, D. and E. Guild (1996), *Free Movement of Persons in the EU*, London, Butterworth.

Martin, P. (1993), 'The migration issue', in R. King (ed.), *The New Geography of European Migrations*, London, Belhaven Press, pp. 1–16.

Martiniello, M. (1994), 'Citizenship of the European Union: a critical view', in R. Baübock (ed.), *From Aliens to Citizens: Redefining the Status of Immigrants in Europe*, Vienna/Aldershot, European Centre/Avebury, pp. 29–47.

Mazey, S. and J. Richardson (eds) (1993), *Lobbying in the European Community*, Oxford, Oxford University Press.

McAdam, D. (1982), *The Political Process and the Development of Black Insurgency*, Chicago, IL, University of Chicago Press.

Meehan, E. (1993), *Citizenship and the European Community*, London, Sage.

Messina, A. (1992), 'The two tiers of ethnic conflict in Western Europe', *Fletcher Forum of World Affairs*, 16:2, 51–64.

Miles, R. and A. Phizacklea (1979), *Racism and Political Action in Britain*, London, Routledge and Kegan Paul.

Milward, A. (1992), *The European Rescue of the Nation State*, London, Routledge.

Mitrany, D. (1943), *A Working Peace System*, Chicago, IL, Quadrangle.

Monar, J. (1994), 'The evolving role of the Union institutions in the framework of the third pillar', in J. Monar and R. Morgan (eds), *The Third Pillar of the European Union*, Brussels, European Interuniversity Press, pp. 69–83.

Monar, J. (1998), 'Justice and home affairs', *Journal of Common Market Studies*, 36: annual review, 131–42.

Monar, J. and R. Morgan (eds) (1994), *The Third Pillar of the European Union*, Brussels, European Interuniversity Press.

Moravcsik, A. (1991), 'Negotiating the Single European Act', in R. Keohane and S. Hoffmann (eds), *The New European Community: Decision-Making and Institutional Change*, Boulder, CO, Westview, pp. 41–84.

Moravcsik, A. (1993), 'Preferences and power in the European Community: a liberal intergovernmentalist approach', *Journal of Common Market Studies*, 31:4, 473–524.

Moravcsik, A. (1998), *The Choice for Europe: Social Purpose and State Power from Messina to Maastricht*, Ithaca, NY, Cornell University Press.

Moravcsik, A. and K. Nicolaïdis (1998), 'Federal ideals and constitutional realities in the Treaty of Amsterdam', *Journal of Common Market Studies*, 36: annual review, 13–38.

Morawska, E. (1998), *Structuring Migration in Historical Perspective: The Case of Travelling East Europeans*, Working Paper No. 98/3, Florence, European University Institute.

Morgenthau, K. (1967), *Politics Among Nations: The Struggle for Power and Peace*, New York, Knopf.

Müller-Graff, P-C. (1994), 'The legal basis of the third pillar and its position in the framework of the Union Treaty', in J. Monar and R. Morgan (eds), *The Third Pillar of the European Union*, Brussels, European Interuniversity Press, pp. 21–36.

Muus, P. (1997), 'A study on the expected effects of free movement for legally residing workers from third countries within the European Community', in P. Muus and C. Curtin (eds), *Free Movement for Non-EC Workers Within the European Community*, Utrecht, Centrum Buitenlanders, pp. 6–28.

Nielsen, R. and E. Szyszcak (1991), *The Social Dimension of the European Community*, Copenhagen, Handelshøjskolens Forlag.

Niessen, J. (1994), 'The role of non-governmental organisations in standard setting and promoting ratification', in J. Cator and J. Niessen (eds), *The Use of International Conventions to Protect the Rights of Migrants and Ethnic Minorities*, Brussels, Churches Commission for Migrants in Europe.

Noiriel, G. (1988), *Le creuset Français: Histoire de l'immigration XIXe–XXe siècles*, Paris, Seuil.

North, D. (1990), *Institutions, Institutional Change and Economic Performance*, Cambridge, Cambridge University Press.

O'Keeffe, D. (1992), 'The free movement of persons and the single market', *European Law Review*, 17:1, 3–19.

O'Keeffe, D. (1994), 'Citizenship of the Union', in D. O'Keeffe and P. Twomey (eds), *Legal Issues of the Maastricht Treaty*, Chichester, Wiley, pp. 87–107.

O'Leary, S. (1996), *The Evolving Concept of Community Citizenship: From the Free Movement of Persons to Union Citizenship*, Den Haag, Kluwer.

Papademetriou, D. (1996), *Coming Together or Pulling Apart? The European Union's Struggle with Immigration and Asylum*, Washington, DC, Carnegie Endowment for International Peace.

Peers, S. (1996), 'Towards equality: actual and potential rights of third country nationals in the European Union', *Common Market Law Review*, 33:1, 7–50.

Peterson, J. (1995), 'Decision-making in the European Union: towards a framework for analysis', *Journal of European Public Policy*, 2:1, 69–93.

Phizacklea, A. (1998), 'Migration and globalisation: a feminist perspective', in K. Koser and H. Lutz (eds), *The New Migration in Europe: Social Constructions and Social Realities*, London, Macmillan, pp. 21–38.

Pierson, C. (1998), 'Contemporary challenges to welfare state development', *Political Studies*, 46:4, 777–94.

Pierson, P. (1994), *Dismantling the Welfare State. Reagan, Thatcher and the Politics of Retrenchment*, Cambridge, Cambridge University Press.

Pierson, P. (1996), 'The path to European integration: an historical institutionalist approach', *Comparative Political Studies*, 29:2, 123–63.

Pierson, P. and S. Liebfried (1995), 'Multitiered institutions and the making of social policy', in S. Liebfried and P. Pierson (eds), *European Social Policy: Between Integration and Fragmentation*, Washington, DC, Brookings Institution, pp. 1–40.

Plender, J. (1988), *International Migration Law*, second edition, Dordrecht, Martinus Nijhoff.

Pollack, M. (1996), 'Delegation, agency and agenda-setting', *International Organization*, 51:1, 99–134.

Portes, A. and J. Borocz (1989), 'Contemporary immigration: theoretical perspectives on its determinants and modes of incorporation', *International Migration Review*, 23:3, 606–30.

Powell, M. and P. DiMaggio (1991), *The New Institutionalism in Organizational Analysis*, Chicago, IL, Chicago University Press.

Pressman, J. and A. Wildavsky (1973), *Implementation. How Great Expectations in Washington Are Dashed in Oakland; or Why It's Amazing That Federal Programs Work At All*, Berkeley, CA, University of California Press.

Putnam, R. (1988), 'Diplomacy and domestic politics', *International Organization*, 42:3, 427–61.

Race and Class (1997), 'Europe: the wages of racism', *Race and Class* (special edition), 39:1.

Reid, E. and H. Reich (1992), *Breaking the Boundaries: Migrant Workers' Children in the EC*, Philadelphia, Multilingual Matters.

Rex, J. and B. Drury (eds) (1994), *Ethnic Mobilisation in a Multi-cultural Europe*, Aldershot, Avebury.

Rhodes, M. and B. van Apeldoorn (1998), 'Does migration from less developed countries erode the welfare state?', paper presented to the conference 'Migration and the Welfare State in Contemporary Europe', European University Institute, Florence, 21–23 May.

Richardson, J. (1996a), 'Policy-making in the EU: interests, ideas and garbage cans of primeval soup', in J. Richardson (ed.), *European Union: Power and Policy-Making*, London, Routledge, pp. 3–23.

Richardson, J. (1996b), 'Eroding EU policies: implementation, gaps, cheating and re-steering', in J. Richardson (ed.), *European Union: Power and Policy-Making*, London, Routledge, pp. 278–94.

Risse-Kappen, T. (ed.) (1995), *Bringing Transnational Relations Back In: Non-State Actors, Domestic Structures and International Institutions*, Cambridge, Cambridge University Press.

Risse-Kappen, T. (1996), 'Exploring the nature of the beast: international relations theory and comparative policy analysis meet the European Union', *Journal of Common Market Studies*, 34:1, 53–80.

Robertson, R. (1992), *Globalization, Social Theory and Global Culture*, London, Sage.

Rogers, R. (ed.) (1985), *Guests Come to Stay: The Effects of European Labor Migration on Sending and Receiving Countries*, Boulder, CO, Westview.

Rosamond, B. (1999), 'Discourses of globalisation and the social construction of European identities', *Journal of European Public Policy*, forthcoming.

Rosenau, J. and E-O. Czempiel (1992), *Governance Without Government: Order and Change in World Politics*, Cambridge, Cambridge University Press.

Ross, G. (1995), *Jacques Delors and European Integration*, Cambridge, Polity Press.

Ruggie, J. (1982), 'International regimes, transactions and change: embedded liberalism in the post-war economic order', *International Organization*, 36:2, 379–415.

Runnymede Trust (1997), *Islamophobia*, London, Runnymede Trust.

Saggar, S. (1992), *Race and Politics in Britain*, Hemel Hempstead, Harvester Wheatsheaf.

Salt, J. (1992), 'Migration processes among the highly skilled', *International Migration Review*, 26:2, 484–505.

Sandholtz, W. and J. Zysman (1989), '1992: recasting the European bargain', *World Politics*, 27:4, 496–520.

Sassen, S. (1996), *Losing Control*, New York, Columbia University Press.

Scharpf, F. (1996), 'Negative and positive integration in the political economy of European welfare states', in G. Marks, F. Scharpf, P. Schmitter and W. Streeck (eds), *Governance in the European Union*, London, Sage, pp. 15–39.

Schmitter, P. (1996), 'Examining the present Euro-polity with the help of past theories', in G. Marks, F. Scharpf, P. Schmitter and W. Streeck (eds), *Governance in the European Union*, London, Sage, pp. 1–14.

Snyder, F. (1994), 'Institutional development in the European Union: some implications of the third pillar', in J. Monar and R. Morgan (eds), *The Third Pillar of the European Union*, Brussels, Interuniversity Press, pp. 85–95.

Soysal, Y. N. (1994), *Limits of Citizenship: Migrants and Postnational Membership in Europe*, Chicago, IL, Chicago University Press.

Soysal, Y. N. (1998), 'Towards a post-national model of membership', in G. Shafir (ed.), *The Citizenship Debates: A Reader*, Minneapolis, MN, University of Minnesota Press, pp. 189–220.

Statewatch (1997), *Key Texts on Justice and Home Affairs in the European Union Volume I (1976–1993): From Trevi to Maastricht*, London, Statewatch.

Steinmo, S., K. Thelen and F. Longstreth (eds) (1992), *Structuring Politics: Historical Institutionalism in Comparative Analysis*, Cambridge, Cambridge University Press.

Stone-Sweet, A. and W. Sandholtz (eds) (1998), *European Integration and Supranational Governance*, Oxford, Oxford University Press.

Streeck, W. (1995), 'From market-making to state-building? Reflections on the political economy of European social policy', in S. Liebfried and P. Pierson (eds), *European Social Policy: Between Fragmentation and Integration*, Washington, DC, Brookings Institution, pp. 389–431.

Streeck, W. (1996), 'Neo-voluntarism: a new European social policy regime?', in G. Marks, F. Scharpf, P. Schmitter and W. Streeck (eds), *Governance in the European Union*, London, Sage, pp. 64–94.

Stubb, A. (1996), 'A categorization of differentiated integration', *Journal of Common Market Studies*, 34:2, 283–95.

Tarrow, S. (1994), *Power in Movement: Social Movements, Collective Action and Politics*, Cambridge, Cambridge University Press.

Tarrow, S. (1998), 'The Europeanization of conflict: reflections from a social movements perspective', *West European Politics*, 18:2, 223–51.

Travis, A. (1998), 'Fortress Europe's four circles of purgatory', *The Guardian*, 20 October, p. 19.

Twomey, P. (1994), 'Title VI of the Union treaty: "matters of common interest" as a question of human rights', in J. Monar and R. Morgan (eds), *The Third Pillar of the European Union*, Brussels, European Interuniversity Press, pp. 49–66.

Uçarer, E. and D. Puchala (1997), *Immigration into Western Societies: Problems and Policies*, London, Pinter.

Wæver, O. (1996), 'European security identities', *Journal of Common Market Studies*, 34:1, 103–32.

Wæver, O., B. Buzan, M. Kelstrup and P. Lemaitre (eds) (1993), *Identity, Migration and the New Security Agenda in Europe*, New York, St Martin's Press.

Wallace, H. (1996), 'Politics and policy in the EU: the challenge of governance', in H. Wallace and W. Wallace (eds), *Policy-Making in the European Union*, Oxford, Oxford University Press, pp. 3–36.

Wallace, W. (1990), *The Transformation of Western Europe*, London, Pinter.

Weil, P. (1991), *La France et ses étrangers: l'aventure d'une politique de l'immigration*, Paris, Calmann-Lévy.

Weil, P. (1996), 'Nationalities and citizenships: the lessons of the French experience for Germany and Europe', in D. Cesarani and M. Fulbrook (eds), *Citizenship, Nationality and Migration in Europe*, London, Routledge, pp. 74–87.

Weiler, J. (1982), 'The community system: the dual character of supranationalism', *Yearbook of European Law*, Oxford, Clarendon Press, pp. 267–306.

Weiner, M. (1995), *The Global Migration Crisis: Challenges to States and to Human Rights*, New York, Harper Collins.

Wiener, A. (1997), *European Citizenship Practice: Building Institutions of a Non-State*, Boulder, CO, Westview.

Wiener, A. and V. Della Sala (1997), 'Constitution making and citizenship practice – bridging the democracy gap in the EU', *Journal of Common Market Studies*, 35:4, 595–614.

Wincott, D. (1995), 'Institutional interaction and European integration: towards an everyday critique of liberal intergovernmentalism', *Journal of Common Market Studies*, 33:4, 597–609.

Wrench, J. and J. Solomos (eds) (1992), *Racism and Migration in Western Europe*, Oxford, Berg.

Zolberg, A., A. Suhkre and S. Aguayo (1989), *Escape from Violence: Conflict and the Refugee Crisis in the Developing World*, Oxford, Oxford University Press.

Index

191